CRISIS
IN
CREDIBILITY

CRISIS
IN
CREDIBILITY

BRUCE LADD

THE NEW AMERICAN LIBRARY

**To my girls—
Dolly, Laura, and Diane**

Published by The New American Library, Inc.
1301 Avenue of the Americas,
New York, New York 10019
Published simultaneously in Canada by
General Publishing Company, Ltd.
Library of Congress Catalog Card Number: 68–17057
Printed in the United States of America

Acknowledgments

This book grew out of a concern for the people's right to know about their national government. This concern was first stimulated while I was a newspaper reporter and editor in Illinois, and was heightened by insights gained as a press secretary to a candidate for government office, as a Congressional Fellow in Washington, D.C., and as a staff assistant to a member of Congress who believes in the necessity of honest reporting by the government. The aim of this book is to discuss the credibility problem in a manner which will enable the reader to comprehend its broad scope. The writing is intended neither as the "last word" on the subject nor as a treatment of every facet of the problem. It deals exclusively with three practices of the executive branch—secrecy, lying, and news management. No attempt has been made to discuss the communications failures of the Congress and the press.

I am indebted to the many who contributed their experiences and encouragement to this effort. It is not possible—in fact, in some cases, not appropriate—to identify all of them here. I would, however, like to express my deep gratitude to the following: Robert A. Gutwillig, my editor, and Edward T. Chase of The New American Library; Congressman Donald Rumsfeld; Miss Estelle B. Hunter; Dr. Ray E. Hiebert; Robert D. Novak; Stephen I. Danzansky; Walter Lippmann; David S. Broder; Samuel J. Archibald; Charles E. Nicodemus, Jr.; Congressman Albert H. Quie; Nick Kotz; Senator J. William Fulbright; Robert R. Carr; Dr. Hoke Smith; Dr. Roy D. Morey; and to my friends and associates on Capitol Hill and among the Washington press corps. I also want to acknowledge the invaluable assistance received from the members of my family. Without their patience and understanding, this book never would have been written.

There may be some who will try to minimize the thesis of this book. That is fine. I hope there will be disagreement. Out of honest differences of opinion may come solutions for this most incredible problem.

BRUCE C. LADD, JR.

Washington, D.C.
February, 1968

Contents

CHAPTER 1

Would You Believe . . . ?

*The credibility of our government has been assailed.
We have a great problem here maintaining our credibility with our own people.* —ARTHUR GOLDBERG

"It's a hell of a way to learn things," President John F. Kennedy declared after the Bay of Pigs invasion in 1961.

"But I have learned one thing from this business—that is, that we will have to deal with the CIA."

President Kennedy had learned an important lesson the hard way. Unfortunately, the President's enlightenment concerning the United States' top-secret intelligence organization, the Central Intelligence Agency, was shared by only a few of his closest advisers.

Thus, when it was first disclosed in February, 1967, that for two decades the CIA had been covertly subsidizing numerous educational, labor, philanthropic, and student groups, the nation and the world expressed shock. Commented Supreme Court Justice William O. Douglas: "This kind of activity results in a loss of confidence and this is disastrous in a free society. The damage is incalculable." A Tokyo newspaper editorialized: "It is not pleasant to know that this or that

American visitor traveling abroad might be a secret espionage agent."

The initial disclosures of the CIA's far-flung activities, along with subsequent revelations, have undoubtedly placed a severe limitation on the ability of the agency to operate as the chief undercover unit of the federal government. As one CIA official admitted: "These disclosures have been a greater disaster and have done more damage to the interests of the United States than the Bay of Pigs. What these disclosures have cost us is far greater than anything we got for our money."

The official was referring to the CIA's loss of face, to its "blown cover." He was suggesting that the trust and confidence formerly enjoyed by the CIA had been replaced by suspicion and doubt. He was saying that the credibility of the CIA, as well as the credibility of the United States government and of many private organizations, had been seriously compromised.

Regrettably, the case of the CIA's diminished reputation is not an isolated one; it is one of a great number of such episodes and certainly one of the most dramatic. Too often in recent years the federal government has sacrificed its credibility in the name of expediency. The government's veracity has come under question. Accelerating instances of government secrecy, outright lying, and news management have contributed to wide public skepticism. Terms such as "credibility gap," "crisis in confidence," and "truth in government" have become commonplace. Indeed, the crisis in credibility today is considered to be one of the nation's major governmental problems.

Former President Dwight D. Eisenhower alluded to the growing credibility problem when he acknowledged: "In the diplomatic field it was routine practice to deny responsibility for an embarrassing occurrence when there is even one percent chance of being believed, but when the world can entertain not the slightest doubt of the facts there is no point in trying to evade the issue."[1] Eisenhower cannot forget the

1960 discovery of the United States' U-2 spy plane deep inside Russia. The Russians smugly kept silent about the capture and confession of pilot Francis Gary Powers until after the United States government had released a contrived story stating the plane was on a weather reconnaisance flight for the National Aeronautics and Space Administration. "The big error we made was, of course, in the issuance of a premature and erroneous cover story," Eisenhower reflected. "Allowing myself to be persuaded on this score is my principal regret—except for the U-2 failure itself—regarding the whole affair."[2] He added: "Credibility in our informational programs is the first essential, and it cannot be achieved by falsehood and hypocrisy, which would be promptly exposed by a free press."[3]

In the post-Eisenhower years, the credibility dilemma was heightened by influential government officials like Arthur Sylvester, who from 1961 to 1967 was in charge of dispensing information for the Department of Defense. Sylvester contended that "information is a weapon, a very important weapon, to be used or withheld." He denied any intent to fabricate or distort the news, but he defended the government's "inherent right . . . to lie to save itself when faced with nuclear disaster."[4] When summoned to testify in 1963 before the United States Senate's Permanent Subcommittee on Investigations, Sylvester moderated his opinion only a little, saying: "The government does not have a right to lie to the people, but it does have a right in facing an enemy [to disseminate information which] is not accurate and is intended to mislead the enemy."[5]

In his published memoirs, *A Thousand Days: John F. Kennedy in The White House,* former White House aide Arthur Schlesinger, Jr., presents a different set of facts about the Bay of Pigs than he originally gave the *New York Times* in 1961. When the *Times* pointed out to him that his earlier statement about the size of the invasion force did not coincide with data in his book, Schlesinger said: "Did I say that? Well, I was lying. That was a cover story."

Doubts about the United States government's candor have been voiced abroad with increasing frequency. In a rare display of undiplomatic language in 1966, United Nations Secretary-General U Thant said that an offer to enter into peace talks with the North Vietnamese had been rejected by the United States in 1964, and that the American people were not getting all the facts. The White House had previously denied receiving any "meaningful" peace feeler. However, the State Department reluctantly acknowledged that the peace feeler had been made, but claimed the offer was "too nebulous" to have been taken seriously. Remarked Australian Denis Warner, a correspondent with twenty-five years of experience in covering Far Eastern wars: "What no one will accept indefinitely, especially in a war of this sort, is a persistent attempt to win by pretense what has not been won on the ground. United States information officers are engaged in the business of turning defeat into victory."[6]

The truth was late in coming when the United States sent troops to the Dominican Republic in 1965 under the guise of "protecting American lives." As it later turned out, the United States force was in Santo Domingo to squelch a takeover of the Dominican government by nationalist elements alleged to include Communists. As if the United States' relations with General Charles de Gaulle's French government were not already sensitive enough, the United States government lied when a United States plane was detected in an overflight of France's atomic installations in 1965. A Pentagon spokesman said we had no involvement in the incident. When irrefutable evidence was presented, the United States retracted its denial and apologized to the French. In the summer of 1965, when the Prime Minister of Singapore charged that the CIA had offered him a $3.3 million bribe, the United States vehemently denied it. The Prime Minister then produced a letter of apology for the bribe attempt from Secretary of State Dean Rusk, whereupon the State Department backtracked, saying: "Those who were consulted yesterday were not fully aware of the background of the incident which occurred four and one-half years ago."

An international drama took place in early 1966 when a Strategic Air Command (SAC) B-52 bomber and a KC-135 tanker collided while refueling over Palomares, Spain. Eight American airmen were killed and four "nuclear devices" were lost, although three were soon recovered. The fourth was eventually recovered too, but as *The Nation* reported: "For forty-four days, Washington kept the incident wrapped in a blanket of impenetrable secrecy during which Department of Defense officials engaged in colloquies with newsmen such as the one quoted by Tad Szulc in the *New York Times:*

> REPORTER: Can you tell me whether you've located the missing bomb?
> BRIEFING OFFICER: I don't know of any missing bomb, but we have not positively identified what I think you think we are looking for."

The great concern of Spanish officials turned to outrage when the United States refused to give straight answers concerning the danger posed by the lost H-bomb, a 1.1-megaton device somewhere beneath the Mediterranean Sea. As the truth became known, the eight-ton bomb had come dangerously close to slipping into a canyon 4,000 feet below the sea and beyond the reach of retrieval equipment. The eighty-day search and recovery operation cost the United States government several million dollars and involved eighteen Navy vessels and 3,200 men. Yet, judging solely from the public statements of United States officials, the United States had no knowledge of any missing bomb and, therefore, no idea as to the gravity of the situation. The world knew better.

A measure of the impact of the credibility problem on the American people can be seen in the results of polls taken regularly by members of Congress. Congressman Jack Edwards of Alabama asked his constituents: "Do you believe that the government gives the people reliable information on what is going on?" Of those responding, more than 86 percent answered "No." A similar question posed by Congressman John N. Erlenborn of Illinois resulted in 75 percent answering "No." An examination of polls taken by other members of Congress shows the Edwards and Erlenborn results to be typical.

The federal government's credibility has suffered particularly as a result of the war in Vietnam. In a poll taken for the Columbia Broadcasting System in December, 1965, the Opinion Research Corporation asked a question concerning the truthfulness of official United States information about Vietnam. Sixty-seven percent of those answering said Government pronouncements about Vietnam are "sometimes" truthful; 13 percent said "almost never" truthful; and 15 percent said "always" truthful. In a poll conducted by National Analysts, Incorporated, for the National Broadcasting Company, more than 59 percent of those answering said "No" when asked, "Has the White House been giving us all the truth about Vietnam?" In a poll for the Republican National Committee, also conducted by the Opinion Research Corporation, a total of 72 percent of all persons—Democrats, Independents and Republicans—expressed the belief that the government tries to present information in its most favorable light and holds back the truth or slants facts it considers unfavorable. The poll indicated that even though the government insists the United States is making progress in Vietnam, three out of five persons believe we are only holding our own there in spite of official pronouncements to the contrary.

For all practical purposes, the decline of the government's credibility had its beginnings in the censorship that the Roosevelt administration necessarily imposed during World War II. Government officials became accustomed to secrecy, and after the war was over they found it difficult to return to prewar policies of frankness and openness. The introduction of a new dimension, the Cold War, presented the government with an additional challenge—a no-war status which seemed to demand war policies relating to government information.

The Truman administration met the challenge in the late 1940's by twitting newsmen who were considered too inquisitive and by invoking excuses of crises in order to withhold information. The demise of the government's credibility continued during the Eisenhower years. The U-2 episode capped an eight-year record of the government withholding much more information than it had a right to and of the indiscriminate use of "executive privilege" as a means of secrecy. Following a brief respite in 1961, the government's credibility continued downward under the regime of President Kennedy. The problem has reached alarming proportions under the leadership of President Johnson.

The current crisis in credibility is attributed to three basic factors:

1. The government's unwarranted and unjustified concern with secrecy; its refusal to reveal information which is properly in the public domain.

2. Lying by government officials.

3. The government's adeptness at devising new ways to mislead the public and the press through manipulation of information or news management.

To date, the government has made some attempt to limit the use of its "right to lie" to occasions of special sensitivity, but these occasions have come more and more frequently in recent years and the special nature of the occasions has magnified the impact of the lie.

The discussion of government information policy, to a very large degree, has been conducted by journalists and others connected with the communications media. Newspapers in the United States, accepted as "The Fourth Estate" or the fourth branch of government, have served as the public's watchdog over government since the first days of the republic. The task of the press in this country has been to take the place of the citizen who is unable to be present, to be the people's eyes and ears. The role of the press in reflecting the actions of government is more important than much of the government itself. It is the role of making the people's government the people's business. Without constant probing of government by the press, the people will remain uninformed and misinformed.

The relationship of the press to the government was defined by *The Times of London* in 1851: "The purposes and duties of the [Ministers of the Crown and of the Press] are constantly separate, generally independent, sometimes diametrically opposite. . . . The Press can enter into no close or binding alliances with the statesmen of the day, nor can it surrender its permanent interests to the convenience of the ephemeral powers of the Government. The first duty of the Press is to obtain the earliest and most correct intelligence of the events of the time, and instantly, by disclosing them, to make them the common property of the nation. The statesman collects his information secretly and by secret means; he keeps back even the current intelligence of the day with ludicrous precautions. . . . The Press lives by disclosures."

Operating from a base independent of government, the communications media—newspapers, radio, television, magazines, and others—relay to the people the substance of the government's decisions, policies, and goals. The media are not interested in relaying propaganda or partisan facts, but rather in reporting the truth. The media, therefore, have a vital stake in the authenticity and accuracy of government information. It has been the media that have taken the initiative over the years to oppose secrecy and deceit by the government. The media, too, have a constituency to which they are responsible, a constituency of over 200 million Americans eager to learn as much as they can about the conduct of their government.

Pierre Salinger, who served as press secretary to President Kennedy, has observed: "No two institutions in the country have a more important relationship than the government of the United States and the press. Each is powerful and each has almost inexhaustible resources. . . . The basic reason for the controversy between press and President is the fact that the objectives of the two institutions collide. The press, rooted in American history and a tradition of freedom, attempts to find and report every single piece of information. The government naturally wishes to present its programs and positions in the best possible light. It therefore resists—sometimes rightly and sometimes wrongly—the pressures brought on it by the press."[7]

While some criticism has been leveled at the Congress with regard to closed sessions of committees, and to a lesser degree at the courts, the major problem has been and is with information generated by the more than sixty agencies of the executive branch of the federal government, including the office of the President. The credibility problem is particularly serious in the executive branch because of the extension of the executive into many new fields since World War II. The increased powers of the President, the development of new techniques for influencing public opinion, and the growing complexity of political events have given the executive branch much greater responsibility for keeping the public adequately and accurately informed. In the current age of Presidential power, the control of information possessed by the executive branch is of more consequence than in any other period of our history. Most of the information about government is in the hands of the executive and is not available outside the agencies directly concerned. Even the Congress is often unable to secure information it deems necessary to its successful operation.

Access to information about the government is required for the democratic system to work successfully. The Founding Fathers gambled when they placed their faith in the principle that, given sufficient information, the people could choose and operate their own government. The gamble has been successful. It will remain successful as long as the people are well informed. In order to maintain a government run by an informed people, secrecy must be minimized and the flow of accurate facts maximized. A government whose leaders cannot be believed runs the risk of losing the privilege of representing the people, and the people risk losing the contest between democracy and despotism. In a democracy, it is essential that the people possess and exercise the right to criticize the actions of the government. Unless there is information available which may reflect unfavorably upon government, the right to criticize is meaningless.

The credibility of a nation's government is absolutely crucial. To the extent that a government is believed, it will function effectively. To the extent that a government is doubted, it will inevitably fall short of its goals. The widening scope of government secrecy, lying, and news management, therefore, contributes to a trend that threatens the basis of democracy. When the government's credibility is impeached, democracy is diminished.

NOTES TO CHAPTER 1

1. Dwight D. Eisenhower, *The White House Years: Waging Peace, 1956–1961* (Garden City, N.Y.: Doubleday & Company, 1965), p. 551.
2. *Ibid.*, p. 558.
3. *Ibid.*, p. 627.
4. Address by Sylvester before The Deadline Club, New York Chapter of Sigma Delta Chi, New York, December 6, 1962.
5. Hearings of the Committee on Government Operations, United States Senate, 89th Congress, First Session, March 12, 1963, pp. 301–302.
6. Alden H. Sypher, "You Can't Fool All the People Even Some of the Time," *Nation's Business*, February, 1966, p. 32.
7. Pierre Salinger, *With Kennedy* (Garden City, N.Y.: Doubleday & Company, 1966), p 109.

CHAPTER 2

The Problem in Perspective

Wherever any public business is transacted, wherever plans affecting the public are laid . . . over that place a voice must speak, with the divine prerogative of a people's will, the words: "Let there be light." —WOODROW WILSON

Our government came into existence because of a widespread distrust of the British governors, whose words could not be believed and whose actions caused apprehension and disdain. While preparing to throw off British authority in the Revolutionary War (1775–1783), our earliest leaders adopted a policy of secrecy which guided the Continental Congress and established a precedent for the federal government to operate behind closed doors. The Continental Congress, on November 9, 1775, resolved:

> . . . That every member of this Congress considers himself under the ties of virtue, honour, and love of his country, not to divulge, directly or indirectly, any matter or thing agitated or debated in Congress, before the same shall have been determined, without leave of the Congress; nor any matter or thing determined in Congress, which a majority of the Congress shall order to be kept secret. And that if any member shall violate this agreement, he shall be expelled this

Congress, and deemed an enemy of the liberties of America, and liable to be treated as such.[1]

In prohibiting its members from informing the people on matters of public concern, the Congress sowed the seed of doubt. As the nation was to mature, the seed sprouted. A major factor in today's credibility problem is the early established tradition that the President has a right, in the absence of any statutory authority to the contrary, to determine which records of the executive branch may be opened to public scrutiny and which may be withheld from public view. On May 13, 1790, when the federal government was hardly a year old, United States Senator William Maclay of Pennsylvania requested that the United States Treasury Department produce receipts which Baron von Steuben had presented for funds advanced to him by the government. Secretary of the Treasury Alexander Hamilton refused to show the receipts, and Maclay told him: "The papers I wanted belonged to the public and to no private gentleman whatever, nor would it do for him to refuse information to a committee of Congress."[2] When Hamilton continued to refuse to give up the receipts, Maclay wrote in his diary: "I told him any member of Congress had a right to any papers in any office whatever; that as chairman of the committee I had promised to procure what papers were necessary."[3] Maclay never saw the receipts.

In 1796, the House of Representatives asked President George Washington to produce certain papers relating to the negotiations of the Jay Treaty with the King of Great Britain. Washington demurred, pointing out that the consent of the House was not necessary to the validity of the treaty and that the treaty exhibited in itself all information which might be of importance to the legislative branch. Washington explained: "As it is essential to the due administration of the government that the boundaries fixed by the Constitution between the different Departments should be preserved, a just regard to the Constitution and to the duty of my office . . . forbids a compliance with your request."[4]

Later, in 1807, President Thomas Jefferson kept confidential information and letters relating to the treason trial of Aaron Burr. In refusing to give the Burr papers to Chief Justice John Marshall, Jefferson reasoned: "With respect to papers, there is certainly a public and private side to our offices. To the former belong grants of land, patents for inventions, certain commissions, proclamations, and other papers patent in their nature. To the other belong mere executive proceedings. All nations have found it necessary, that for the advantageous conduct of their affairs, some of these proceedings, at least, should remain known to their executive functionary only. He, of course, from the nature of the case, must be the sole judge of which of them the public interests will permit publication. Hence, under our Constitution, in requests of papers, from the legislative to the executive branch, an exception is carefully expressed, as to those which he may deem the public welfare may require not to be disclosed; as you will see in the inclosed resolution of the House of Representatives, which produced the message of January 22nd, respecting this case."[5]

Justice Marshall seemed at a loss to disagree with Jefferson's argument. In the Burr trial, Marshall said: "In no case of this kind would the court be required to proceed against the President as against an ordinary individual. The objections to such a course are so strong and so obvious that all must acknowledge them. . . . Of the weight of the reasons for and against producing it he himself [the President] is the judge."

Instances of the executive branch refusing to disclose records to Congress or to other federal authority are numerous throughout history. They include refusal of requests for: documents relating to the conduct of naval officers in the Pacific Ocean (President James Monroe, 1825); a list of all appointments made without the consent of the Senate between 1829 and 1836 (President Andrew Jackson, 1836); a report to the War Department dealing with frauds practiced on Indians (President John Tyler, 1843); evidence of payments made through the State Department on President's certificates by a prior administration (President James Polk, 1846); official information concerning a proposition made by the King of the Sandwich Islands to transfer the islands to the United States (President Millard Fillmore, 1852); and a refusal of a message of protest to the House against a resolution to investigate attempts by the executive branch to influence legislation (President James Buchanan, 1860).

An effort by Congress to overcome the barriers of secrecy was successful during the administration of President Abraham Lincoln. By concurrent action of both the House and the Senate on December 9, 1861, a joint committee was authorized to investigate the conduct of the Civil War. Ignoring executive branch pleas that its investigations constituted a serious infringement of the powers of the President as Commander-in-Chief of the Army, the joint committee investigated battles, disloyal employees, surrenders at sea, military supplies, and war contracts. The secrecy which had always accompanied wars was temporarily broken. Congress was able to legislate with adequate knowledge and to hold the Lincoln administration to strict accountability.

Lincoln was one of the first Presidents to exhibit skill in managing events so as to guarantee their maximum impact on the people. Drawing on his keen sense of timing, Lincoln waited two months for the appropriate moment to announce his signing of the Emancipation Proclamation. He later wrote: "Finally, came the week of the battle of Antietam. I determined to wait no longer. The news came on Wednesday that the advantage was on our side. . . . The Proclamation was published the following Monday."[6] Lincoln broke a policy of his predecessors when he refused to designate a Washington newspaper as the official administration organ, recognizing that he would lose more than he would gain by tying himself to only one newspaper. With the help of Joseph Medill of the Chicago *Tribune,* Lincoln used the press to great advantage in winning the Presidential nomination at Chicago in 1860. His close relationship with Medill required that he be especially sensitive to the needs of Horace Greeley of the New York *Tribune,* the most influential editor of the day. Lincoln gave exclusive information to Greeley "for the use or guidance of the *Tribune*" by feeding it through a Treasury Department official.

In the days of President William McKinley (1897–1901), the first of the Presidential press secretaries came into prominence. He was George B. Cortelyou, an intelligent and handsome young aide who had served as stenographer for President Grover Cleveland. Cortelyou quickly grasped the importance of serving as a go-between in representing the President in dealing with the press. In an age when Washington correspondents lived by their wits and the scramble for news was a free-for-all, McKinley steadfastly shunned publicity. A President who failed to establish personal relationships with correspondents was opening himself to scandalous attacks against which he had no defense. Cortelyou perceived the problem and began to shape a press program. He was the first presidential assistant to send for correspondents and distribute statements in the President's name. He established the custom of catering to the big press associations. He became known to the newspaper profession as the man to whom to apply and from whom to expect honest and courteous answers. But Cortelyou's talent for press relations did little to reduce secrecy in the executive branch. When the treaty ending the Spanish-American War was signed on August 12, 1898, newspapermen and photographers were excluded. A free flow of information about the conduct of government was nonexistent. The government took special precautions to protect information about the official conduct of its business.*

---

* Unusually tight security measures were taken in March, 1898, to prevent leakage of the text of a report on the cause of the sinking of the battleship *Maine.* The secret report was carefully placed in a safe in the executive offices on Friday, March 25, to await its delivery to Congress at noon on Monday, March 28. To the dismay of all concerned, the Monday morning newspapers carried an Associated Press story which gave full and accurate details of the report. Colonel Charles A. Boynton, chief of

Historians have generously treated the fact that President Woodrow Wilson frequently voiced his belief in the freedom of the press. But insufficient attention has been given to the authoritarian rule imposed on newsmen by the Wilson administrations and very little mention has been made of the ill-advised information policies adopted by the government during World War I.

In 1917, Wilson was trying to get Congress to incorporate in the espionage bill the legal power to curb free speech. Without waiting for Congress' decision, the Department of Justice organized a group of special agents to stamp out agitation against compulsory military service. Attorney General Thomas W. Gregory warned: "Any spoken or written word, uttered or written for the purpose of interfering with the purpose of the Selective Service Act, will result in prompt arrest of the person or persons responsible." Three students were taken into custody in New York for setting up a protest against conscription. A Socialist meeting was raided in Topeka, Kansas. In Columbus, Ohio, a printer was arrested and charged with treason for preparing an anti-war poster. Scores were jailed for exercising the right to dissent.

Meanwhile, on Capitol Hill, the House rejected Wilson's request for authority to censor the newspapers. The mood of the public was angrily opposed to censorship. Joseph P. Tumulty, Wilson's private secretary and trusted advisor, told him: "I know how strongly you feel on the matter of a strict censorship, but I would not be doing my full duty to you . . . if I did not say . . . that there is growing a feeling of bitter resentment against the whole business."[8] Wilson never did get censorship power, but, as it turned out, the additional powers conferred on him by the mass of wartime legislation were so extensive that specific authority for censorship was unnecessary.

---

the AP Washington bureau, testified that AP had access to the report for a full day and that it had not been obtained from the White House. This penetration of the secrecy barrier remained an unsolved mystery of the *Maine* affair.[7]

While Wilson sulked over his failure to win censorship rights, he received at the White House a document summing up the arguments for and against censorship. The document suggested that what was needed was not suppression, but expression—a publicity campaign to sell the war to the nation. Creator of this idea was George Creel, a Colorado journalist who was characterized chiefly by his belief that Woodrow Wilson was the greatest man that ever lived. Wilson summoned Creel to Washington, briefly interviewed him, and appointed him chairman of the new Committee on Public Information (CPI).

After setting up the CPI office across the street from the White House, Creel proceeded to exercise the President's powers to suppress and express, to coordinate the activities of military censors, to establish subsidiary offices in large cities, and, generally, to shape all information coming from the executive branch. Throughout the war, most of the material published in the newspapers was piped to them through Creel. A picture and film division was established, special matter was prepared for the foreign press, speeches were written for 75,000 volunteer orators, and posters and bulletins were distributed far and wide. In an incredibly short time, Creel had the vast majority of the American people reciting slogans in support of the war to "make the world safe for democracy."

Wilson was pleased with it all. He delighted in denying the existence of censorship or news management, and he conducted press conferences as if he were the leader of an orchestra. A British diplomat wrote: "The President . . . is as mysterious as ever. When he summons the newspapermen he talks to them at length and in excellent language, but when they leave his presence they say to each other, What on earth did he say? When he sees the members of Congress he reads them a lecture and tells them what he thinks is good for them to know, which appears to them to be very little. He asks the advice of no one."[9] One day Wilson lashed out during a press conference at newsmen who had been accurately reporting the romantic escapades of his daughters, Jessie and Eleanor. "If this continues," the President glowered, "I shall deal with you, not as President, but as man to man."

As time wore on, Wilson lost all vestiges of a favorable press. Newsmen had long protested Creel's heavy-handed practices, but they had remained respectful of the President. However, three days after the armistice ending World War I was signed, Wilson destroyed any remaining press support by using wartime power to seize the Atlantic news cables. Some editorial writers attributed this move to Creel and his "Committee on Public Misinformation," which, it was contended, was planning to use the cables to censor and distort news of the peace conference. But Wilson was the loser, pure and simple.

President Franklin D. Roosevelt was unsurpassed in the uses to which he put the news media. The severe economic situation in the 1930's and the involvement of the United States in World War II resulted in Roosevelt's inheriting sweeping powers and authority, including new opportunities for "educating" the public. Debate continues today as to whether or not the people were honestly informed about Roosevelt's illnesses, his extended absences from the White House, the events leading up to United States involvement in World War II, the conduct of the war itself, and the negotiations that were held during the closing months of the war. The calculated government leak was polished under Roosevelt, as was perfection of the technique of launching trial balloons for testing public opinion. Leaks were often denied despite their origination with the White House. If public reaction to a trial balloon was negative, the balloon was hauled down and a new policy formulated.

At the start of the war in 1939, Roosevelt said America would be "neutral in fact, if not in spirit," but the country was neither. Roosevelt was the first President to make "nonpolitical" inspection tours of defense facilities, using that ploy with great effect in 1940. He made the White House press conference and the "Fireside Chats"* over radio efficient instruments for communicating an impression of the government. Whenever possible, Roosevelt relied on direct means of communication with the people because he was distrustful of the ability of newspapers and congressional leaders to get his messages across. The war compounded secrecy in government and prompted the installation of public relations and publicity specialists on a grand scale. Hundreds of public information officers were put on the federal payroll to disseminate information construed to be "in the public interest." Career diplomat Robert Murphy recalls: "There had been practically no security precautions in the State Department prior to the war. Suddenly we had too much. Every report seemed to contain secrets; the most innocuous information was 'classified'; a swollen staff of security agents hampered the work of everybody."[10]

Roosevelt was an evangelist capable of making public issues come alive. He gripped the attention of the people when he spoke. Author John Dos Passos described his radio voice as "the patroon voice, the headmaster's admonishing voice, the bedside doctor's voice that spoke to each man and to all of us." This newsman's account is illustrative of the command that Roosevelt had over a majority of the people:

> In July, 1933, riding into New York on the Long Island Railroad, I fell into conversation with a fellow commuter—a New York businessman whose name is not unknown to fame. . . . I ventured to criticize Mr. Roosevelt's course and to my surprise my companion—a businessman, a Republican businessman who had voted for Hoover—turned on me indignantly. He ended by saying that he had voted for Hoover but that he hoped God would forgive him and that he believed Franklin D. Roosevelt was the greatest leader since Jesus Christ.[11]

Merriman Smith, the veteran Washington correspondent for United Press International, added this perspective:

* There was a total of eight Fireside Chats: four in 1933, two in 1934, and one each in 1935 and 1936.

He would have been a wonderful actor. He probably would have been a Shakespearean star who wore fur-collared overcoats, carried a gold-headed cane and lorded it over the rest of the troupe. . . . He knew he could thrill a crowded stadium by just this simple wave of a hand, or his brown felt hat. That was all it took to jerk a hundred thousand people to their feet in screaming frenzy.[12]

As early as 1938, Roosevelt had expressed himself privately as favoring preparation for a defense of the western hemisphere from Fascism. He did not doubt the inevitability of war in the light of confidential reports received through diplomatic channels. But he judged the American people were not yet psychologically prepared for war, and when hostilities in Europe began with the German invasion of Poland, he issued a proclamation of neutrality. The Japanese attack at Pearl Harbor on December 7, 1941, provided the emotional shock that Roosevelt believed the American people needed if the government was to execute effectively a major war. His strategy was successful, though his means of handling information of war and peace were open to question.

Allegations that Roosevelt had specific advance knowledge of the impending attack on Pearl Harbor are probably without foundation. Nevertheless, certain facts were clearly known to the United States government in 1941: we knew Japan had been in a warlike state since 1931; we knew Japanese naval vessels were on the move in the Pacific Ocean; we knew negotiations with the Japanese government were going badly; and we knew the U.S. Pacific fleet nestled at Pearl Harbor provided an ideal target for an enemy attack. It is evident that that responsibility for the United States' defenseless position on December 7 was shifted from shoulder to shoulder and that U.S. government officials lied to the people in the mistaken belief that the truth would be too painful. A 1942 probe headed by Supreme Court Justice Owen J. Roberts placed the blame on Admiral Husband E.

Kimmel,* who was commander of the Pacific fleet. Others defended Kimmel, saying he was being made a scapegoat by politicians seeking to protect their own reputations. Whatever the case, Roosevelt's many prewar statements about the United States being "opposed to armed intervention" and against involvement in "wars between other nations" had lulled the American people into a false sense of neutrality. Peace, of course, had a popular appeal. During the campaign of 1940, Roosevelt pledged: "I repeat again that I stand on the platform of our party: 'We will not participate in foreign wars and we will not send our army, naval or air force to fight in foreign lands outside of the Americas . . .'" After the election of 1940, Roosevelt said: "There is no demand for sending an American expeditionary force outside our own borders. There is no intention by any member of your government to send such a force. You can, therefore, nail any talk about sending armies to Europe as deliberate untruth."

Roosevelt was at times totally out of touch with the people and the press. At the time of his historic Atlantic Charter meeting with Winston Churchill off the Maine coast in August, 1941, connection with the United States press was completely severed for thirteen days, and there was considerable irritation when it was learned that accredited British journalists had accompanied Churchill. Consternation also developed over the conditions imposed upon newsmen at the Quebec, Cairo, and Tehran conferences. Roosevelt was necessarily away from Washington from time to time on official business during the war, but he disappeared once for a month

*Admiral Kimmel, now 84 and a resident of Groton, Conn., was "retired" from the Navy three months after Pearl Harbor. Historian Samuel Eliot Morison maintains Kimmel might have anticipated the attack had officials in Washington communicated to him the text of intercepted Japanese dispatches. "But he never had the chance," Morison says. Of the claim that Kimmel should have interpreted a November 27 "war warning" from Washington as evidence of imminent attack, author Roberta Wohlstetter says: "There seems little doubt that if the sender had been more alarmed, the warning itself would have been more alarming."

and it was discovered later that he had been at Bernard Baruch's estate in South Carolina for his health. He went to great lengths to conceal from anyone outside his official family how much time he spent at his home in Hyde Park. During the campaign of 1944, elaborate staging was used to give the impression the President was holding his own physically. Columnist Arthur Krock noted that the administration used "more ruthlessness, intelligence and subtlety in trying to suppress legitimate unfavorable comment than any I know." In the wake of reassurances from the President's physician, the world was stunned by an announcement on April 12, 1945, that the President was dead. The facts of his declining health were never known to the people.

On August 6, 1945, President Harry S. Truman disclosed to the nation: "Sixteen hours ago an American airplane dropped one bomb on Hiroshima. . . . It is an atomic bomb. . . . The fact that we can release atomic energy ushers in a new era in man's understanding of nature's forces. . . . Normally, everything about the work with atomic energy would be made public. But under present circumstances it is not intended to divulge the technical processes of production or all the military applications, pending further examination of possible methods of protecting us and the rest of the world from the danger of sudden destruction."* The bomb ushered in a new age. It was to be accompanied by new departures in government secrecy and deceit.

A warning of the developing information problem came from Zechariah Chafee, Jr., author and professor of law at Harvard University. He said: "The controversy over atomic bomb control shows how the claim of military security may possibly be used to hamper civilians in proper scientific activity, the progress of which depends on public communication in lectures and learned periodicals. In short, official

---

* The bomb dropped from the *Enola Gay* killed more than 78,000 people and demolished nearly every building within a three-mile radius. An even more powerful bomb was dropped over Nagasaki two days later.

encroachments on freedom of the press will be increased unless the boundary line between secrecy and publicity is very carefully demarcated. And officials must not do the demarcating."[13]

The post-bomb period was a particularly difficult one because the public was reluctant to accept the word of civilian authorities that secrecy must be maintained even though the war was ended. This difficulty was pinpointed by David E. Lilienthal, chairman of the Atomic Energy Commission: "During the war the American people knew nothing of the atomic project; indeed public money was spent to see to it that they did not know. Over two billion dollars were spent without public knowledge or a chance by Congress to stipulate, or even examine, the manner of spending. But that was in wartime. It was not the normal situation of a federal enterprise. The fact is, and we must face it—that it has yet to be demonstrated that in peacetime the cumbersome and time-consuming normal process of our federal government can make a success or insure leadership, world leadership, of such a complex scientific and technical undertaking as this."[14]

The press vigorously resisted what it considered to be unnecessary restrictions on postwar government information. When Truman attempted to implement a program of peacetime censorship of news in the executive branch, it was exposed by Nat Finney, a reporter for the Minneapolis *Tribune*. The program was quickly abandoned. When the Security Advisory Board prepared a draft of information guidelines barring public access to facts which might embarrass government officials, the American Society of Newspaper Editors blasted it. The plan was scuttled. When Secretary of Defense James Forrestal attempted to induce the news media to become "partners" with the government in determining what information about military matters the public should have, news media representatives rejected the notion, saying: "We do not believe that any type of censorship in peacetime is workable or desirable in the public interest. If any exists, we would not be sympathetic with an intent, on the part of the Military Establishment, to propose peacetime censorship."[15]

The Truman administration did not hesitate to employ the lie. In September of 1946, Truman and Secretary of State James F. Byrnes were trying to fashion a new "get tough" policy toward Russia. On September 10, Secretary of Commerce Henry Wallace went to the White House to get Truman's approval of a speech he was to deliver two days later in New York at a rally for Soviet-United States friendship. The Wallace speech was critical of the Western Powers for their failure to recognize and accommodate themselves to Russian suspicions of the capitalist world. The speech was obviously out of step with Truman-Byrnes thinking. However, Truman did not object to the speech's content and Wallace left the White House in good spirits. On September 12, three hours before Wallace was to speak in New York, Truman was asked at his press conference if he had approved the text of the speech and if it accurately reflected administration policy. Truman answered firmly "Yes" to both questions. Wallace delivered the speech and a great uproar ensued. At issue was Truman's mistaken public endorsement of a policy he did not support. The President had to be rescued. On September 14, reporters were called to the White House to hear Truman read a statement: "There has been a natural misunderstanding regarding the answer I made to a question asked at the press conference on Thursday, September 12, with reference to the speech of the Secretary of Commerce delivered in New York later that day. The question was answered extemporaneously and my answer did not convey the thought that I intended to convey. It was my intention to express the thought that I approved the right of the Secretary of Commerce to deliver the speech. I did not intend to indicate that I approved the speech as indicating a statement of the foreign policy of this country. . . ."[16] This transparent fabrication further confused the Russians and made Truman look foolish. It was branded "a clumsy lie" by *Time* magazine. Six days later, on September 20, Wallace was dismissed from the Cabinet.

Truman irreparably damaged his credibility with issuance of an order on September 25, 1951, that extended to all government agencies handling military information the same security measures already in force in the Defense and State Departments. The President insisted the order was designed to prevent "disclosure harmful to the security of the United States," but the loud and numerous protests were based on the concern that it might lead to unreasonable suppression of legitimate information. The fear mounted when the Office of Price Stabilization (OPS) issued a staff memorandum ordering that information which might embarrass OPS be withheld from the public. Truman immediately ordered the OPS directive withdrawn, though his controversial order of September 25 remained in effect. The public reaction was expressed by the president of the American Society of Newspaper Editors, Alexander F. Jones: "Any time you give a government department head authority to classify material as top secret on a security basis, you are placing a potent weapon in his hands. The result, invariably, is further suppression of the news." James S. Pope, chairman of the ASNE Committee on Freedom of Information, contended the "ill-advised" order would "smother legitimate information about the operation of government."

Despite all opposition, however, the government followed a distinct path toward secrecy. The term "secret" was applied to much information having no relation to national defense. Secrecy began to be used to cover up mistakes and inefficiency on the part of government officials. Hanson W. Baldwin, special correspondent for the *New York Times,* commented: "The reasons for this trend are many. One is the carry-over into peacetime of wartime security regulations; it is difficult in bureaucratic Washington to rid the government of standards and rules established during the war. Another is obviously the tense international situation and the danger, ever-present in the official mind, of Communist 'boring from within' and of espionage. A third is the technological revolution in weapons through which we are passing. . . . A fourth reason is the increasing influence of the military in Washington; they probably wield today greater power than in any prior peacetime period in American history."[17] Baldwin proposed some general rules for easing the secrecy problem. His first rule was, simply, the less censorship in peacetime the better. Another was that no censorship which acts solely to protect government against criticism is justifiable. A third rule was that the few secrets which could be legitimately termed "secrets"—precisely how the atomic bomb works, for instance—should be real secrets, not subject to careless or deliberate revelations.

The Truman administration refused to heed such suggestions. The blanket of secrecy covered more and more information in the executive branch. Luther Evans, the scholarly head of the Library of Congress, felt constrained to tell the National Association of State Librarians: "There seems to be a tendency among bureaucrats . . . to keep away from the public, and even scholars, information which might in any way be misconstrued if published, or which might by any chance make it more difficult to have their way free of the annoyances of public opinion or the constituted representatives of the people in Congress."[18] Harold D. Lasswell, professor of law at Yale University, wrote: "In some ways the most insidious effect of continuing crisis is the undermining of the press and public opinion. The process resembles death by slow strangulation more than heart failure."[19] He added: "If public information dries up, and the level of suspiciousness goes up, the first casualty is the man of independent mind. When the caliber of the news in the media is reduced, the honest man finds the ground slipping out from under his feet. He sees that he does not have the raw material of judgment. As the fog deepens from the progressive blackout of information, it is apparent to the citizen that he is less and less qualified for effective citizenship."[20]

During Truman's second term, a ray of hope glimmered in

the approach to government information taken by Stuart Symington of Missouri. Truman asked the former Secretary of the Air Force to step in and direct rehabilitation of the Reconstruction Finance Corporation (RFC), the multimillion-dollar government lending agency which had suffered from mismanagement and talk of "favoritism" and "influence." Not only had the RFC fallen to a record low in public esteem, but it was also the subject of a withering investigation from a Senate committee headed by Senator J. W. Fulbright of Arkansas. Upon surveying the situation, Symington acknowledged: "This is a really horrible mess. I've seen some bad ones, but this is the worst in my experience."[21] He asked for and received full authority from Truman to clean up the RFC as he saw fit. Symington accomplished the job in a matter of months by instituting the so-called Goldfish Bowl policy which gave the fullest information on every loan granted and on other transactions of the agency. A register was established requiring every person calling at the agency about a loan to sign his name and to give details of his connection with the loan. Unhappily, Symington's enlightened performance represented an isolated departure from the government's general policy of keeping the public in the dark.

By the end of Truman's Presidency, the propaganda machinery he inherited from Roosevelt had doubled. The executive branch had 3,632 employees classified by the Civil Service Commission as "Editorial" and "Information" specialists. Untold others carried such titles as "Deputy Assistant Secretary for Public Affairs" and "Executive Assistant to the Assistant Secretary." Congressman Christian Herter of Massachusetts complained: "Our federal bureaucracy revealed itself as the most powerful and potentially dangerous lobby of all. It fought, bureau by bureau, every Congressional move to curb its innate desire to expand. Backed by its vast, tax-supported propaganda machine . . ." Herter was reflecting the concern of the public and the press.

Shortly after World War II, Dwight D. Eisenhower— General of the Army—expressed his opposition to peacetime censorship and proved his sincerity by opening up large amounts of war documents previously kept secret. After the election of 1952, Dwight D. Eisenhower—President of the United States—failed to carry out the same farsighted information policy.

Eisenhower reiterated his belief in a free flow of information but permitted federal officials to use the so-called "housekeeping statute" (5 U.S.C. 22) as justification for maintaining secrecy. The "housekeeping statute" was passed during the administration of George Washington in order to require government departments to keep and safeguard their official records. The statute was distorted by government lawyers and interpreted as authorization for withholding information from the public. Eisenhower allowed accelerated use of the statute by permitting secondary bureaucrats to invoke it. In a memorandum to Eisenhower in 1954, Attorney General Herbert Brownell gave the government's justification: "For over 150 years . . . our Presidents have established, by precedent, that they and members of their Cabinets, and other heads of executive departments, have an undoubted privilege and discretion to keep confidential, in the public interest, papers and information which require secrecy." All arguments against this logic were futile.

The Eisenhower administration first claimed "executive privilege" during the Army-McCarthy hearings in 1954 to bar testimony involving high administration officials.* Then, in a long series of cases, the claim was used by a score of executive agencies. It was used to protect Sherman Adams when his relationship with Bernard Goldfine began to surface; to cover up some aspects of the Dixon-Yates case; to withhold facts

---

* Senator Joseph McCarthy of Wisconsin charged in 1954 that the Army promoted a dentist, Dr. Irving Peress, from captain to major and honorably discharged him although it had information he was a Communist. McCarthy implied subversion in the military was responsible for Peress being treated so well. Secretary of the Army Robert Stevens refused to permit Brigadier General Ralph Zwicker, commandant of Camp Kilmer, N.J., where Peress was stationed, to testify before McCarthy's investigating committee.

concerning foreign aid programs in Laos and Peru; and to prevent the General Accounting Office (GAO) from reviewing records of the Air Force ballistic missile program. In the last case, the administration was working at cross purposes with its own appointee, Joseph Campbell, head of the GAO. When Campbell requested Air Force reports on inspections and audits of the missile program in 1958, the Air Force refused to produce them. Security was not a consideration in the refusal because GAO employees had top security clearance. The requested reports did not contain war plans, the names of confidential informants, results of criminal or personnel investigations, or other sensitive information. There was no acceptable excuse for the secrecy.

The Eisenhower administration tried to sidestep growing sentiment against secrecy by creating such designations as "For Air Force Eyes Only," "Administratively Confidential," "Not for Public Distribution," and "Submitted in Confidence." When one government official was asked for his solution to the secrecy pattern, he confided: "The best answer is a big bonfire." Another official suggested that all rubber stamps used by censors be gathered up and declared forbidden in government offices. In 1957, it was estimated that nearly one million federal employees were withholding information in one form or another, and that the greatest amount of this withheld data had no connection with internal security whatsoever. That year the Civil Service Commission listed 6,878 "Information and Editorial Employees" in the executive branch.

One of the first indications of the style to be adopted under Eisenhower came when a White House assistant boasted: "We're going to merchandise the hell out of the Eisenhower administration." Chief of the merchandisers was to be James Hagerty, the President's press secretary, who had an extraordinary grasp of modern communications techniques. It was Hagerty who devised the gimmick of the "work and play" vacation. Eisenhower had a penchant for taking frequent vacations, and, in order to distract the focus of public attention from them, Hagerty made them appear to be "working" trips. Once, while the President golfed at Augusta, Georgia, Hagerty announced the President's decision to appoint three ambassadors. The decision had been made weeks earlier. On another occasion, Hagerty disclosed that Secretary of Labor James Mitchell was joining the President in Augusta to discuss a bill having to do with labor welfare funds. The bill had been before Congress for several months. Thus, the impression was made that the President was continuing to struggle with problems of state on his trips away from Washington. As columnist Russell Baker saw it: "Hagerty's enduring contribution to the White House was his demonstration of how to exploit the weakness of the American newsgathering system for the promotion of his boss. . . . If editors demanded a Presidential story a day, it follows that reporters will be found to satisfy them one way or another. On days when there is no news, they will poke around darkened rooms, look under the carpet, or start staring at the west wall and adding two and two in news stories. When that sort of thing happens, the White House is in trouble. Hagerty prevented this by seeing to it that there was rarely a newsless day. If there was no news, he made a little."[22]

The credibility of the State Department was especially shaky during the Eisenhower years, in part because of the "brinkmanship" policies of Secretary of State John Foster Dulles. Newsmen in Washington hardly knew whether to believe what Dulles told them because they could not be sure if he was speaking to them as reporters or seeking to use them as instruments of psychological warfare. In the spring of 1955, at the time of one of the crises with the Chinese Communists over the islands in the Formosa Strait, one newsman counted five basic contradictions in the information put out by the State Department. James Reston of the *New York Times* said: "There has been a growing tendency . . . to put out not what government knows to be true, but what it wants the people to believe is true." Columnists Joseph and Stewart Alsop commented: "A whole elaborate system of secrecy has been developed, charged with limiting the people's knowledge in these areas [defense and foreign policy]. And the habit of secrecy has now spread, by a sort of noxious contagion, to other government agencies and departments that have no shadow of an excuse for secretiveness. . . . The country as a whole does not yet understand the country's situation, because the country's leaders have thus far persisted in concealing or misrepresenting the hard facts known to the experts."[23]

Eisenhower's Cabinet officials freely managed the news to their advantage through leaks to favored reporters. After Attorney General Brownell had leaked to a few reporters the important news that Earl Warren had been chosen to head the Supreme Court, a distressed newsman asked the President at his next press conference if the administration would continue to favor selected reporters. Eisenhower answered: "I think I have trusted subordinates who may occasionally leak news for purposes they consider proper."

Because of unnecessary government secrecy, a campaign issue developed in 1960 that harmed the President's party at the polls. Eisenhower had established the Gaither Committee* to examine the nation's defense system. The committee made its report but it was kept under wraps. Newsmen fitted various pieces of information together and concluded that the country was threatened by a "missile gap." The government vigorously denied the existence of such a gap, but it continued to withhold the Gaither report. Doubts as to the administration's credibility came into prominence, the people voted in November of 1960, and it was left for the next administration to discover the truth in the Gaither report and to acknowledge that there had been no missile gap after all. Another charge during the 1960 campaign was that the United States' prestige abroad was declining rapidly. Eisenhower might have proven

* Technically titled "The Security Resources Panel of the Office of Defense Mobilization Science Advisory Committee," the committee was established in April, 1957, under the chairmanship of H. Rowan Gaither, Jr., then chairman of the board of the Ford Foundation.

this charge to be less than accurate had he released surveys conducted by the United States Information Agency (USIA). The surveys were kept secret, however, and the secrecy worked its will to the jeopardy of the incumbent party.

The most damaging blow to the credibility of the Eisenhower administration was struck when the U-2 spy plane plunged onto the Russian countryside in 1960, wrecking the impending summit conference in Paris and setting back Soviet-United States relations considerably. Our government deliberately lied about what happened. In the words of one official: "We were, to put it bluntly, caught lying in our teeth." A measure of the everlasting harm of this lie can be seen in remarks made nearly six years later by Robert Shaw, manager of the Minnesota Newspaper Association:

> We were told, way back in 1960, that the U-2 plane shot down in Russia was an "upper altitude weather research plane" which had mistakenly flown over Pakistan. . . . It was shocking to learn—from the Premier of Russia, if you please—that our government was lying. Now . . . why was this clumsy falsehood necessary? Why didn't the U.S. government simply say "no comment"? Certainly the American public is grown up enough to know that we are competing with dangerous adversaries, that we need espionage. But the Russians knew, the whole world knew, everyone but the American public knew that the United States government was telling a whole series of baldfaced lies. It took Khrushchev to spill the beans.[24]

President John F. Kennedy came into office in January, 1961, amidst great expectations that his administration would reform the unsatisfactory information policies of the Eisenhower regime. Such was not to be the case.

As a candidate for President, Kennedy had promised to end unlimited secrecy in government and to tell the truth to the American people. For a time it appeared he might be trying to live up to his pledge. Then, during his first year in office, Kennedy authorized the use of "executive privilege" to block the Senate Armed Services Committee from questioning administration officials. He declared that he would not allow the questioning of "subordinate officials of our career service" concerning their official acts. Newsmen began to detect disturbing trends in the handling of information by government employees, prompting them to request a meeting with the President. The meeting, held May 9, 1961, was friendly but unproductive. An agreement was made to hold a second meeting. It was never held.

Word went out early in the Kennedy administration for government spokesmen and their public relations personnel to give the President credit for various projects being announced and to accentuate favorable publicity. When the bureaucracy was slow to implement these orders, reminders were issued. A memo circulated in the Commerce Department said: "At a White House meeting we have been advised again that speeches of Cabinet and sub-Cabinet officers do not contain sufficient reference to the President. It is to be kept in mind that, in announcing local projects, the President should be given a credit line in the lead paragraph."[25] Memos of this kind turned up time and time again, but no one would ever admit to ordering their circulation.

Kennedy was determined that his administration would speak with one voice. Tight restrictions were clamped on federal employees—particularly those in the Defense and State Departments—whose duties normally involved exposure to newsmen. Defense employees were prohibited from talking to reporters unless a third person was present or unless written reports were submitted after all interviews. The State Department adopted similar rules, though they were soon rescinded by Assistant Secretary of State Robert Manning, who felt strongly that they inhibited "the fullest possible dialogue between policy officials and newsmen." Through necessity, therefore, Pentagon officials became expert in the use of the unauthorized leak. Ideas, opinions, and plans were "floated" to newsmen willing to write stories describing what unidentified officials "think" or "feel." The substance of leaks often ran counter to official Pentagon policy, and the FBI was called in on several occasions to assist in detecting those responsible for releasing "unauthorized" material. Once a leak was out, its purveyor remained aloof, in readiness to deny, accept credit, or charge "foul," depending on reaction to the thrust of the leak.

Kennedy administration officials frequently found it more convenient to lie than to tell the truth. In 1961, when Presidential press secretary Pierre Salinger was negotiating a television exchange involving Kennedy and Nikita Khrushchev, he arranged to go to Paris to meet with Russian representative Mikhail Kharlamov. Instead of announcing the true purpose of his trip, Salinger lied. He said the visit to the French capital was to confer with USIA Director Edward R. Murrow and American information specialists from London, Bonn, Rome, and Paris. However, the press was tipped that both Salinger and Kharlamov would be in Paris at the same time, and speculation arose that a summit conference was in the offing. Rather than divulge the real purpose of his trip in order to dispel the summit rumors, Salinger stuck to his lie.

It was widely known in 1961 that the Central Intelligence Agency was training Cuban exiles in preparation for an invasion of the Caribbean island. In his book, *With Kennedy,* Salinger points out that reports of the United States training a brigade for military action against Fidel Castro were published as early as October, 1960, and that when Kennedy read them he was livid. Salinger quotes Kennedy as saying: "I can't believe what I'm reading! Castro doesn't need agents over here. All he has to do is read our papers. It's all laid out for him." Yet, the United States government consistently denied any knowledge of invasion preparations. The Bay of Pigs became history and questioning of the Kennedy administration's credibility increased. *Fortune* magazine's Washington correspondent, Charles J. V. Murphy, filed a complete account of the Bay of Pigs fiasco for the *Fortune* edition of September, 1961. Kennedy personally denounced the account at a press conference and sent an emmissary to complain—unsuccessfully—to publisher Henry Luce. Murphy, a colonel in the Air Force Reserve, soon found himself shifted to a minor post. This "reassignment" was Murphy's slap on the wrist for reporting data unfavorable to the administration. The paradoxical nature of Kennedy's reaction to press treatment of the Cuban venture was revealed by Clifton Daniel, managing editor of the *New York Times,* who reported that after the invasion attempt Kennedy told the *Times'* executive editor, Turner Catledge: "If you had printed more about the operation you would have saved us from a colossal mistake."[26] Kennedy is also reliably reported to have said to Orvil Dryfoos, publisher of the *Times:* "I wish you had run everything on Cuba. . . . I am just sorry you didn't tell it at the time."[27] The fallout from the Bay of Pigs episode was summed up by the Baltimore *Sun*'s Paul W. Ward: "Since the Cuban affair, which taught us that even categorical denials or assertions by U.S. government officials are no longer trustworthy, most of the reporters assigned to the State Department have maintained a highly skeptical attitude toward all major formal pronouncements there."

The weaknesses of the Kennedy administration's information policies were described in a speech by Carl T. Rowan, assistant to the Secretary of State for Public Affairs: "In an organization as big and complex as the federal government there are public officials who want to hide their inefficiency and mistakes. . . . There are individuals who regard the press only as a vehicle to be used when they want to dispense self-serving propaganda. There is a great deal of information that the public does not get because that information gets lost in the maze of bureaucracy, or it is filed away by an individual whose inexperience or ignorance makes that individual unaware of the serious need to educate the public." Lawrence Fanning, a former executive of the Chicago *Daily News* and *Sun-Times,* was more explicit:

> The President of the United States, as an individual, is one
> of the most gifted, spectacular men in the world today. . . .
> As a citizen, I voted for Mr. Kennedy and I voted for him

with real enthusiasm. As a professional journalist . . . I am troubled.

The people of my country—and I was one of them—asked for a master politician. . . . In John F. Kennedy we got that man. But we got something else too. Along with the fantastically accomplished leader, along with the Master Politician, we got a Master Manipulator—a man who has managed with impressive artistry to apply the tools of power to the task at hand. . . .

Shortly after President Kennedy was inaugurated, many of the men whose task it is to report the activities of government thought they perceived a substantial improvement in the accessibility of information. . . . The disaster of the Bay of Pigs ended the honeymoon. . . .

Some of us are troubled by the signs and portents. For example, Secretary of Defense McNamara, a brilliant administrator, gives every impression of distrusting the intelligence of the people and, in a corollary sense, the intelligence of the Congress and the press. . . .

One can raise, I think, legitimate questions about such a system if it becomes an established precedent. It boils down to government by an intellectual elite and the policies can only be as good as the members of the elite. What happens if the elite is replaced by a venal, arrogant, or power-mad cabal? What happens if it is replaced by an elite of the stupid?[28]

Fanning's deep personal liking for Kennedy did not prevent his criticizing information policies he felt impaired the government's relationship with the people. The points raised by Fanning were well worth serious thought, but they received little consideration from the Kennedy administration.

In October, 1962, one week before the Cuban missile crisis became known to the public, McGeorge Bundy, special assistant to the President, stated: "I know there is no present evidence and I think there is no present likelihood that Cubans and the Cuban government and the Soviet government would in combination attempt to install a major offensive capability."[29] The interim report of the Senate Preparedness Subcommittee, published after the 1962 elections, disclosed that the government knew as early as September, 1962, that a medium range missile site existed in Cuba's Pinar del Rio Province. There was reason to believe that additional missile capabilities existed in Cuba as well.

During the missile crisis, restrictions on news coverage and centralization of authority for releasing information enabled government spokesmen to withhold or slant news at will. The passing of the first Soviet ship through the United States Navy blockade was originally announced by a member of Congress. Photographs of the missile sites in Cuba were first released in London. The Pentagon refused to confirm the fact that forty-two Soviet missiles had been removed from Cuba even though newsmen knew most of the details of the removal.

A newspaper editor from the Midwest, who attended a special State Department briefing a few days before the missile crisis reached its peak, recalls high-ranking government officials taking the podium to minimize the danger in Cuba and to point with great alarm to the situation in Berlin. The editor termed the briefing "a well rehearsed mockery." He asked: "What did the government hope to gain by staging this elaborate fraud? And what did Secretary of Defense McNamara hope to gain when he had his flackman Arthur Sylvester say, 'News is part of the weaponry of international diplomacy, and the results justify the methods we use.' What was to be gained by making such an arrogant statement? It is a wide-open announcement to the whole wide world that 'Of course we tell lies. Those are the rules of the game we're playing. And we'll do it again.' How can we trust any statement McNamara makes—or has his flackman make for him—ever again?"

What especially disturbed newsmen was their distinct impression that the Kennedy administration really believed that news management, as a principle, was good. It had been accepted for some time that government will manage the news in times of crisis, but the great concern under Kennedy was that news management in tranquil times was becoming the rule rather than the exception. When news unfavorable to the administration was discovered, the procedure was to cover up, then to fog up, and then to counter with some sort of denial. During the Cuban crisis, the Kennedy administration set the pattern for sophisticated and carefully planned control of all news relating to both military and political actions. By 1963, the pattern was being perpetuated throughout government with the assistance of five hundred full-time employees described as "Congressional Liaison Officers," whose sole duty was to pacify members and committees of Congress, to sell them the official administration line.

Kennedy pioneered a number of techniques for trying to win the allegiance of reporters. These techniques included, among others: frequent "backgrounder" news conferences in which sources of information were intentionally blurred; exclusive chats with the President for favorite newsmen; small, informal gatherings with Washington correspondents, usually in private homes; White House meetings for publishers of small daily and weekly newspapers; and increased authority for White House staffers to talk with reporters, though here again identification of source was usually prohibited. Kennedy worked diligently to make reporters feel that their critical reports might endanger their relationship with him and with his subordinates. The President's carrot-and-stick routine was explained by one White House correspondent: "Today one newsman is given an exclusive story, yesterday it was another, tomorrow there will be another, and so on. A warm feeling goes far and wide and is stimulated either by memory of favors past or hopes of favors to come. To be critical is to court exclusion." Kennedy gave every indication of believing that the Washington press corps ought to consider itself an adjunct of the federal government, a sort of Public Relations Bureau under the guidance of the executive branch.

There is no doubt that Kennedy was the most able shaper of public opinion in Presidential history. A Gallup poll published in the spring of 1963 showed that less than one fourth of the American people disapproved of the way Kennedy was performing as President. He was distinguished from other Presidents by the youth and wit and charm which he delighted in exploiting at every possible opportunity. A majority of the people simply chose to overlook his failures and to concentrate on his captivating personality, beautiful family, and graceful manner. Upon reading the 1963 Gallup findings, a newspaper publisher exclaimed: "I just can't understand it. We've exposed Kennedy. We've shown that he's been failing and lying to the American people. . . . And yet they're making a god of him."

NOTES TO CHAPTER 2

1. Quoted from *Secret Journals of the Acts and Proceedings of U.S. Congress,* Vol. 1, p. 34.

2. William Maclay, *Journal of William Maclay* (New York: D. Appleton & Co., 1890), p. 262.

3. *Ibid.*

4. J. D. Richards, *Messages of the Presidents,* p. 196.

5. Henry S. Randall, *Life of Thomas Jefferson* (New York: Derby & Jackson, 1858), Vol. 3, p. 211.

6. William L. Rivers, *The Opinionmakers* (Boston: Beacon Press, 1965), p. 131.

7. Margaret Leech, *In the Days of McKinley* (New York: Harper & Brothers, 1959), p. 177.

8. John Dos Passos, *Mr. Wilson's War* (Garden City, N.Y.: Doubleday & Company, 1962), p. 218.

9. *Ibid.,* p. 88.

10. Robert Murphy, *Diplomat Among Warriors* (Garden City, N.Y.: Doubleday & Company, 1964), p. 452.

11. John T. Flynn, "Other People's Money," *New Republic,* December 11, 1935, p. 12.

12. Merriman Smith, *Thank You, Mr. President* (New York: Harper & Brothers, 1946), pp. 63–64.

13. Zechariah Chafee, Jr., *Freedom of the Press in the United States* (Chicago: University of Chicago Press, 1947), p. 29.

14. Address to New York State Publishers Association, Albany, N.Y., January 19, 1948.

15. Resolution adopted by news media representatives. Released to the press by Office of the Secretary of Defense, March 29, 1948.

16. Cabell Phillips, *The Truman Presidency* (New York: The Macmillan Company, 1966), p. 152.

17. *New York Times,* November 16, 1947, Section 4, p. 4.

18. Quoted in remarks of United States Senator Homer Ferguson, "The Iron Curtain at Home," *Congressional Record,* August 7, 1948.

19. Harold D. Lasswell, *National Security and Individual Freedom* (New York: McGraw-Hill Book Company, 1950), p. 33.

20. *Ibid.,* p. 36.

21. Paul I. Wellman, *Stuart Symington* (Garden City, N.Y.: Doubleday & Company, 1960), p. 140.

22. As quoted in Rivers, *The Opinionmakers,* p. 144.

23. Joseph and Stewart Alsop, *The Reporter's Trade* (New York: Reynal & Company, 1958), p. 30.

24. Quoted in remarks of United States Representative Archer Nelsen, "The Dangers of Getting Used to Lies," *Congressional Record,* February 9, 1966.

25. Raymond Moley, *The Republican Opportunity* (New York: Duell, Sloan and Pearce, 1962), p. 86.

26. *Washington Post,* June 2, 1966, p. 5.

27. *Ibid.*

28. Address at International Press Institute, Paris, France, May 2, 1962.

29. In remarks on "Issues and Answers," ABC-TV, October 14, 1962.

CHAPTER 3

The President

Credibility Gap is located in the Great Society Mountain Range somewhere between Johnson City and Washington, D.C. . . . Thousands of newspapermen have not only seen the Credibility Gap and gone through it, but have come out of it badly battered, suffering from frostbite and shock. They bear witness to the fact that the Credibility Gap exists.
                                        —ART BUCHWALD

The host: The President of the United States.

The place: 1600 Pennsylvania Avenue, Washington, D.C.

The occasion: A high-level briefing for congressmen and senators.

As the members of Congress and their wives arrive, their coats are checked downstairs and they are ushered to a large room on the second floor. There, amidst the impressive trappings of the White House, drinks and hors d'oeuvres are served, and the guests, both Democrats and Republicans, mingle sociably.

Soon, the President enters the room. He claps his hands loudly and says, "Attention, ladies and gentlemen. We are going to ask the ladies to go with Lady Bird up to look at the rooms and the men will come with me." The guests obediently divide, the men following the President into an adjoining room where chairs have been arranged in neat rows. Everyone takes a seat.

Standing in front, the President opens with a word of welcome. He alludes to the "many difficulties" facing him and issues a plea for "cooperation." "Your President is mindful of the bipartisan assistance he has received in the past, but he is also mindful of who his friends are," he notes.

It is at these periodic briefing sessions that the multi-faceted, often paradoxical personality of Lyndon B. Johnson is at full bloom. The avowed purpose of the briefings is to enable congressmen and senators to directly question the President and members of his Cabinet on matters of national concern, to permit them "to be in on the takeoff as well as the landing." More often than not, however, the briefings serve as forums for the President's use in lecturing, admonishing, and misleading his captive audiences. It is at these briefings that the President challenges the credulity of those whose under-standing he seeks and vividly demonstrates his personal ambivalence.

The usual briefing format is for President Johnson and Vice President Humphrey, Secretary of State Rusk, Secretary of Defense McNamara, and perhaps one or two other high-ranking administration officials to be joined at the White House by from fifty to a hundred or more congressmen and senators. The briefings, which last about two hours, begin at 6 P.M. or 7 P.M. on Tuesdays, Wednesdays, or Thursdays, the days most members of Congress are available in Washington. The guests are sometimes photographed with the President. The proceedings are always tape-recorded.

Upon concluding his opening remarks, the President calls on a Cabinet official—Humphrey first, as a rule—and then seats himself in a front row chair where a Scotch and water has been placed. Humphrey comments about administration plans for three or four minutes and then invites questions. The first question no sooner leaves a congressman's lips than Johnson, not Humphrey, is on his feet to answer it. Striding back and forth across the room, his hands and arms waving in the air, his voice pitching high and low, the President razzle-dazzles his audience. His language leaves nothing to the imagination. His lips alternatingly drawn back in irritation and then melting into a smile, he rambles on. All at once he pulls up short, as if suddenly remembering the interrupted Cabinet officer who remains standing at the front of the room. Johnson returns to his seat and the questioning is resumed Another member of the Cabinet takes the floor and the process is repeated.

After attending a recent briefing at the White House, one senator went directly to his Capitol Hill office to record what took place "so that my grandchildren will know how it actually was." He dictated a lengthy memorandum which, in part, read: "The President opened the briefing with short remarks about his pleasure at having us there. Then the Vice President told of his trips about the country. During the remainder of the time, the Vice President supposedly chaired the meeting but with the almost continuous assistance and interruption of the President. The President was up and down like a yo-yo all evening long. He gave the impression of a man sitting on the lid of a volcano, and he kept erupting. He made at least three direct jabs at Senator Robert Kennedy's position (without using Kennedy's name) on negotiations with the Viet Cong. . . . White House aides circulated throughout the audience planting questions. I personally saw questions planted with a Senate colleague, with Congressman Jack Brooks of Texas, and with another congressman sitting two rows in front of me. The President closed the briefing by saying, 'And don't any of you ever say you have not been briefed.' Some briefing!"

If a Cabinet officer's answer to a question is not to his liking, Johnson may offer a rebuttal or indulge in undisguised sarcasm. He does not hesitate to ridicule his guests. He once told Senator Frank Church of Idaho, a critic of the Vietnam war: "Okay, Frank, next time you need a dam in Idaho, ask Walter Lippmann for one." In the next breath, he may appeal for "understanding" in the spirit of "Come, let us reason together." He may then turn on a staff aide to administer a blue-toned chewing out for all to hear.

With few exceptions, members of Congress leave the briefings feeling no better informed than when they came. "These meetings are just used for propagandizing us, for 'conning' us," a Democratic congressman explained. "We can't believe half of what we're told. The funniest thing about them is that they're secret, everything is supposed to be off the record. Actually, nothing worth repeating is said." Another congressman said he attended one briefing but would never attend another. "I was mad as hell when it was over," he recalled. "We just sat there to listen to a bunch of stuff that only made us more suspicious. There was no hard information given out at all." Congressman Peter H. B. Frelinghuysen remarked: "I found the meeting disappointing. Although virtually nothing was said which had not already been said publicly in considerably more detail, the President warned us not to divulge details of the discussion. If the purpose of these briefings is to inform Congress, why should a gag be imposed on what we may have learned? And how ignominious for these important Cabinet officials to have to terminate their remarks when an alarm bell rings. It was all too reminiscent of the old days in the classrooms, with a strict but well-meaning teacher firmly in charge."[1] Others agree that the White House briefings are of value chiefly to the President for aiding the development of a consensus or for selling a particular administration line.

To be sure, Johnson's approach to the Presidency is complicated by his preoccupation with self and by his dependence on secrecy. While it is accepted that government leaders by their nature incline to secrecy, and that this inclination is heightened by the ever-present danger of nuclear conflict, Johnson's application of secrecy stretches far beyond issues of the Cold War. He is the most intensely secretive President in history. His insistence on secrecy covers the biggest and the smallest matters. His predilection for "protecting options" deprives national goals of the support they require and seriously hinders the President's ability to serve as an effective molder of public opinion. And, importantly, Johnson's penchant for secrecy runs counter to the traditional American concept of openness in government.

Life columnist Hugh Sidey, author of a weekly feature on "The Presidency," describes Johnson as "a living, breathing contradiction of proportions rarely seen before. . . . His public life is a testimony to this singular ambivalence. Part of the problem no doubt stems from the fact that his techniques worked well in Texas politics and served him magnificently in the Senate. The White House is different."[2] The accuracy of Sidey's assessment is reflected in today's public impression of Johnson as cunning, petulant, insincere, and, most of all, unbelievable. He is seen as a "politician's politician," as one who will say what he had to say to gain an end. As a result of the image he projects, Johnson finds it very difficult to win the trust and confidence of others. His credibility is buried under a mountain of doubt.

In an attempt to explain what he termed the President's "studied impulsiveness" and "planned spontaneity," former White House press secretary Bill D. Moyers said: "It's very important for the President to keep the element of surprise as a tactical weapon in the arsenal of moving his government forward. If his moves are known in advance, if his options are identified prior to actual implementation, then his opponents . . . can move to choke off his options." Moyers failed to point out that by employing secrecy as a "tactical weapon," the President sometimes interferes with the orderly process of government. The President has become furious when information he believes should be secret has been reported by the news media. His anger over "premature" publication of information has led to investigations by the Federal Bureau of Investigation and to punitive measures being taken against government officials and newsmen.

Johnson became enraged in March of 1966 when the *Washington Post* reported that a decision had been made to appoint Deputy Under Secretary of State U. Alexis Johnson as ambassador to Japan. The same day the *Post* story was published, Johnson unexpectedly strode into a briefing being held in the White House by Secretary of Agriculture Orville Freeman. He took a seat and remained silent until Freeman finished speaking. Then he stood up and called attention to the *Post* story. He admonished the startled reporters to keep in mind that decisions on appointments are made by him and not by "some kid over at the State Department." He said no decision had been made about the post in Japan. This denial made headlines in the evening newspapers. Four months later, his anger at being scooped by the *Post* having subsided, Johnson announced his appointment of U. Alexis Johnson as ambassador to Japan. The decision had, of course, been made earlier. The delay in disclosing the appointment allowed Johnson to maintain the element of surprise and to preserve his options.

At a press conference on March 9, 1967, Johnson stated that there was "no truth" to press reports that he was looking for a successor to Henry Cabot Lodge as ambassador to South Vietnam. Five days later, Johnson announced his appointment of Ellsworth Bunker as Lodge's successor. White House press secretary George Christian explained that Johnson's statement of March 9 was absolutely accurate—the President had already picked Bunker to succeed Lodge and therefore he was not "looking" for a replacement.

In at least two cases, speculation in the press prompted Johnson to scrap plans to name highly competent men to federal office, thereby aggravating the already serious problem of attracting top-calibre people to government service. A member of the White House staff told a reporter that the quickest way to kill a particular candidate's chances for appointment to a sub-Cabinet job was to print the name of the candidate ahead of Johnson's formal announcement. (The newsman refrained from printing the name.) Stories sprang up in Washington that individuals being coaxed by Johnson to fill government posts were approaching reporters and begging them to print speculative stories, thereby causing the President to stop pursuing them.

This state of affairs led to the "Oshkosh Rule" which

Johnson spelled out himself in a discussion with newsmen in September, 1966: "When you see on the ticker that Oshkosh says that Bob Pierpoint [CBS News correspondent Robert Pierpoint] may be named Chairman of the Joint Chiefs of Staff you don't necessarily give much credence to it, because the very fact that it is on there is the best indication that it is not likely to happen." He continued: "I would say, generally speaking, you can count their [press] speculations as totally unreliable and uninformed. . . . The day will come when regularly employed speculators will find that their speculations are just pure speculation and nothing else, because we don't appoint men on that basis."[3] To Johnson, those who "speculate" are not serving the best interests of their country. Nevertheless, newsmen continue to anticipate Presidential actions and to report their early findings. However, the "Oshkosh Rule" has forced government officials to refrain from discussing pending appointments and programs before they are officially approved by the President.

The secrecy syndrome applies to foreign policy deliberations, legislative plans, political undertakings, and a wide variety of other subjects. Government employees speak to reporters at the risk of losing their jobs. A correspondent for a weekly news magazine related: "I telephoned a fellow I had once worked with who was involved in making a decision in the State Department. I asked him to fill me in on details of the decision-making process so I could better understand what was decided. I assured him I'd protect his anonymity in anything I wrote. He said, 'I can't tell you a thing. I'd like to, but policy has not finally been made on this.' Nothing I could say would change his mind. I think he was scared to death to even be talking to me." A White House correspondent explained: "Nowadays everybody is afraid to talk about how a decision was made. I ask long-time acquaintances in the government to tell me about events leading up to a major government policy and they respond by saying that there's no use in talking about 'what might have been.' After policy is declared, it's too late to inquire about it." The result of the embargo on information both before and after government decisions are made is that the public rarely finds out exactly what happened, much less why and how it happened. Johnson argues that public awareness of alternatives in advance will reduce his freedom of choice, bring about pressures in behalf of one approach or another, and prevent him from fashioning a consensus. Once a policy is decided upon, Johnson reasons, any discussion of alternatives is unnecessary, divisive, and "harmful to the national interest."

"What's amazing to newsmen is the secrecy of the President's objectives," said Philip Potter of the Baltimore *Sun,* one of the few correspondents in Johnson's good graces. "He learned this [secrecy] in Congress, where you have to protect yourself."[4] A former Senate aide pointed out that Johnson's acute sense of secrecy doubtless served him well as a Senate leader. "He 'kept book' on everybody and used the information he gathered to get certain things accomplished. Information was power and you didn't share the wealth. This was the only way to operate." But Johnson is no longer leader of a handful of senators; he is leader of the nation and of the free world. Yet, he labors to keep others in the dark until he is ready to turn on the lights.

In June of 1966, the imminent United States bombing of oil installations around the North Vietnamese cities of Hanoi and Haiphong was the worst-kept secret in Washington. Hints of the attack had been seeping out for months. Rather than confirming or denying word of the planned attack, Johnson talked in veiled terms such as citing the necessity "to raise the cost of aggression [in Vietnam] at its source." He exploded in anger when the press reported that the oil dumps were to be hit. He set the FBI on the trail of those responsible for "security leaks." As the FBI discovered, British Prime Minister Harold Wilson lent credence to rumors of the attack when he spoke in Parliament against United States extension of bombing in North Vietnam. The United States had been alerting friendly governments to the likelihood of escalated bombing for several days and Johnson himself had forewarned a number of congressional leaders, not all of whom supported the bombing decision. Johnson's anger reached a new height on June 24 when a story on the Dow Jones News Service reported: "The decision [has] been made. . . . The air attacks are expected to begin within the next several days." Under Secretary of State George W. Ball was sent on NBC's "Meet the Press" on June 26 to assure the world that no decision to bomb Hanoi and Haiphong had been made. When the oil dumps were bombed during the first week in July, another mark was chalked up against the President's credibility.

The blanket of secrecy has been thrown over relatively unimportant matters. After hearing numerous references to a gushy film biography of Johnson's life in Texas, Vera Glaser of the North American Newspaper Alliance telephoned the USIA for information about its contents and cost. She got nowhere. At a news conference on August 24, 1966, Mrs. Glaser put the question directly to Johnson:

MRS. GLASER: Has there been any instruction from the White House to keep this information under wraps and, if not, could you give us the cost and content of the film?

THE PRESIDENT: No, there's been no instruction. I do not have the information, although I'm sure that it's publicly available to the proper committees. I've seen a story on it. It's been published. If you get out the clip sheets I'll ask Mr. Moyers to try to help you.

MRS. GLASER: Can we ask the USIA to give us the information?

THE PRESIDENT: Well, I'll give it to you if we have it. I think it's been published. The USIA has made a number of films of that nature. And I first knew of this film when I read it in the front page of the papers. So if you'd just read your papers, I think you'd have the information.

Moyers said after the news conference that he had called the USIA and "tanned their hides" for refusing to disclose details of the film. He reported the film was entitled *The President's Country* and that it cost $89,000 to produce. Several days later, Mrs. Glaser contacted the USIA and scheduled a viewing of the film, but at the last minute the showing was canceled. She appealed to Howard Cernoff, assistant to USIA Director Leonard Marks, who barked: "That's the way it's going to be. Don't try to blackjack me. When the President tells me to release information, I'll release it."[5] The blackout remained in force.

Johnson's seemingly insatiable appetite for secrecy extends to his travel plans. He embarrassed Indiana Governor Roger Branigan, a fellow Democrat, when he went to Indiana to speak in the summer of 1966 without ever notifying the governor's office. Other Democratic Party leaders have been similarly insulted. The most grumbling has come, however, from the reporters assigned to cover the President's trips away from Washington. Newsmen are often given only a few minutes' notice that a trip is being made, thus preventing news coverage at airports and playing havoc with working schedules. Destinations sometimes are kept secret until after the press plane is in the air. "More than once I've taken off to cover the President without being able to tell my office or my family where I was going," one reporter complained. Johnson's unannounced departure for New York in March, 1966, to attend a funeral caused the wire services to distribute stories saying he was flying on a "mystery trip." After Luci Johnson Nugent's baby was born in 1967, reporters asked the First Lady if she and the President would soon visit their grandson. "I don't know," Mrs. Johnson replied. "I never know until he's airborne."

Johnson is secretive about weekends and vacations at his Texas ranch, though the "Pedernales Press Service" (weekend record: 42 press releases) continues to give uninterrupted service. At times the President bans reporters from the ranch and at other times invites them in for sumptuous barbecues, rambling tours, and fast boat rides. On election night in 1964, Johnson secretly left his headquarters in Texas to drive to a nearby civic center to make a victory statement. A newscaster reported over the limousine radio that he was en route.

Johnson fumed. His secrecy had been violated. Upon arriving at the civic center he noisily accused Malcolm Kilduff, assistant press secretary, of leaking his travel plans to the press. Kilduff was innocent. Newsmen at the Austin Civic Center had seen the President's special rostrum being installed and correctly concluded that he was coming to make a statement.

Johnson has allowed unnecessary secrecy to short-circuit his legislative program and to strain his association with congressional leaders. Only a few close aides knew he was going to propose in the 1966 State of the Union message that Congress pass a Constitutional amendment to increase the term of House members from two to four years. Even though many congressmen were in favor of the proposal, it died. No basis of support had been built for it on Capitol Hill. Johnson similarly erred in 1967 when he failed to notify congressional leaders that he was planning to ask for a 6 percent surtax on corporate and personal incomes. To insure the secrecy of this proposal, he assigned only one trusted assistant to draft the State of the Union speech. Then, at a press conference on December 31, 1966, he went out of his way to give the impression that he had decided against asking for a tax increase. He said: "I read in the papers in retrospect some people feel very strongly there should have been another tax increase. But in the light of developments of the economy at this moment, I do not think so." When a reporter asked if this meant the President would forego seeking a tax increase, a White House aide answered: "You may be reading his mind correctly, but I wouldn't bet on it." The secrecy in this instance extended to the chairman of the congressional tax-writing committees, the Ways and Means Committee in the House and the Finance Committee in the Senate. Congressman Wilbur Mills of Arkansas was notified of the proposal only three hours before it was made public, and Senator Russell Long of Louisiana was informed one hour in advance. The 1967 State of the Union message also contained an unexpected proposal that the Commerce and Labor Departments be combined into a single unit. Again, in the absence of congressional support, the plan never got off the ground.

The doctrine that the President has the power to withhold information successfully and to refuse inspection of records in the executive branch is considered to stem from precedents set early in United States history. The doctrine is based upon:

1. *The duties and powers of the President granted by the Constitution.* These include the duty to "take care that the laws be faithfully executed," the duties as Commander-in-Chief of the Army and Navy, and the power to make treaties. As the court said in 1803 in the landmark case of Marbury vs. Madison: "By the Constitution of the United States, the President is invested with certain important political powers, in the exercise of which he is to use his own discretion, and is accountable only to the country in his political character and to his own conscience . . . and whatever opinion may be entertained of the manner in which executive discretion may be used, still there exists, and can exist, no power to control that discretion."[6]

2. *The separation of governmental powers.* As amplified in 1880 in the case of Kilbourn vs. Thompson: "It is believed to be one of the chief merits of the American system of written constitutional law, that all the powers entrusted to government, whether state or national, are divided into the three grand departments, the executive, the legislative, and the judicial. . . . It is also essential to the successful working of this system that the persons entrusted with power in any one of these branches shall not be permitted to encroach upon the powers confided to the others."

3. *The absence of procedure for forcing the President to take a particular course of action.* The legislative and judicial branches recognize, for example, the extreme consequences of their trying to force a President to release information against his will. Even though all others say yield, there is no procedure for forcing the President to yield. There is no practical way to compel favorable action.

Since George Washington's day, requests for information have been denied by Presidents. But it has been only in recent years that secrecy in the executive branch has negatively affected public policy. Most of the conflict in this area has been between the President and Congress. This growing conflict was noted in a recent study by the Attorney General:

> An examination of the history of Congressional demands upon the Executive for confidential documents during the past six years discloses that more has been said in Congress and the press during this period than in the preceding 60 years. Not since the famous debate in 1886 in the first administration of President Cleveland has there been such extensive public discussion of this question.[7]

The major importance of the President's right to refuse official (congressional) requests for information is in the license it gives him to adopt across-the-board secrecy. The President has the power to withhold any information he wishes to withhold no matter how frivolous the reason. There is no appeal to higher authority. The fear of ultimately arousing a hostile public opinion is the only consideration which may cause the President to release information against his better judgment.

In addition to an unwarranted degree of secrecy, other restrictive practices followed by the Johnson administration include: (1) unresponsive treatment of questions put to officials; (2) refusal to discuss certain matters for illegitimate "security" reasons; (3) release of information only through a few administration spokesmen; and (4) publication of reports which are incomplete, tardy, distorted, politically motivated, or unnecessarily censored.

Less than two months after assuming the Presidency, Johnson instructed his press secretary, Pierre Salinger, to assemble the information directors of a dozen federal departments for a meeting in the White House. With the information officers gathered in the Fish Room, Johnson entered, and, flanked by a glum-looking Salinger, intoned: "Pierre here tells me what you guys do. Frankly, I don't think you do a goddamn thing."[8] He complained that during the preceding week the only story to receive significant treatment from the news media was the lighting of the President's Christmas tree. He laid down a law that each member of the group was to produce a "page one" story every day to describe the administration's accomplishments. He said that he had checked the budget and found that the government was spending a billion dollars on "people like you." In departing, he warned: "We are not going to be paying you on space rates, but we'll be judging you that way."

This incident marked the beginning of the end of Johnson's honeymoon with the press. In the eight weeks following John F. Kennedy's death, the new President had been treated generously and understandingly by the news media, not to mention lavishly. As a new year approached, however, his activities began to have less news value. The press was beginning to assume its customary role as adversary. Johnson became distressed over his diminishing press coverage. He blamed others. He felt he had gone out of his way to make friends with newsmen and believed they were now returning his kindnesses with venom.

True, after the assassination, Johnson had applied the buddy-buddy treatment to newsmen. He courted them with zeal. He drank with them on New Year's Eve, invited them into his office for friendly chats, entertained them at the LBJ ranch, promised them status and fame (in return for "cooperation"), took them skinny-dipping in the White House pool, and, in general, showered them with Johnson-sized affection. "He tried killing the press with what he regarded as kindness," said Paul Healy of the New York *Daily News*. "He has been very clever in his attempts to get reporters obligated to him," another correspondent observed.

The President's best efforts to influence the press were bound to fail because, in a very real sense, the President and the press are natural antagonists. Reporters know full well that the closer their relationships are with government officials, the greater the danger is of their being compromised. James Reston of the *New York Times* stayed away from the White House for twenty years because, as he explained: "It is hard to go into that House that means so much to us historically and not be impressed with it and the terrible burdens that the President has to carry. How could you help but be sympathetic? Once you become sympathetic it becomes increasingly difficult to employ the critical faculties."

When Johnson recognized in early 1964 that his relations with newsmen were deteriorating despite his most earnest wooing, he fell into a period of alternating love-hate cycles which lasted through the November election. One day he would shower the White House press corps with attention; the next day he would refuse to comment on any subject. He could not understand why his techniques of persuasion were not working on reporters. He failed to comprehend that he could not continue indefinitely to dispense occasional "inside" news items in exchange for favorable press coverage. "The President just can't understand how a reporter can write a critical story after he's been down on the ranch," a newspaperman noted. As Johnson was to learn, the fifty White House correspondents are a breed far different from the dozen "regulars" he had known in the Senate. His relations with the press were to become characterized by mutual distrust. The most significant aspect of the President's failure with the press was not the absence of a warm romance, but rather the disintegration of the favorable image of him which had been projected in the early post-Kennedy days.

Johnson began his Presidency with an ambivalent approach to formal press conferences. He welcomed them as forums for expressing himself, but he knew he lacked the personal magnetism of his predecessor and therefore was leery of their all-revealing nature. He appreciated the televized press conference as a means of reaching millions of Americans who never see a newspaper, but he doubted his ability to project favorably over the television screen. He also realized that full-fledged press conferences brought embarrassing questions.

Johnson's approach to press conferences was apparent two weeks after he became President. When twenty-five White House reporters went to press secretary Salinger's office for a routine briefing, they were suddenly whisked into the Oval Office of the President. Coffee was served. Johnson sat in a rocking chair. Everything was quite informal. Between sips of coffee, the reporters asked questions and the President answered them at length. Ten days later a similar "conference" was held—no advance notice was given, only a few correspondents attended. The pattern was set. Johnson preferred this informal conference because he could control it, adjourning it as quickly as he had convened it. There was no opportunity to install equipment for television coverage or to make use of broadcasting equipment already installed. It was a forum that Johnson could dominate.

The Washington press corps became highly agitated when it was clear that the formal press conference was falling into disuse. The formal conference permitted newsmen to ask searching questions and to study the President's appearance, his moods, his reactions. The press and the public had become accustomed to conferences announced a day or two in advance, attended by 200 to 400 newsmen, and equipped for radio and television coverage. Such conferences were recognized as excellent vehicles for explaining complicated government issues through question and answer exchanges. Commented the *Christian Science Monitor*'s Richard L. Strout: "His [Johnson's] ideal is a private audience with selected reporters where he can talk and they can listen, and nobody asks too many unexpected questions. It is a habit, an approach, an instinct that he cannot break. . . . News by osmosis may be successful for a while, but in time it produces, I believe, a credibility gap; the kind of gap which some think they see at present."[9]

Next, the President became enthusiastically experimental with his news conferences. He held them between bales of hay on his ranch, in the crowded White House theater and in the spacious East Room, in seven laps around the White House grounds (while trotting along and trying to take notes, one reporter ran into a post and split his head open), and in *Air Force One*. Once Johnson staged a conference at a picnic-like gathering to which reporters' wives and children were invited. "If you think that doesn't obligate you, you have another think coming," a radio broadcaster quipped. A syndicated columnist wrote that the President had "now held press conferences almost everywhere except in Lincoln's bed and underwater." The common thread among these conferences was that they enhanced Johnson's reputation as an unpredictable person who relished surprise.

The President's growing estrangement with the press was heightened by his efforts at intimidation. He once criticized a reporter for asking a "chicken-shit" question. To a team of magazine reporters, he said: "Someone ought to do an article on you and your damn profession, your First Amendment." When a Johnson critic, James Deakin of the St. Louis *Post-Dispatch,* took a place at a news conference behind Tom Johnson, an assistant White House press secretary, the President noted with sarcasm: "Mr. Johnson, you're standing in front of Mr. Deakin. We wouldn't want that." At an informal conference in 1964, Johnson made a few announcements and then teased reporters: "Don't run out of here if you have questions to ask. Ask them. I will answer them. This is not a quickie news conference. I don't know what you call a formal one. I guess I ought to wear a white tie. I came to work this morning and I didn't think it was formal. I just thought I was supposed to be here, and if you are all here, I will give you anything I know at any time."[10] Another injunction was: "If you want to know anything, just ask. Ask George Reedy, and if he doesn't know, ask Jack Valenti. If Jack doesn't know, ask Bill Moyers. If Bill doesn't know, then ask me." And: "Why don't you fellows do what the Baltimore *Sun* does? Now the *Sun* always checks out its stories."

Johnson is extremely sensitive about what is written about him. (Today, he is sensitive about being called sensitive.) Yet, the more he tries to "put them in their place," the more newsmen respond with suspicion and closer, more critical coverage. Johnson is the ultimate loser as a result of his confrontations with the press. He fails to heed his own advice: "When you crawl out on a limb, you always have to find another one to crawl back on."

Any discussion of the President's press relations would be incomplete without mention of his press secretaries. The turnover has been impressive. They have included:

Pierre Salinger—Served less than four months, November 22, 1963, to March 18, 1964. Resigned because he was unable to orchestrate the news to Johnson's satisfaction.

George Reedy—Served just under sixteen months, March 18, 1964, to July 9, 1965. Johnson never took Reedy into his confidence, thus preventing his serving as an effective conduit to the press.

Bill D. Moyers—Served slightly less than nineteen months, July 9, 1965, to February 1, 1967. Resigned because of downgrading by Johnson and disappointment over building bridges the President didn't care to use.

Robert H. Fleming—Announced by Johnson as successor to Moyers, but was never actually more than deputy press secretary, in which capacity he still serves.

George Christian—Incumbent whose service began February 1, 1967. Former press secretary to Governor John Connally of Texas.

Johnson's predecessors managed to get one good press secretary and keep him. Eisenhower, for example, was served by James Hagerty for eight consecutive years. Johnson's rotation of press secretaries is symptomatic of his press problems. He demands too much of them. A Johnson press secretary must be brave, self-effacing, serious, deceitful, sturdy, wise, obedient, tight-lipped, and lucky. Salinger was happy and outgoing, but not wise or tight-lipped. Reedy was imperturbable and hardworking, but he lacked bravery and luck. (Reedy will be remembered in Washington long after his time as the man who said of Johnson's relationship with Bobby Baker: "I'm going to be completely frank. . . . They hardly knew each other.") Moyers was a straight-shooting combination of Boy Scout and Baptist minister, but neither sufficiently deceitful nor adequately obedient. Fleming is untried and, therefore, must be rated as lucky. Christian is professional, devoutly loyal, and fully informed; he may be the best of the lot. "The common denominator among these men is that they've worked for a boss who is damn near impossible to satisfy, no matter how good a job is done," a White House reporter said. He cited as another "press-area unfortunate," White House photographer Yoichi Okamoto, who was discharged (but later rehired) by Johnson when he admitted to a newsman that he had taken 11,000 photos of the President in a two-month period.

Nowhere in the broad spectrum of government is Johnson's duplicity more apparent than in his handling of the federal budget. For four consecutive years (1964–1968), his budget presentations have served as tuning exercises in the legerdemain with which he has become so closely identified. Through deft manipulation of the budget, Johnson has painted a false picture of government economics. He has attempted to convince the people that the federal government is practicing maximum restraint in domestic spending in deference to the heavy demands of the war in Vietnam.

Until 1921, agencies of the federal government transmitted their spending proposals to the Treasury Department, where they were gathered together and sent to Congress. President Warren Harding observed that this procedure failed to take into consideration the need for associating spending with income and the need for a coordinated approach to government economics. Harding got Congress to pass the Budget and Accounting Act establishing the Bureau of the Budget under the President's office, and he appointed a Chicago banker, Charles G. Dawes, as the first director of the new bureau. Dawes closely examined agencies' requests for funds and freely lopped off items he considered to be unnecessary. On one occasion, he summoned high Navy officials to his office, where they stood open-mouthed and watched him sweep the carpet with two brooms. Dawes demanded to know why, since each broom did the job satisfactorily, the Navy was paying thirty-two cents more than the Army for its brooms.

The duty of the Budget Bureau Director today is to interpret for the President what the figures mean and what the choices are. This is one of the most demanding and difficult jobs in government. The finances of the federal government are so complex that one former Budget Bureau Director finds it necessary to return to Washington regularly for informal "short courses" which enable him to give sound advice as a private financial consultant. The Budget Bureau begins assembling data six months before the annual budget is presented to Congress (January) and a year before the beginning of the next fiscal year (July 1 to June 30).

When he assumed the presidency in November, 1963, Johnson knew next to nothing about the federal budget. It did not take him long to learn. Within twenty-four hours after President Kennedy's assassination, Budget Bureau Director Kermit Gordon had a one-page budget memo on Johnson's desk. It made two points: first, it outlined how the Bureau of the Budget operates, and second, it pointed out that there was still time to make the next budget a Johnson budget. It was Saturday; by Sunday at 6 P.M. the President and Gordon were meeting to discuss a document which, Johnson knew, touched the lives of more people than ever before in history. For the next month, the budget was Johnson's main preoccupation. Applying all his political antennae, he mastered the complexities of federal finances virtually overnight.

At his first press conference as President, on December 7, 1963, Johnson was asked about anticipated federal spending for fiscal 1965. He observed that Kennedy's last budget had been $98.8 billion and that $3.5 billion would have to be added to cover built-in increases in spending. Newsmen came away with the distinct impresion that the budget would be between $102 and $103 billion. But the prospectus had changed by December 18 when Johnson told a news conference: "I am working from a budget of $98.8 billion this year. It appears that we will expend about that amount, and maybe a little under or a little over, but substantially $99 billion will be the expenditure this year. That was the amount of Mr. Kennedy's budget." Johnson noted, however, that the United States population had increased. "When we have an increase in population, we are going to have an increase in the budget," he explained. So the budget figure still seemed to hover around the $102-103 billion mark. Then, in the State of the Union message on January 21, 1964, Johnson disclosed: "My proposals call for administrative budget expenditures in 1965 of $97.9 billion—$900 million less than requested in the 1964 budget. . . . This marks an important step toward a balanced budget."

Important to Johnson was what looked like his success in maintaining—indeed, reducing—the level of federal spending. As finally submitted, the budget was $97.7 billion, just under the mythical $100 billion limit. The President had declared the brook was too broad for leaping and then had leaped it. To newsmen, who had been fooled into reporting the budget would exceed $100 billion, Johnson was no saint. The year 1965 showed an eventual deficit of $3.4 billion, far from the "balanced budget" promised by Johnson in the State of the Union message.

In unveiling his budget, Johnson had his eye firmly on the 1964 election only ten months off. He sought to build an appeal to the South as an economizer and to the North as a compassionate spender. His budget reflected a reduction in defense spending in favor of accelerated domestic spending. While this shift in spending emphasis failed to square with developing events in Vietnam, it did enable Johnson to campaign against Senator Barry Goldwater as the man of peace and the champion of the underprivileged. Johnson had an ace up his sleeve to cover Vietnam: supplemental financing. He knew Congress could not turn him down if he later sought additional funds for conducting the war.

When budget time came around in 1965, Johnson was back

at the same stand. He instructed a White House aide to tell reporters that "in the normal course of things" the budget for fiscal 1966 would be between $104 and $106 billion. Newsmen were reluctant to believe it. On January 4, 1965, the President told Congress: "We will continue along the path toward a balanced budget in a balanced economy." The implication that the budget had been balanced and that it would "continue" in balance was misleading. The eventual deficit for 1966 was $2.3 billion.

The President's sleight-of-hand in budget-making is abetted by the existence of three separate budgets, each for a different purpose and each showing different figures. That is one reason why the budget can be easily manipulated. The three budgets are:

The Administrative Budget—Best known and most widely quoted, this budget covers the general activities of the government. Its receipts represent expected cash inflow and its expenditures are keyed to programs approved by Congress. But large items such as trust funds (Social Security Funds, Highway Trust Fund, and Unemployment Trust Fund, among others) are not included in this budget.

The Cash Budget—Includes practically all items, including trust funds. It excludes borrowing between the government and the public. The deficit shown in this budget is usually smaller than in the other two budgets.

The National Income Accounts Budget—Little known to the public, this budget is considered to be the most precise indicator of federal fiscal activities. It covers all transactions except loans, mortgages, and purchase and sale of existing assets. It adds up all debts as they are incurred.

Johnson is not the first President to juggle the three budgets in order to achieve political goals, but he has done it more openly and on a grander scale. In the middle of the 1966 State of the Union address, he switched from one budget to another, alternately citing the budget which showed the least spending, or the most income, or the smallest deficit. The three budgets also allow Johnson to "save" money by shifting expenditures from one account to another. He moved $110 million from the 1967 administrative budget and placed it in the highway trust fund in order to convince the public he had reduced spending. His budget showmanship was again apparent when he forecast that appropriations for disaster relief in 1967 could be reduced by $115 million. The President surely has great powers, but it is extremely doubtful that he is able to exert control over the number of disasters caused by the forces of nature. Remarked Joseph D. Ardleigh, executive vice president of the Research Institute of America: "The budget counts on savings that won't be made and receipts that won't be gotten."[11]

In presenting the budget for fiscal 1967, Johnson estimated that the deficit would be $1.8 billion. Senator John J. Williams of Delaware, ranking minority member of the Senate Finance Committee, put the deficit at $9.2 billion. Senator Everett M. Dirksen of Illinois, an old friend of Johnson's, also felt compelled to challenge the President's estimate. "He talks about a $1.8 billion deficit," Dirksen said, "but that's completely phony. The deficit is likely to be somewhere between $5 billion and $6 billion." The minority senators were closer to the truth than the President. The official deficit was $9.9 billion. The budget chicanery continues today.

The overall damage done by Johnson's budget juggling is unknown. It is known, however, that businesses and industries take their cues from the annual budget. Economists rely on it for projecting economic plans. Foreign countries judge the United States' ability to meet its commitments around the world on the basis of budgeted funds. There is ample evidence that the country is wearying of playing peekaboo with the budget each year. After attempting to analyze Johnson's statements about the 1968 budget, the *Washington Post* told its readers: "If the foregoing exercise in conjecture appears bizarre . . . remember that strange things happen to shrewd men during the annual budget circus." Columnist David Lawrence wrote: "It's bad enough to run deficits of $8 billion or $9 billion . . . but when there are 'gimmicks' used that hide the true nature of the red figure, confidence in the dollar is bound to be affected."

By relying on murky maneuverings rather than on clear, straightforward explanations, the President is contributing to the federal government's credibility problem. As Douglas Kiker of NBC News has charged, the President too often "mixes truth, half-truth and non-truth and dares you to isolate them." The public has taken cognizance of this; the people no longer accept at face value what the President says. Following the President's State of the Union address in 1967, James Reston noted: "This city [Washington, D.C.] is constantly looking for the other motive. . . . There is reason for this. It is a very serious problem. It is the President's most serious problem." Reston was intimating that secrecy, deceit, and manipulation of fact work against the interests of the President, as well as against the interests of the country. James Deakin concluded: "As the President knows from the fate that has befallen other public servants, any politician so clever as to meet himself coming around the corner always finds someone waiting there to remind him where he has been."[12]

Until such time as Lyndon Johnson recognizes that being President of the United States demands honesty, candor, and a certain amount of grace, his hopes for America will be unfulfilled. The President's credibility can be restored only by the President himself.

NOTES TO CHAPTER 3

1. From Frelinghuysen's "Washington Letter" to his constituents, August 19, 1965.

2. Hugh Sidey, "The President," *Life,* June 24, 1966.

3. Remarks at impromptu press conference following Cabinet meeting of September 22, 1966.

4. Remarks on "The Great Society: LBJ's Own Brand," WETA-TV (Washington, D.C.), June 6, 1966.

5. Annual Report of the Advancement of Freedom of Information Committee, Sigma Delta Chi, 1966, p. 9.

6. As cited in Harold L. Cross, *The People's Right to Know* (New York: Columbia University Press, 1953), p. 203.

7. As quoted in *The Power of the President to Withhold Information from the Congress,* Memorandums [sic] of the Attorney-General, compiled by the Subcommittee on Constitutional Rights of the Senate Committee on the Judiciary, 85th Congress, Second Session, February 6, 1958, p. 90.

8. Jim Faber, "How News Gets Managed," *Seattle Magazine,* January, 1967, p. 37.

9. From George Polk Memorial Lecture delivered at the 18th annual Awards Luncheon of Long Island University, March 29, 1966.

10. As quoted in James E. Pollard, *The Presidents and the Press* (Washington, D.C.: Public Affairs Press, 1964), p. 115.

11. "Reading the Budget for Fun and Profit," *Time,* February 18, 1966, p. 36.

12. James Deakin, "I've Got a Secret: President Johnson and the Press," *New Republic,* January 30, 1965, p. 13.

CHAPTER 4

The Postmaster's Secrets

Where the access to facts about government is open and unobstructed . . . misrepresentation is perilous. . . . But when there are no independent means of verifying official accounts of public transactions, an invaluable check is removed. . . . Government then can manage the news to its taste. It will speak with one voice and, however that voice may err, there will be none to say it nay.

—J. RUSSELL WIGGINS

Nick Kotz wheeled half-circle in his swivel chair and reached for the telephone ringing on the desk. He punched a button marked "Intercom" and picked up the receiver.

"Nick, this is Wilson. The Vice President is holding a news conference tomorrow in the Capitol to talk about the administration's 'Youth Opportunity Campaign.' I think we should cover this."

"I'll be there," the young newspaperman promised.

It was Thursday, May 27, 1965.

What Nick Kotz did not know was that the seemingly routine assignment he had just accepted from Richard L. Wilson, Washington bureau chief of Cowles Publications, was to trigger events that would dominate his life for the next eight months.

He was about to become a leading protagonist in a drama that was to include the President and the Vice President of the United States, the United States Congress, the Postmaster General, scores of federal officials, and thousands of high school and college students. He was on the brink of uncovering one of the most blatant and far-reaching cases of government secrecy in recent years.

Nathan K. (Nick) Kotz is perhaps typical of the emerging new breed of news correspondent in Washington, D.C. A sturdy six-footer with straight brown hair, he is self-effacing and industrious. Born in 1932, less than a month before Franklin D. Roosevelt was first elected President, he is a Phi Betta Kappa and magna cum laude graduate of Dartmouth College. After serving two years in the United States Marine Corps, he joined the staff of the Des Moines *Register,* which, along with the Minneapolis *Star* and *Tribune* and *Look* and *Harper's* magazines, is a property of Cowles Publications. In June, 1964, Kotz was transferred to the Cowles Washington bureau, where he became the fifth man on a staff which included two Pulitzer Prize winners, a nationally syndicated columnist, and a prominent White House correspondent.

At 3:30 P.M. on Friday, May 28, Nick Kotz entered the white-domed Capitol and proceeded to the second floor office of Vice President Hubert H. Humphrey. Twenty reporters were already gathered in the Vice President's ornately furnished reception room.

Friday afternoon is not the best time to hold a news conference in Washington. It is the practice of both the House and the Senate to cut short Friday afternoon sessions so that congressmen and senators can depart as early as possible for weekend forays into their home states. Over the years, this abbreviated Friday schedule has been accepted by virtually everyone in Washington, including the news media.

But Kotz and his colleagues were on hand this particular Friday afternoon because they realized government officials were worried that the approaching "long, hot summer" spelled trouble if more job opportunities could not be found for youths from low-income families. If serious disorders in slum areas were to be prevented, the federal government had to act fast. Jobs could be the answer.

Vice President Humphrey opened the news conference by

reiterating what President Johnson had announced five days earlier: the federal government was sponsoring a "Youth Opportunity Campaign" aimed at finding 500,000 summer jobs for high school and college-age youths. Humphrey, who had been placed in charge of the campaign by the President, hinted that the President's original announcement had failed to receive the "desired" media treatment, and that he therefore hoped this second announcement would be given prime attention in news columns and broadcasts on Sunday, May 30.

In order to get the summer job campaign off the ground, Humphrey explained, the federal government was immediately making available 25,000 government jobs for "boys and girls through twenty-one who need them the most because of economic and educational disadvantages." Special "Youth Opportunity" registers were being established in State Employment Service offices and youths needing jobs could apply by merely going to the offices nearest their homes. Private businesses and industries were being asked to provide 475,000 additional jobs.

When the news conference ended, Kotz caught a taxi back to the National Press Building and, at his desk in Suite 852, wrote a story reflecting the importance and urgency of the "Youth Opportunity Campaign." The story was printed on the front pages of Cowles' Sunday morning editions.

Three days later, on Wednesday, June 2, Kotz kept a luncheon date at The Assembly restaurant with a United States senator and one of the senator's aides. As coffee was being served, Kotz remembered the "Youth Opportunity Campaign" and asked the senator what he thought about it. The senator turned to his assistant and asked: "Is that the program that Mike Manatos called us about and offered us some jobs?"

The assistant shrugged. He said he wasn't sure. He looked a little ill at ease.

That's strange, Kotz thought. Mike N. Manatos is the Presidential aide whose duties include congressional patronage. Certainly Manatos wasn't "offering" jobs to a United

States senator under the "Youth Opportunity Campaign." Or was he?

Kotz posed several follow-up questions. The answers made it clear that the programs were the same. The White House and patronage were involved in the campaign to assist needy youths. Was the "Youth Opportunity Campaign" being subverted into a program for dispensing patronage jobs? The thirty-five-year-old newsman knew he was onto something.

Kotz slept on the story Wednesday night. When he arrived at the office the morning of Thursday, June 3, he had reached two conclusions. First, if the government announces a program with noble motives to meet a national problem, and that program is turned into a patronage scheme at the expense of the original goal, it is clearly wrong. Second, the question warranted further investigation.

Kotz knew at least one senator had been offered a quota of jobs under the "Youth Opportunity Campaign." Had other members of Congress been similarly approached? He had to find out.

At 2 P.M., he began telephoning congressmen and senators from Iowa and Minnesota, the major circulation areas of Cowles' Des Moines and Minneapolis papers. In the course of the next hour, he learned that White House aide Manatos and two high-level officials in the Post Office Department had been contacting Democratic members of Congress to advise them of the number of post office jobs "assigned" to them. No Republicans called by Kotz had been contacted by administration officials.

At 3:10 P.M., Kotz telephoned the office of Postmaster General John Gronouski.* He was referred to Ira Kapenstein, a special assistant to Gronouski. Kapenstein acknowledged that Michael Monroney, post office congressional liaison officer, and Frederick Belen, deputy postmaster general, had been contacting congressmen and senators "who previously told us they were looking for jobs." Only four Republicans had been

* Gronouski is currently serving as United States Ambassador to Poland.

contacted—two congressmen and two senators. (Three of the four were ranking minority members of the House and Senate Post Office and Civil Service Committees, and the fourth more often than not voted for administration programs.)

At 4 P.M., barely thirty minutes after he had finished talking with Kapenstein, Kotz began receiving return calls from Iowa and Minnesota Republicans he had talked to previously. They reported that within the last half hour they had been called by regional post office directors in their home areas and invited to submit the names of youths wanting summer employment. No mention whatsoever had been made of "quotas" or "economic need."

The fact of the matter was obvious: a patronage program was under full steam. It was also apparent that the Post Office Department was hurriedly trying to cover its tracks by making fast calls to Republicans whom Kotz was most likely to contact.

A page-one headline in the June 4, 1965, editions of the Des Moines *Register* and the Minneapolis *Tribune* read: YOUTHS GET U.S. JOBS ON PATRONAGE BASIS. Under the Kotz byline, *Register* and *Tribune* readers learned that the federal government's "Youth Opportunity Campaign" was being used by the Post Office Department to distribute summer jobs to politicians.

Congressman Albert H. Quie of Minnesota's First Congressional District paid close attention to the *Tribune* story. He was aware of the administration's campaign to locate jobs for needy youths and he supported it. But his curiosity had been aroused when he received a phone call from Kotz alerting him to the questionable hiring practices in the Post Office Department. Then the regional postal director in Minneapolis called to invite him to submit the names of job seekers. Now came the revelation in the *Tribune*.

Ruggedly handsome and athletic in appearance, Congressman Quie was a dairy farmer and a state senator before his election to Congress in 1958 at the age of thirty-four. His Norwegian ancestry and imposing six-foot-two, 205-pound frame provide the physical stamina demanded of him as one of the House's hardest working members. Now the second ranking Republican on the House Education and Labor Committee, he played important roles in such landmark legislative successes as the Manpower Development and Training Act (1962), the Higher Education Academic Facilities Act (1963), and the Economic Opportunity Act (1964). He has led his party's efforts to improve the administration's "War on Poverty" by accentuating preschool training and vocational education.

On Saturday, June 5, the *Register* and the *Tribune* carried Nick Kotz' second story about post office hiring. It pointed out that distribution of jobs as patronage was in direct violation of a Presidential directive which said the jobs should go to disadvantaged youths.

Quie read the *Tribune* story and went into action. He personally contacted as many of his fellow legislators as possible to determine the scope of the Post Office Department's activities, and, on June 10, fired off a 300-word telegram to Postmaster General Gronouski. He demanded to know:

—Why post office officials were ignoring the President's order that summer jobs be given to economically and educationally deprived youths?

—Why post office officials restricted their job quota calls to Democrats, contacting Republicans days later and only after a newspaperman began asking questions?

—Why post office jobs were not being filled through State Employment Service offices?

The answers came from a Gronouski assistant, Monroney, who reported the Postmaster General was out of town. Monroney pretended no partisan favoritism existed. He dismissed the President's "need" directive by stating: "The Postal Service is primarily interested in obtaining the highest qualified young people available." He said the authority for selecting summer employees had been placed in the hands of regional postal directors because local postmasters were too "susceptible to political influence." His response was evasive and contradictory.

Monroney's most damaging comment was made in a letter to a senator who had complained of not being notified of the availability of post office jobs. Monroney remarked: "You know, Senator, it is ironic that, *when the Department attempts to assist Members of the House and Senate,* we end up being criticized." There, in one sentence, Monroney got to the truth: the Post Office Department's real aim was to win friends in Congress through patronage rather than to assist underprivileged youths.

Meanwhile, Nick Kotz was building the case through continuing stories in the *Register* and *Tribune.* A dispatch of June 12 reported Quie's exchange of letters with Monroney. Another story on June 16, based on an interview with Vice President Humphrey, quoted Humphrey as saying the Post Office Department was using "bad judgment" in its hiring practices and that the summer job program was not intended "as a way to take care of the family."

It was mid-June and the fat was in the fire. The Post Office Department was coming under attack from members of Congress from both sides of the aisle, reporters, and concerned citizens. In an effort to learn how and where post office jobs had been distributed in Minnesota, Quie wrote to the Minneapolis regional postal director, Adrian P. Winkel. He asked for full details, including the names, addresses, and political sponsors of summer employees. Winkel refused to divulge the identities of employees, but he did send statistics which showed that about two-thirds of the youths referred by members of Congress and only one out of fifteen recommended by State Employment Service offices had been hired. Kotz reported this news on July 16 and, at this point, events began to develop rapidly.

On July 20, the White House and the United States Civil Service Commission ordered an end to the use of political patronage in summer hiring.

On July 21, a story by Kotz presented State Employment

Service rebuttal to the Post Office Department's tale that the Service had been bypassed because it was "too slow" in producing job candidates.

On July 23, Quie sent a telegram to John W. Macy, Jr., chairman of the Civil Service Commission, asking for a national investigation. (Similar requests were made by Congressman H. R. Gross of Iowa and Senator Milward Simpson of Wyoming, both Republicans.)

On July 26, Kotz revealed in a news story and Quie disclosed in a House speech that hiring on a patronage basis was continuing despite the prohibition of July 20. In addition, Quie pointed out that 50 of the 140 Republicians in the House never had been contacted by the Post Office Department even though the department was claiming it had contacted every member of Congress.

The Post Office Department's attempt to bolster the sagging amount of patronage available to politicians, particularly Democrats, had become a national issue. The press wire services were carrying the story to every state in the nation. Scores of relatives of Democratic politicians were discovered in postal patronage jobs. Members of Congress were demanding congressional inquiries. Local postmasters and newsmen were being drawn into bitter arguments. Vice President Humphrey was personally stung when Kotz revealed Humphrey's nephew was working in the Huron, South Dakota, post office.

Industrious reporting uncovered the fact that post office jobs had been handed to the sons of six congressmen and one senator: Congressman Charles C. Diggs, Jr., Democrat of Michigan; Senator Hiram Fong, Republican of Hawaii (Fong is a millionaire); Congressman Richard Fulton, Democrat of Tennessee; Congressman Henry Gonzalez, Democrat of Texas; Congressman Clarence D. Long, Democrat of Maryland; Congressman L. Mendel Rivers, Democrat of South Carolina; and Congressman Stanley R. Tupper, Republican of Maine.

But the most devastating aspect of the patronage hiring

was the impact it had within the postal service itself. A father protested that his son had been pushed to bankruptcy after losing his postal job because of an alleged "lack of funds" in a Massachusetts post office. Several women in Wisconsin lost their jobs because the postmaster had to make room for political appointees. A State Employment Service officer in Vermont was fired for speaking out against nepotism. The morale of postal employees dropped dramatically as more incidents were reported.

Now, with the scandal full blown, the controversy centered on one basic issue: secrecy in government. Did the public have a right to know the identities of employees hired by the Post Office Department?

The position of the Post Office was spelled out on August 6 in a sharply worded letter to Quie from Assistant Postmaster General Richard J. Murphy, who said:

> For many years the Post Office Department has had a regulation providing that lists of employees, including their designations, salaries or addresses, shall not be furnished to any individual, commercial firm, or other non-Federal organization. . . .
> This regulation serves to protect Postal employees from harassment or invasion of their privacy. . . . I do not feel I can release a list of names as you requested.

The regulation (744.444, United States Postal Manual) cited by Murphy had been a source of conflict since 1959 when it was adopted under the Eisenhower administration. Its original use was to prevent commercial firms from acquiring lists of post office employees for solicitation purposes, but it had often been used as a cover-up by fearful bureaucrats. The Post Office Department chose to rely on the regulation while ignoring the instruction in its final sentence: "Refer doubtful cases to the Regional Director for decision." Regional directors were not being permitted to decide this issue; the shots were being called by the Postmaster General in Washington. The Post Office Department was hiding behind a regulation of secrecy conceived by its own legal staff. It had no foundation in law or moral principle.

Dissatisfied with Murphy's distortions, Quie wrote back to him:

> . . . As a Member of Congress of the United States, I am surprised that I am considered in this case "an individual, commercial firm, or non-Federal organization." I note that Regulation 744.444 also states that "A single name or a list of names may be furnished on the written request of another Federal agency, when properly justified and its preparation would not involve excessive expense."
>
> I believe that the interest of Members of Congress in regard to the operation of certain programs of the Federal Government is certainly a "proper justification" and is, in fact, essential if we are to function effectively as the elected Representatives of the people.
>
> Certainly, I am not to construe from your letter that you believe I intend the harassment or invasion of the privacy of Post Office employees? I assure you, I am not.
>
> . . . I respectfully request that you immediately provide me with a list of the names of those young people placed in summer post office jobs under the President's Youth Opportunity Campaign.

Six days later, on August 16, Murphy responded. He again rejected Quie's request, saying:

> In answer to the specific points raised in your letter regarding the regulation:
>
> (1) Although you are a Member of Congress, you are certainly an "individual";
>
> (2) Under no interpretation could you be considered to be "another Federal agency";
>
> (3) The preparation of a list of approximately 8,500 names would, indeed, "involve an excessive expense";
>
> (4) While I have no doubt that you do not intend the harassment or invasion of privacy of post office employees, I call to your attention that recently in your area certain newspaper stories concerning the summer employment program have resulted in a number of our summer employees

having their names printed in newspapers as though they were guilty of some serious offense rather than performing a job for the government in a creditable fashion;

(5) If I were to accede to your request and grant you a list of employees, summer or otherwise, there would be no grounds on which to refuse similar requests from others, some of whom may not have the same motives as yourself, and who may wish to make use of such lists for political or other purposes.

Quie was thus denied access to the information on the grounds that: he was an "individual"; he was not "another Federal agency"; compilation of the names would cause "excessive expense"; newspapers had published the names of some summer employees; and release of the data in this instance would prevent denials in future cases. Absurd though these reasons were, it was obvious that the Post Office Department intended to stand on them. More pressure was needed.

Upon arriving at his office in the Longworth House Office Building on Tuesday, August 17, Quie was greeted by another Kotz exclusive. Headlined VOW TO HALT PATRONAGE IN POSTAL WORK, the story reported a joint statement issued the day before by Postmaster General Gronouski and Civil Service Commission chairman Macy. The statement attributed the patronage scandal to a "misunderstanding" and pledged the situation would not recur. Carefully written in generalities, it never mentioned the word "patronage" and revealed no names of employees.

Turning to the morning's mail, Quie found a copy of the joint statement and a covering note from Macy. The note said:

The Civil Service Commission made a review of summer employment in the Post Office Department in cooperation with the Post Office Department. Attached is a statement reflecting the findings made in this review.

The Department and the Civil Service Commission have agreed to conduct a thorough study of summer employment procedures in the Department to be completed in time for use in the summer of 1966. The purpose of this study, as indicated in the statement, is to establish a program for future summer employment which will meet the operating needs of the Department on a full merit basis.

Quie had served in government long enough to recognize a whitewash when he saw one. He immediately dictated a letter to Congressman John E. Moss of California, chairman of the House Subcommittee on Government Information, sending him copies of his correspondence with Murphy and Macy and a copy of the Gronouski-Macy statement. He expressed the strong hope that these documents would assist Moss in investigating the matter.

Also in Quie's August 17 mail delivery was a letter from Monroney on another matter. Monroney had scrawled a postscript which said: "Now that summer is drawing to a close, I must admit you've made it interesting!" Quie was determined to make the fall months equally interesting.

When Speaker John McCormack called the House to order that afternoon, Quie was in the chamber. He stood and addressed the House: "I have asked of the Post Office Department a list of the names of people hired under the so-called Youth Opportunity Campaign. I have received the evasion of blatant bureaucratic secrecy. . . . I cannot see how congressmen can carry out their duties as the elected representatives of the people if they are to be denied the most harmless information. Therefore, Mr. Speaker, I intend to introduce a House resolution requiring the United States Post Office Department to provide in full the names of its employees to Members of Congress upon written request."

Quie had hit upon a means of forcing disclosure of the names through a rarely used, privileged resolution. The resolution would have to be reported to the House from committee within seven days. It would force a vote of the full House, thereby putting each congressman on public record for or against secrecy in the Post Office Department.

Quie ordered his staff to prepare the resolution.

On Wednesday, August 25, Gronouski rejected an appeal for release of the names made by the Subcommittee on Government Information. In a letter to chairman Moss, Gronouski repeated the excuses employed by his aide, Murphy. But there was a new ingredient added. Gronouski said he would release the names to the congressional committees "having jurisdiction over the post office" if either of the committees requested them. Congressman Tom Murray of Tennessee and Senator A. S. Mike Monroney of Oklahoma,* chairmen of the House and Senate Post Office and Civil Service Committees respectively, were contacted and asked to help.

While Quie wrestled with the case in the House, Kotz provided day-to-day coverage of events. He also stirred greater interest in the matter in the Senate and assisted other reporters in their investigative efforts. More and more anonymous tips were being received; more and more high-ranking Democrats were being embarrassed.

On Monday, August 30, Quie brought the issue to the attention of the President. In a letter to President Johnson asking him to direct Gronouski to release the names, Quie said: "If we are to establish by precedent that the people have no right to know who sorts their mail, there is no basis on which to contend that the people have a right to know who makes major policy decisions that affect their day-to-day lives. If this is the case, it appears to me that representative government is dead."

On Thursday, September 2, Quie appealed to Lawrence F. O'Brien, whom Johnson had appointed to succeed Gronouski as Postmaster General. Quie reminded O'Brien of his testimony of September 1 before the Senate Post Office and Civil Service Committee:

> SENATOR SIMPSON: Do you feel that Members of Congress, in the performance of their duties, are entitled to know who works for the Post Office Department, and will you supply such information to them when they request it?

* Senator Monroney is the father of Michael Monroney, the post office assistant who had called Democratic congressmen to offer them jobs.

MR. O'BRIEN: I can see no reason why the employees of the Post Office Department should not be in the public domain.

On the basis of this testimony, Quie was hopeful Gronouski would, as one of his last official acts, change his position and release the names. The optimism was premature.

In a letter of September 3, Gronouski told Quie he was responding in behalf of the President. He again denied the existence of patronage in post office hiring and refused to reveal any employees' names. A letter received the same day from Macy also glossed over the entire affair, noting that a hiring program would be used "next year which should avoid any misunderstanding."

Quie saw no alternative other than to force the issue in the House. He dropped his resolution into the hopper on Wednesday, September 8. It called on the Postmaster General to provide the requested information.

On Monday, September 13, the first crack in the solid wall of secrecy came when Gronouski unexpectedly announced he was permitting local postmasters to release the names. But Quie quickly pointed out the uselessness of this gesture. It would be an impossible task to individually query 34,000 local postmasters. Quie said: "Gronouski is admitting we are right in asking for public disclosure of the names of public employees and yet is making it virtually impossible for one to examine the department's handling of the 'Youth Opportunity Campaign.'"

Kotz contacted the Postmaster General's office and asked why the names could not be released by the fifteen regional post office directors since, by the department's own statements, the regional directors had actually been in charge of the summer hiring program. A spokesman for Gronouski answered that the regional directors kept no records of summer employees. (This answer later proved to be false.)

The Congress of the United States has been described as "the world's greatest deliberative body." For a bill to become law, it must pass the inspection of a subcommittee, then a committee, and finally the full House and Senate. This procedure often takes months and even years. The process is painstakingly slow because experience has shown that hasty legislation is almost certainly bad legislation.

Careful study and deliberation were noticeably absent in the United States House of Representatives on Thursday, September 16, 1965. On that day, the Democratic majority on the House Post Office and Civil Service Committee silently rushed the Quie resolution through a subcommittee and through the full committee, each time recommending that it be rejected by the House. The Democrats carefully rigged notice of the committee meetings so that Republicans were unable to attend. Employing every legislative stratagem at its disposal, the House Democratic leadership set out to kill the resolution once and for all.

The issue in the floor debate on September 16 was secrecy in government. Quie, with the assistance of Republicans Gross of Iowa, Thomas B. Curtis of Missouri, and Paul Findley of Illinois, took on an opposition which outnumbered them two-to-one. Congressman James H. Morrison of Louisiana, second-ranking Democrat on the Post Office and Civil Service Committee, led the argument for the majority. By calling up the resolution for debate himself, Morrison was able to effectively control it. He permitted Quie only eight minutes to speak.

In the end, the most telling remarks were made by Congressman Moss, whose Government Information Subcommittee had been "cooperative" in trying to pry loose the postal employees' names. On the House floor that day, Moss spoke out strongly against the Quie resolution. He said he favored free access to government information, but felt that the resolution was not the "appropriate procedure" for securing the names. He offered no better procedure. Moss carried the day for the administration, but only after three Democrats were convinced to switch their votes. In so doing, Moss tarnished his reputation as the leading advocate in the House of the public's right-to-know.

The final vote was 186–180 against the resolution. Sixty-four Democrats had joined 116 Republicans in voting for an end to secrecy in the Post Office Department. A battle was lost, but the war was far from over.

Kotz and Quie persisted. They concentrated on securing the names from the regional post office directors. Kotz kept after the Civil Service Commission and the Senate Post Office and Civil Service Committee. He succeeded in getting the commission to declare that summer hiring in 1966 would be done entirely on the strength of merit examinations, and he convinced the Post Office Committee chairman, Senator Monroney, to make a formal request for the names. Quie directed his attentions to the regional postal directors and the House Government Information Subcommittee. He wrote the regional directors individually to ask that they produce the names, and he discreetly prodded the subcommittee into accelerating its investigation.

By early October, the toll was beginning to tell on Gronouski. He had fewer apologists within the administration and he was receiving pleas from embarrassed Democrats all across the country urging him to put an end to the scandal by releasing the names. On October 5, Gronouski took a swipe at Macy by saying: "I asked for the merit exam last Frebruary but the Civil Service Commission turned it down as too expensive for temporary employees working a short period. After what happened this summer, I asked again and they approved." But Gronouski still refused to release the names.

After completing a six-week study, the Civil Service Commission announced on November 19 that it had tentatively approved guidelines requiring the Post Office Department and all other federal agencies to make public the names of their employees. Macy said he initiated the study because of the furor over the Post Office Department's hiring practices.

Macy's tune had changed dramatically. In mid-August he had shrugged off Quie's requests, but now he declared: "I start off with the view that basic facts about public employees are public business. The public is entitled to know the names, salaries, job titles, and addresses of its federal employees.

Such information should be given out on requests of legitimate public interest. The privacy of employees should be protected, but I think we also need to consider the public because the public is paying the bill."

Now O'Brien had taken over as Postmaster General. Having been in charge of relations with Congress for both Presidents Kennedy and Johnson, he had a good grasp of the problem. One of his first acts was to order the regional postal directors to forward the names to Quie. He then moved to scrap postal regulation 744.444 in conformity with the new Civil Service Commission guidelines.

The victory was in sight.

On Thursday, January 20, 1966, Congressman Quie entered the Republican cloakroom adjoining the House chamber. There was a gleam in his eye. His deep sense of personal satisfaction was shared by Nick Kotz, who sat in the House press gallery a floor above. On the floor of the House, Quie was recognized for sixty minutes. He began:

"Mr. Speaker, I gained personal insight last summer into some of the ways in which a federal program, however outstanding its motives, can go astray and thus endanger public confidence because ethical standards 'falter or appear to falter.'

"It was in the first week of June that I received the first inkling that the manner in which the Post Office Department was distributing its share of jobs might give the appearance that ethical standards were faltering. I received a telephone call from a newspaper reporter. . . ."

Then Quie recounted his many attempts to gain access to the postal employees' names, noting the five House speeches he had made on the subject and the hundreds of newspaper stories which had discussed it. He continued:

"A few days ago, my efforts were finally finished, as I obtained the final list of names.

"Mr. Speaker, I am going to include all of these names in the *Record* today. I do so for two important reasons.

"First, I believe that nonsecurity information concerning

any department or agency of the federal government should be in the public domain.

"Second, I believe that the American people have a right to examine this information themselves, to determine whether or not the Post Office Department administered this portion of the President's 'Youth Opportunity Campaign' according to the intent of the program and the will of the people."

Quie concluded by voicing the hope that his experience would serve to reinforce two simple truths which should guide the actions of government officials:

"First, when a program is devised and presented to the public as a means of helping the disadvantaged, the disadvantaged should be helped; second, any attempt to withhold from the Congress and the people information regarding nonsecurity matters of the executive branch, should be opposed.

"Mr. Speaker, following are the names of those employed in the Post Office Department during the summer of 1965 under the President's so-called 'Youth Opportunity Campaign.' "

The *Congressional Record* of January 20, 1966,* contains 52 pages of names and addresses of summer postal employees.

There are no rewards given to members of Congress who serve the people well. Their moment of recognition comes once every two years on election day. On Tuesday, November 8, 1966, Congressman Quie was reelected by the voters of Minnesota's First Congressional District by a margin of 52,765 votes, or 65.9 percent.

There *are* some rewards for enterprising and dedicated newspapermen. In May, 1966, Nick Kotz was presented the Sigma Delta Chi journalism society's Award for Outstanding Washington Correspondence. A few weeks later, at the annual meeting of the American Society of Newspaper Editors, he received the twenty-second annual Raymond Clapper Memorial Award for "comprehensive and discerning reporting."

* See pages 759–811 of the *Congressional Record*.

What were the characteristics of the 1965 post office secrecy case which distinguished it from other cases of secrecy in the executive branch?

It proved that the barriers of secrecy can be overcome.

It led to the adoption of permanent improvements in Post Office Department hiring practices and in Civil Service Commission employment policies.

It served as the last major episode in a ten-year-old drive to win congressional approval of "Freedom of Information" legislation.

It reminded the executive branch that secrecy cannot be reliably depended upon to shield government actions from public scrutiny.

CHAPTER 5

To Tell the Truth

*A shepherd boy, who tended his flock not far from
a village, used to amuse himself at times in crying
out "Wolf! Wolf!" Twice or thrice his trick succeeded. The whole village came running out to his
assistance; when all the return they got was to be
laughed at for their pains. At last one day the Wolf
came indeed. The boy cried out in earnest. But no
heed to his cries, and the Wolf devoured the sheep.
So the boy learned, when it was too late, that liars
are not believed even when they tell the truth.*

—ÆSOP

One lie can destroy a thousand truths.

A democratic government which resorts to the use of the lie
as an instrument of official policy not only risks the loss of
international trust, but—more importantly—courts disaster
through the loss of confidence of its own people.

In lying about circumstances surrounding the U-2 incident
in 1960, the Bay of Pigs invasion in 1961, the Cuban missile
crisis in 1962, and about numerous other of its undertakings,
the United States government has consistently jeopardized its
integrity in quests for political gains. The government has
dealt carelessly with the truth, and in the process, has contributed significantly to the demise of its own credibility.

Illustrative of the federal government's tendency to resort
to deceit at times of stress was its handling of events leading
up to and during the revolution which racked the Dominican
Republic in the spring of 1965. As more and more facts have
come to light concerning the Dominican uprising, it has

become indelibly clear that the United States government perpetuated three basic lies in the defense of its intervention. Subject to disbelief were the government's claims that:

1) The United States dispatched troops to the Dominican Republic for the sole purpose of protecting the lives of American citizens;

2) The United States maintained a strict neutrality in the rebel (pro-constitution) versus loyalist (military junta) conflict; and

3) The revolution was part of a Communist plot to gain control of the Dominican government.

It was on the strength of these contentions that the United States hoped to convince the world, and especially other Latin nations, that United States intervention in the internal affairs of a sovereign state was prompted not by political self-interest but by the highest and most fundamental concerns for human life and freedom. Such was not the case.

Even if it were to be granted that the United States acted correctly in the Dominican crisis, it is not possible to justify the government's deceit in explaining its actions to the world. As author Theodore Draper has observed: "What was done cannot be separated from how it was done, how it was conceived and executed, how it was justified to the American people and the world at large. For this reason, I will be concerned as much with the *how* as with the *what*—not only with the nature of the policy but with the way it was managed and rationalized."[1] If we, as a nation, are to weigh the future with an eye to avoiding the repetition of past mistakes, we surely must consider the *how* of the Dominican affair. From the standpoint of the degree of candor accompanying the United States government's involvement, it is not a proud record.

The history of the Dominican Republic is an unenviable one. The Republic occupies the eastern two-thirds of the Caribbean island of Hispaniola, sharing it with Haiti to the west. The island was discovered in 1492 by Christopher Columbus, whose brother, Bartholomew, founded the

Dominican capital of Santo Domingo, the first permanent settlement in the New World. The Dominican people are poor and largely uneducated. Of mixed Spanish, Indian, and Negro blood, they have become accustomed to a succession of tyrannical leaders, military dictators, starry-eyed reformers, and meddling foreigners.

For well over a century, the United States has been instrumental in determining the fate of the Dominican people. The administration of President Ulysses S. Grant flirted with the idea of annexing the Republic to the United States; the United States entered into an agreement in 1905 to collect and distribute Dominican customs revenues; President Woodrow Wilson authorized a United States Marine occupation which lasted from 1916 to 1924; three United States Presidents helped prop up dictator Rafael Trujillo from 1930 to 1961. At the same time the United States was supporting Trujillo, the CIA was giving financial assistance to Trujillo's arch-enemy, Juan D. Bosch, who had been sent into exile in 1937. After Trujillo was assassinated in 1961, it was learned the CIA had provided the weapons used by his assassins.

In view of the United States' long and intimate involvement in Dominican affairs, many Dominicans believe the United States will never be entirely free of entanglements in the Republic. A leading Dominican diplomat explained: "As much as we all wish it could be so, the United States will never completely disassociate itself from Dominican problems. There is too much at stake, both in terms of hemispheric and United States interests." An influential United States senator agrees, reasoning that the United States is not about to cast off its "welfare imperialism," a modern version of the "white man's burden" which governed British foreign policy for many years. To be sure, if the United States ever does decide to extricate itself from burdensome commitments in the Dominican Republic, the task will be neither simple nor without loss to United States investments.

The 1965 revolution in the Dominican Republic could not have come as a total surprise to the United States. A loud warning was sounded in September, 1963, when military leaders, political conservatives, and former Trujillo advocates combined to overthrow the government of Juan Bosch, who had been the first freely elected president of the Dominican Republic in nearly forty years. The ouster of Bosch represented a major setback for the Kennedy administration's Alliance for Progress, a program based on the principle that all people have a right to elect their own governments. Kennedy reacted by withdrawing diplomatic recognition and severing economic aid to the Republic.

When Bosch was elected president in December, 1962, the United States pledged its full assistance in making the Dominican Republic "a showcase of democracy." It was a difficult pledge to fulfill. Kennedy and most of his policymakers worked toward the establishment of a lasting democratic system under Bosch, but other United States officials, numerous anti-Bosch Dominicans, and, to an extent, even Bosch himself confounded the Kennedy dream.

Bosch, more a philosopher than a politician, was an ineffective president. He was a poor administrator. He was a dreamer, not a doer. But he was honest, intelligent, and possessed of a strong desire to improve the condition of his people. After three decades of Trujillo's dictatorship, Bosch represented hope.

Despite his desirable traits and his overwhelming election victory,* Bosch was under heavy political attack from the first day he took office. When he spoke out in behalf of free speech, land reforms, and the right of political parties to organize, he was accused of encouraging communism. His political opponents raised the Communist bogeyman time and time again. They considered anybody who favored social reforms, or anybody who expressed reluctance to be beholden to the United States, a Communist. Bosch was vulnerable on both points.

*Bosch's party, the Dominican Revolutionary Party (PRD), received over 58 percent of the vote, twice as many votes as the party finishing second.

Kennedy's ambassador to the Dominican Republic, John Bartlow Martin, a liberal journalist and author, had little confidence in Bosch's ability to govern effectively. In his memoirs, Martin said he noted four days before Bosch was inaugurated: "Bosch is a divider, a splitter, a schemer, a destroyer. Can he build? I doubt it. . . . I said last summer, Bosch won't do. He won't either."[2] Martin's pessimism was to have a profound influence on United States policy toward the Republic. His fatalistic views contributed to an impression in Washington, D.C., that Bosch was unstable, unqualified for leadership, and destined for failure.

While Bosch struggled to establish a government in early 1963, Kennedy was experiencing political difficulties in the United States. The Kennedy myth had begun to fade and Congress was obstructing important administration programs, especially those concerned with foreign aid. Conservatives in Congress stepped up their opposition to Alliance for Progress funds which were earmarked for Bosch.

By spring of 1963, the usually optimistic Newell Williams, head of the United States Agency for International Development (AID) in the Republic, was worried. He told Ambassador Martin that prominent Dominicans were openly lobbying against Bosch in Washington and meeting with a sympathetic response. He said: "We feel a stiffening toward the Dominican Republic in Washington."[3] Martin was aware that Williams had been unable to get thirty thousand tons of wheat under PL-480, the Food for Peace law, and that Washington had again turned down a request for a long overdue loan of $22 million. The ambassador wrote: "He [Williams] said, 'Ever since Bosch has been in, we've been turned down. The fact is, we're just no longer the fair-haired boys up there.' This was highly disturbing. If Washington was really cooling off on Bosch, he had no chance."[4] Martin received word from other sources that certain influential United States officials had decided Bosch would fail and that the United States had no intention of putting more money into the Dominican Republic. Martin detected skepticism everywhere. He noted:

I myself, by my detailed reporting, had probably dis-
abused Washington of any notion that Bosch was an ideal
President. And the CIA's reporting on the Castro/Commu-
nists had hurt him. It is the CIA's duty to collect information—facts, rumors, everything. It also must evaluate the
information. Several times recently I had noticed routine
CIA reports on the Castro/Communists that gave rumors a
credibility far higher than I would have, and I had talked to
the CIA station chief about it. (In reporting a Castro/Com-
munist plot, however wildly implausible, it is obviously safer
to evaluate it as "could be true" than as nonsense.)[5]

Meanwhile, reporters employed by conservative United
States newspapers were magnifying Bosch's problems by writing stories that said he was "soft on communism." Many of
the stories were originated by Bosch's political enemies, who
fed unfavorable and inaccurate information to American reporters, and, once the stories were published in the United
States, caused them to be reprinted and widely distributed in
the Dominican Republic. The "message" in the stories was
always the same: Bosch was unable to cope with communism.

Especially damaging to Bosch were the reports of the late
Jules DuBois of the Chicago *Tribune* and Hal Hendrix of the
Miami *News*. DuBois, a friend of Dominican generals, had
misread Fidel Castro's rise to power in Cuba and, as a result,
was particularly responsive to any mention of Communist
influence in government. Articles by Hendrix were repudiated
by Ambassador Martin as "a vicious hatchet job." Bosch said
that no opponents of democracy in Latin America "cause
such immediate damage as irresponsible United States newspapermen," yet he made no effort to censor them.

On May 31, 1963, Congressman Armistead Selden of
Alabama, chairman of the United States House Subcommittee
on Inter-American Affairs, publicly decried "the advancing
Communist offensive of subversive penetration in the
Dominican Republic." He said in a speech on the floor of the
House that "more than one hundred and fifty Communists"
previously deported from the Republic had been allowed to

return under Bosch, failing to take into account that, over Bosch's objections, the United States government had paved the way for the Communists' return by lifting departure controls on deportees in the United States. Congressman Selden was one of many members of Congress influenced by the Hendrix reports. On June 4, Selden inserted in the *Congressional Record* an article by Hendrix headlined, "Red Tide Rising in Dominican Republic."

Throughout the summer of 1963, Bosch strove to get his government on its feet. He made many mistakes. His deep sense of pride and fierce nationalism forced him to try "going it alone" whenever possible. He asked for outside assistance only when he felt he had no other alternative.

On the eve of his overthrow, Bosch agreed to Ambassador Martin's suggestion that a United States aircraft carrier be permitted to enter Santo Domingo harbor as a public show of solidarity between the United States and Dominican governments. Martin's request for the carrier was rejected by the State Department. Martin explained: "It [State Department cable] said that the Department could do little more to save Bosch in view of his past performance. . . . As for the aircraft carrier, the Department refused to intervene militarily unless a Communist takeover were threatened."[6]

In a predawn coup, Bosch was arrested and stripped of all authority. He had served as the constitutionally-elected president of the Dominican Republic for only seven months. The United States ambassador had never trusted him. The United States government had given him only minimal support. His political opponents had undermined his every effort. The Castro/Communist specter had been constantly raised against him. It was as if he had been poisoned. In the end, Bosch had only one remaining source of political power—the Dominican people, and they were powerless to help him.

The "Communist" case of those who ousted Bosch was unimaginably weak. No important Castro/Communists were found in or out of the administration. Some seven hundred people were arrested, not because they were Communists but because they were loyal to Bosch. The new junta announced that all government employees could keep their jobs, including the "Communists in government" whose supposed existence had precipitated the coup. One junta leader privately admitted that the coup was based more on "the fear of what might have been" than on what actually was. Ambassador Martin acknowledged that the United States placed too much emphasis on the Castro/Communists. He said: "But we had to—a Castro/Communist takeover was the one thing the United States government, and the American people, would not tolerate."

The United States must bear a large part of the responsibility for Bosch's downfall. At the moment of crisis, the United States declined to display even a token amount of confidence in Bosch. Nineteen months later, however, the United States landed 22,000 armed men in support of the right-wing junta which had forcibly removed Bosch from office. This duplicity on the part of the United States was duly noted throughout the world.

On December 14, 1963, less than a month after Kennedy's death, President Johnson officially recognized Bosch's successors. He also appointed a new Assistant Secretary for Inter-American Affairs, Thomas C. Mann, who was given extraordinary authority. On December 18, the President announced: "We expect to speak with one voice on all matters affecting the [Western] Hemisphere. Mr. Mann, with the support of the Secretary of State and the President, will be that voice." Mann, who was on record in favor of United States involvement in overthrowing Latin American leaders who appeared to be too liberal, became the chief architect of United States policy in the developing Dominican crisis.

In February, 1964, President Johnson named W. Tapley Bennett, Jr., as the new United States ambassador to the Dominican Republic. A career diplomat with an undistinguished record, Bennett immediately established a close relationship with the leaders of the anti-Bosch junta, now headed by Donald Reid Cabral, a Dominican businessman. Bennett made no attempt to develop rapport with the leaders of Bosch's PRD or with other pro-Bosch or liberal elements in the Republic. He made no contact with Bosch, then in exile. He dramatically accelerated United States economic assistance to the Republic.*

Notwithstanding Reid Cabral's efforts to stabilize the government, it soon became evident that his standing with the armed forces, upon which the regime was based, was declining. The economy was being overtaken by mismanagement and corruption. In an interview in New York, Bosch observed: "Corruption is so widespread in political and military ranks that it is undermining the politico-military dictatorship. . . . Everything that could be pocketed has been. Given the limited economic possibilities of the country, the looters are falling out among themselves."[7] Ambassador Bennett apparently shared this view. "We are almost on the ropes in the Dominican Republic," he told Assistant Secretary Mann.

But when a warning of the pending rebellion was sent to Bennett, he attributed it to the usual rumors in Santo Domingo, and on Friday, April 23, he departed on a trip to the United States. On Saturday, April 24, the day the revolution started, Bennett was in Georgia visiting his mother. He later said he had flown to Washington to discuss the Dominican unrest with State Department officials, but no one took this transparent excuse seriously. In Bennett's absence, Chargé d'Affaires William B. Connett, Jr., a foreign service officer who had been on the job for five and a half months, was in charge of the United States Embassy.

During the first twenty-four hours of the revolution, the question of Communist influence was never raised. The United States appeared to conclude that the revolt was led by Bosch's PRD and that it was democratic in nature. However,

* In 1963, the year in which Bosch was in office, the United States sent $49,600,000 in aid to the Dominican Republic. Two years later, in 1965, the United States pumped nearly $150,000,000 into the Dominican economy.

as soon as United States officials in Santo Domingo realized the rebels might succeed, their attitude changed. They then began to express fears that "Castro/Communists" were at work.

On the second day of the rebellion, Sunday, April 25, Reid Cabral requested military assistance from the United States. Believing the rebels could be put down without outside intervention, the United States denied Reid's request. Thereupon, Reid resigned and turned the anti-rebel fight over to a military clique headed by General Elias Wessin y Wessin, a professional anti-Communist. Wessin's assumption of control coincided with the rebels' installation of an Acting President, José Rafael Molina Urena, the president of the Chamber of Deputies under Bosch.*

Wessin was at first undecided whether to aid the rebels or to oppose them. Momentarily, he held his troops in check. There is reason to believe that if the United States had moved into this temporary vacuum and declared its support for Molina Urena, the revolution would have been won. But the United States withheld its recognition. Wessin interpreted this failure of the United States to back Molina Urena as the green light he was looking for. He ordered the Dominican air force and navy to begin strafing and shelling the Presidential Palace where Molina Urena was headquartered. "We simply couldn't afford to let Wessin lose," a United States official said. According to Dan Kurzman of the *Washington Post,* the United States Embassy "was rooting for Wessin indeed."

The ambiguity of United States actions during the first crucial hours of the revolution was described by *Wall Street Journal* correspondent Philip Geyelin:

> What the record reveals, in fact, is that from the very outset of the upheaval there was a concerted United States government effort, if not actually a formal decision, to checkmate

* Under Article 131 of the Dominican Constitution, in the absence of the President, Vice President, and President of the Senate, the President of the Chamber of Deputies was in line for the nation's presidency.

the rebel movement by whatever means and whatever cost. Consider these facts:

Item: By Sunday, April 25, just one day after the uprising got under way, while Washington remained openly confused and non-committal, the Santo Domingo embassy had clearly cast its lot with the "loyalist" military cabal and against the rebellion's original aim: the return of Juan Bosch. . . . Restoration of the Bosch regime would be "against United States interests," the embassy counseled. Blocking Bosch could mean further bloodshed, the embassy conceded. Nonetheless, Washington was advised, the embassy military attachés had given "loyalist" leaders a go-ahead to do "everything possible" to prevent what was described as the danger of a "Communist takeover."[8]

Reporter Tad Szulc of the *New York Times* concurred in Geyelin's analysis. Szulc said:

Meanwhile the events of the last twenty-four hours seemed to have convinced the United States Embassy in Santo Domingo of two things. One was that a return of Dr. Bosch would mean "Communism in the Dominican Republic in six months." The second was that United States forces would have to be used in support of General Wessin's troops if the pro-Bosch rebellion was to be defeated.

These two basic judgments, which the embassy arrived at even before the rebellion could be identified politically in any way, went far to shape subsequent United States attitudes and policies. It was Ambassador Bennett who had long felt that the Bosch influence would be pernicious for the Dominican Republic, and in his absence his staff members apparently shared this view. . . .

Thus, in a sense, the situation in terms of Juan Bosch had been prejudged at the embassy before the rebellion erupted.[9]

A distinct anti-Bosch bias was reflected in messages sent to the State Department by Chargé d'Affaires Connett. He reported "armed leftists on street corners" and strongly hinted of a Communist takeover. Embassy reporting to Washington during this period was filled with such terms as "the talk now," "word has reached us," and "our sources report," hardly conclusive evidence of Communist activity. Former Ambassador Martin has since acknowledged that there was a distinct separateness between Bosch and the Communists, that the revolution was launched by Bosch's PRD, and that the "rebellion seems to have taken the Castro/Communists by surprise." Ambassador Bennett also later voiced the belief that the rebellion caught the Communists off guard.

However, it was Martin's conclusion in the early days of the revolution that Communists had taken control. Though this judgment was based on suspicion and unsubstantiated rumor rather than on fact, it was an important factor in shaping policy in the United States. A fatal flaw in United States decision-making was that no distinction was drawn between a few Communists *joining* the revolt and Communists *directing* it.

Under the influence of Thomas Mann, who had been promoted to Under Secretary of State for Economic Affairs, officials in Washington set in motion contingency plans to be used if the rebellion fully developed into "another Cuba." President Johnson personally studied the cables sent from the United States Embassy in Santo Domingo. According to messages received from United States military attachés, who were operating directly from the Wessin command center at San Isidro Air Force Base, the junta forces needed help. The United States provided it. Six troop-laden ships, led by the U.S.S. *Boxer,* were already at anchor off Santo Domingo. While preparations were being made for the landing of troops, the United States swore it was maintaining strict neutrality in the conflict.

At 7 P.M. on Wednesday, April 28, President Johnson summoned the congressional leaders of both parties to the White House. He told them that the decision to land troops had been made because of the need to protect the lives of American citizens in Santo Domingo. He failed to mention administration fears of a Communist take-over. Only when Senator Everett M. Dirksen of Illinois raised the question of communism did Johnson divulge that the CIA had identified three Communists in the rebel leadership. The President was upset when Dirksen left the meeting and alluded to the danger of communism in an interview with newsmen. The Senator had not been alerted to the fact that the administration was not yet ready to make the Communist charge—publicly.

Earlier in the afternoon, when Johnson met with members of his Cabinet and a few key aides, it had been decided to eliminate any mention of communism from a Presidential statement announcing the landing of troops. It was felt that the Communist angle should not be introduced until sufficient evidence was available. The adoption of this position was credited to the late Adlai Stevenson, Ambassador to the United Nations, and Presidential assistants Bill D. Moyers and Richard Goodwin.

One of those attending the April 28 meeting with the President was Senator J. W. Fulbright of Arkansas, chairman of the Senate Foreign Relations Committee. He recalled: "The President told us of the danger to American lives and of the shooting going on. He mentioned the shooting up of the United States Embassy and how Ambassador Bennett had to hide under a desk. He told us several hair-raising tales like that; they were not supported by facts. He said he had ordered troops in to save American lives. He made no mention of the danger of communism. He told us what he was going to do; he didn't ask us." Fulbright expanded his assessment of the Dominican affair in a Senate speech on September 15, 1965:

> United States policy in the Dominican crisis was characterized initially by overtimidity and subsequently by overreaction. Throughout the whole affair, it has been characterized by a lack of candor. . . .
> Very close to the beginning of the revolution, United States policymakers decided that it should not be allowed to succeed. This decision seems to me to have been based on exaggerated estimates of Communist influence in the rebel movement in

the initial stages and on distaste for the return to power of Juan Bosch or of a government controlled by Bosch's party. . . .

The United States intervened in the Dominican Republic for the purpose of preventing the victory of a revolutionary force which was judged to be Communist dominated. On the basis of Ambassador Bennett's messages to Washington, there is no doubt that the threat of communism rather than danger to American lives was his primary reason for recommending military intervention.[10]

Fulbright's contention that the United States intervention was, in fact, prompted by an official fear of Communist involvement in the revolution was supported by another United States senator, a member of the Senate Foreign Relations Committee. Several days after the revolt started, the senator recalled, he encountered Jack Hood Vaughn, a State Department "expert" on Latin America. The senator noticed that Vaughn looked exhausted and suggested that he "rest up for a few days." Vaughn rejected the suggestion, saying he would continue to work "day and night until the Communists are stopped" in the Dominican Republic.

On Wednesday, April 28, President Johnson went on nationwide television to announce the landing of United States troops in Santo Domingo. He said: "The United States government has been informed by military authorities in the Dominican Republic that American lives are in danger. These authorities are no longer able to guarantee their safety, and they have reported that the assistance of military personnel is now needed for that purpose. I have ordered the Secretary of Defense to give protection to hundreds of Americans who are still in the Dominican Republic and to escort them safely to this country."[11]

The President's reference to "military authorities" was to leaders of the anti-rebel junta upon whom the administration was relying for guidance. There was no similar reliance on rebel sources. The United States government had accepted the word of junta leaders that United States military assistance was needed. While the President told the American people the troops were needed to protect American lives, it was clear both in the United States and in the Dominican Republic that the arrival of United States forces would seriously hamper the rebel movement.

In his statement, the President did not mention a threat of a Communist take-over. A more plausible excuse, the protection of American lives, was deemed more appropriate. What American could object to the deployment of troops for the purpose of saving the lives of fellow citizens?

The circumstances that led up to the request by "military authorities" for United States intervention are fraught with overtones of deceit. At mid-afternoon on April 28, Dominican Air Force Colonel Pedro Bartolome Benoit, chief of Wessin's hastily formed military government, asked Ambassador Bennett to send United States troops on the ground that this was the only way to defeat the rebels and to prevent a Communist victory. In response to Benoit's request, Bennett said: "I can't get away with bringing Americans in on that ground because the evidence is not clear. If you will change your request and make it in writing, and ask American forces to intervene in order to protect American lives, then I believe that we can persuade Washington to do it."[12] Benoit obliged, the newly worded request was forwarded to Washington, and the troops were ordered in.

From the time Ambassador Bennett returned to the Dominican Republic on Tuesday, April 27, he pursued a course deliberately calculated to assist the military junta. He was ever mindful of President Johnson's personal reminder that "another Cuba" would be a completely unacceptable solution. His concern was political, not humanitarian. Upon his arrival, Bennett encouraged United States military attachés to coach the Dominican generals at San Isidro Air Force Base, he secured badly needed transportation and communications equipment for the junta, he rejected a rebel plea for peace talks on the ground that he lacked authority to mediate, and, in general, he threw the full weight of United

States prestige and resources against the rebels. A high-ranking administration official expressed belief that Bennett was intent on "killing the revolution from the very beginning." Senator Fulbright understated Bennett's questionable conduct when he said: "I think Mr. Bennett was scared to death. He'd never been in trouble before. He is a nice, polite fellow from a nice home in Georgia. But he just wasn't up to it."

In a briefing for newsmen on Thursday, April 29, Bennett went to great lengths to recount "rebel atrocities," never mentioning atrocities by the junta forces. He said the rebels were shooting people against walls, severing heads and parading them through the streets on spikes, and machine-gunning innocent citizens. Each of these stories was proven false. The ambassador also told reporters that a rebel leader had murdered the junta's Colonel Juan Calderon. The "murdered" colonel, alive and well, was interviewed by newsmen a few hours later.

It was at the April 29 briefing that Bennett released a controversial list of Dominicans whom he identified as Communists in the rebel camp. Reporters quickly discovered that some of those named were out of the country or out of Santo Domingo at the time, others were in jail, and still others were devout nationalists with no Communist inclinations whatsoever. The list described Alfredo Conde Pausa as "a known sympathizer with PSPD (the Communist Dominican Popular Socialist Party)." Conde Pausa was visited by the *Washington Post*'s Dan Kurzman, who wrote: "A Supreme Court Justice for twenty-six years, Conde Pausa said, weeping, that in the last presidential election he had voted for the conservative Civic Union Party."[13] Conde Pausa had worked on the 1963 Dominican Constitution with United States Supreme Court Justice William O. Douglas. He abhorred communism. As it turned out, the list of names had been compiled by combing the "suspect" files of Dominican police, whose leaders did not disguise their militant anti-Communist feelings and their suspicions of the Republic's non-Communist left.

Another incident cited by the United States as proof of "Communists running wild in the streets and threatening the lives of American citizens" was shown to be without foundation. While a thousand or so Americans were awaiting evacuation at the Hotel Embajador on April 27, a group of armed rebels entered the building in search of a hated anti-Bosch newspaper publisher who had been instrumental in Bosch's overthrow. After searching the hotel from top to bottom, the rebels left. Not one American was harmed. In fact, witnesses said the rebels went out of their way to avoid any inconvenience to those in the hotel. When this incident was reported to Washington, however, it was presented as an illustration of the "great peril" to American citizens. Secretary of State Dean Rusk referred to the incident as one of grave danger with "people running around the hotel, shooting it up with tommyguns, and so forth." Again, the damage was to the United States' credibility.

In the final analysis, it was President Johnson, more than any other single individual, who contributed to the crisis in credibility which arose out of the Dominican rebellion. It can be said in the President's behalf that, since he was not personally on the scene in Santo Domingo, his statements merely reflected the views of his subordinates. But the explanation is not that simple. The President was presented with all the options, and yet, in his private and public utterances, he chose to reflect all the worst rumors and suspicions, the darkest descriptions of criminal violence, chaos, and communism. When it became apparent that the President was seriously overstating the degree of danger in the Dominican Republic, public confidence began to slip away.

Although President Johnson has been criticized for his lack of interest in foreign affairs, he has not been accused of lacking a firm conviction as to the main United States goal in Latin America: the prevention of "another Cuba." As the

Vice President, Johnson had discussed the Cuban situation at length with President Kennedy, and they had agreed that any President who allowed another Communist state to develop in the Western Hemisphere would surely be defeated if he sought reelection. In a speech on May 3, 1965, Johnson declared: "What is important is that we know, and that they know, and that everybody knows, that we don't propose to sit here in our rocking chair with our hands folded and let the Communists set up any government in the Western Hemisphere." When faced with the difficult task of assessing events in the Dominican Republic, the President leaned hard to the right. It was not necessary for him to be convinced that the Dominican revolution was Communist-controlled. The point that it *might* be was sufficient. Johnson was unwilling to accept even a remote risk of a Communist regime coming to power.

After announcing the landing of the first four hundred Marines in Santo Domingo, Johnson set out to fashion an absolute consensus. He used the telephone, personal confrontations, anything to communicate the legitimacy of his action. The harder he tried, the more uncertain he seemed. The justification for United States intervention began to be questioned.

On the evening of Friday, April 30, the President went before the television cameras for the second time in three days, and for the first time, he alluded to the Communist menace: "Meanwhile there are signs that people trained outside the Dominican Republic are seeking to gain control. Thus the legitimate aspirations of the Dominican people and most of their leaders for progress, democracy, and social justice are threatened and so are the principles of the inter-American system."[14] He called for the "return of constitutional processes and free elections" in the Republic. There was some preliminary evidence that individual Communists had joined the rebels, but there was no proof that the Dominican government or the inter-American system were threatened by a Communist take-over. The President neglected to mention one of the most basic principles of the inter-American system, that of nonintervention. His call for restoration of "constitutional processes and free elections" was premature; they had not been abandoned. Most importantly, Johnson had switched from the original justification for United States intervention—saving American lives—to the excuse that Communist penetration had to be prevented. At least all the cards were now on the table.

Twenty-four hours later, on May 1, Johnson issued a statement announcing that two battalions of the Eighty-second Airborne Division were being sent to the Dominican Republic for "protecting human life." This time he omitted any direct mention of a Communist threat, referring instead to the necessity of a cease-fire and a return to "political democracy, social justice, and economic progress." The President highlighted United States efforts to achieve a cease-fire, but he failed to note simultaneous United States military moves to crush the rebels.

At 10 P.M. on Sunday, May 2, Johnson again went on television, the third time in four days. In a long, rambling, and emotion-charged speech, he recounted events of the previous week and stated: "The revolutionary movement took a tragic turn. Communist leaders, many of them trained in Cuba, seeing a chance to increase disorder, to gain a foothold, joined the revolution. They took increasing control. And what began as a popular democratic revolution, committed to democracy and social justice, very shortly moved and was taken over and really seized and placed in the hands of a band of Communist conspirators."[15] There was absolutely no evidence and never would be that Communists had "taken over and really seized" the rebellion. In response to heavy criticism of his earlier intimations that the revolution was Communist-dominated from the beginning, Johnson publicly acknowledged that it had begun "as a popular democratic revolution."

The President undercut his position even more when he invited the television audience to contact their ambassador to the Dominican Republic "to get firsthand evidence of the horrors and the hardship, the violence and the terror, and the international conspiracy from which United States servicemen have rescued the people of more than thirty nations from that war-torn land." Certainly Ambassador Bennett, with his hands full in Santo Domingo, was not about to begin answering individual citizen inquiries. When newsmen in the Dominican Republic heard Johnson's description of the situation there, they thought he was talking about another conflict, maybe Vietnam. The President's speech also increased the scope of the "Communist design," now noting the presence of an "international conspiracy" instead of a group of Cuba-trained Communist agents.

In regard to the United States government's political position, the President said: "Let me also make clear tonight that we support no single man or any single group of men in the Dominican Republic." This was simply not true. All the actions of United States officials, both civilian and military, were aimed at bolstering the military junta and defeating the rebels.

In a meeting with members of congressional committees in the White House on May 4, the President evidenced a continued reliance on emotionalism. In discussing the evacuation of American citizens, he said: "It has been necessary for a few Marines to go out and take an old lady and her little belongings and with a crippled hip, carry her down through the streets where the firing is taking place, but we carried three thousand that way without the loss of a single civilian up to now." He added that "six or eight of the embassies have been torn up" and that "we have from a thousand to fifteen hundred bodies that are dead in the street." These conditions never existed; no embassies were destroyed and no more than a few bodies at a time were ever observed in the streets.

In their political biography of Johnson, authors Rowland Evans and Robert Novak concluded that "the President's obsession with criticism embarked him on the most blatant personal campaign to sell the intervention to the country through the White House press corps that any President in history had ever undertaken. It was this campaign . . . that brought about the crisis in credibility that was to heighten, not lessen, tensions."[16] In a book on Johnson's conduct of foreign policy, Philip Geyelin wrote: "His public and extemporaneous description of the carnage in Santo Domingo . . . went so far beyond the demonstrable facts that United States officials on the spot could only throw up their hands when badgered by newsmen for some supporting evidence. Friends dismissed it as Texas hyperbole, but to the war correspondents in Santo Domingo, Presidential hyperbole could only serve to widen an already widening credibility gap about Administration moves and motivations in the Dominican affair."[17]

Whatever the extenuating circumstances may have been, the fact remains that the President of the United States, not to mention scores of lesser United States officials, indulged in the kind of half-truths and exaggerated explanations which invariably result in total falsehoods. United States government statements about the Dominican crisis were so contradictory, inconsistent, and erratic that few believed them for very long and some not at all.

"The administration is more interested in maintaining the false cover story that its intervention was primarily to save lives than in cultivating public understanding of the real reasons for its activities," the *Washington Post* commented in an editorial. A United States senator admitted: "Yes, there were basic lies involved in the Dominican crisis. It [United States intervention] had to be justified to the American people somehow." A Democratic member of Congress observed: "It's difficult to say if the stories told, the half-truths and untruths, were intentional or not. But it doesn't make much difference, does it?" Former Ambassador Martin remarked: "Once we had decided we were in the Republic to stop communism, we should have stopped pretending neutrality."

After the Dominican revolt was ended, the Senate Foreign Relations Committee held exhaustive hearings in an effort to establish the truth. However, the hearings were held in "executive session," closed to the public and the press. In April of 1967, when Senator Joseph S. Clark requested that the hearings be made public, Senator Fulbright told him: "I am inclined to think that it would be premature to reopen this question at this time. There are a good many crucial points in those hearings which I expect the State Department would still be unwilling to declassify . . . and I think if we are going to publish any of the record, we ought to publish all of it." The hearings remain officially secret today.

It is abundantly clear that the United States' reputation for truth and honesty suffered as a result of its involvement in the Dominican revolution. This diminution of our country's credibility was especially unfortunate because it was unnecessary. The full and unfettered truth would have served United States interests just as well—in fact, much better—than did deceit. If the United States' cause in the Dominican intervention was just, as it may have been, there was no need for official lying; the world would have accepted the truth. Deceit breeds distrust, and the world will be much more skeptical the next time a crisis arises.

Americans might well consider a remark made by conservative leader Russell Kirk in a letter to Robert Welch, founder of the John Birch Society: "Cry wolf often enough and everyone takes you for an imbecile or a knave, when after all there *are* wolves in this world."[18]

NOTES TO CHAPTER 5

1. Theodore Draper, "The Dominican Crisis," *Commentary,* December, 1965, p. 33.

2. John Bartlow Martin, *Overtaken by Events* (Garden City, N.Y.: Doubleday & Company, 1966), p. 329.

3. *Ibid.*, p. 389.

4. *Ibid.*

5. *Ibid.*, p. 451.

6. *Ibid.*, p. 570.

7. *Background Information Relating to the Dominican Republic,* Committee on Foreign Relations, United States Senate, July, 1965, p. 14.

8. Philip Geyelin, *Wall Street Journal*, June 25, 1965.

9. Tad Szulc, *Dominican Diary* (New York: Dell Publishing Company, 1965), pp. 29–30.

10. Remarks of United States Senator J. W. Fulbright, "The Situation in the Dominican Republic," *Congressional Record*, September 15, 1965.

11. Statement by President Johnson of April 28, 1965. See *Department of State Bulletin*, May 17, 1965, pp. 738–739.

12. Remarks of United States Senator Joseph S. Clark, quoted by Draper, *Commentary*, December, 1965, p. 50.

13. *Washington Post*, May 9, 1965.

14. Statement by President Johnson of April 30, 1965. See *Department of State Bulletin*, May 17, 1965, p. 742.

15. Statement by President Johnson of May 2, 1965. *Ibid.*, p. 744.

16. Rowland Evans and Robert Novak, *Lyndon B. Johnson: The Exercise of Power* (New York: The New American Library, 1966), p. 520.

17. Philip Geyelin, *Lyndon B. Johnson and the World* (New York: Frederick A. Praeger, Inc., 1966), p. 19.

18. *National Review*, October 19, 1965.

CHAPTER 6

Managing the News

Any reporter or editor who does not take for granted that the government, or any experienced source of news, always tries to manage information is naive.

—BEN H. BAGDIKIAN

The *Washington Post,* one of the most respected and influential newspapers in the United States, published the following page-one story in its editions of April 15, 1967:

SHARP JUMP IN WAR COST IS FORECAST

By Hobart Rowen
Washington Post Staff Writer

A high government official predicted yesterday that the cost of the Vietnam war would spurt sharply above current administration estimates for this year.

Carefully disclaiming inside information, the official nonetheless predicted that after making "some difficult decisions," President Johnson would decide to increase troop strength in Vietnam this year by about 50,000 men over the currently planned ceiling.

. . . The official, *who declined to be identified,* compared the situation to 1965.

. . . *He left the implication* that higher taxes or higher interest rates would be needed to cope with the situation.

[Emphasis added.]

This news article is the equivalent of the anonymous telephone call or the unsigned letter. It is the end product of a calculated "leak" of information by a government official. It is one of the many and varied techniques used by the federal government to manage the news of current events.

The *Post* story illustrates the usefulness of the well-timed release of information by an unidentified government source. This particular leak came at a time when the Johnson administration was publicly denying that it had decided to accelerate the United States effort in Vietnam. While it may have been true that no formal decision had been reached in favor of increasing the number of troops in Vietnam, such a move was under careful and serious consideration at the highest levels of the government. Administration officials were cognizant of the importance of psychologically preparing the public to accept a greater commitment of manpower, but for reasons of political expediency and military strategy, they were not yet ready to openly discuss this eventuality. The guided leak permitted presentation of the matter in an unofficial way.

Note the italicized portions of the *Post* story. The use of the term "high government official" suggests that the "predicted" course of action had the blessing of the administration, or, at least, of one leading representative of the administration. Yet, the refusal of the official to be identified precluded his having to answer embarrassing questions or to confirm or deny the prediction that a change in government policy was in the making. By "carefully disclaiming inside information," the anonymous official was accentuating the personal nature of his belief, and, at the same time, avoiding an outright declaration that the administration knew more than it was telling the public. In essence, the official was having his cake and eating it too. His position in the government carried weight sufficient to prompt reporter Rowen to write the story and the *Post* to publish it on page one. The result of the article was to suggest in the minds of readers the distinct possibility that an increase in both men and money for Vietnam was in the offing.

Unlike secrecy and deceit, two of the major defensive

weapons in the federal government's "arsenal of weaponry," news management is a positive striking force. It is an offensive weapon. With it, government officials are able to seize the initiative in influencing public opinion, projecting ideas, and securing support for federal programs. The goal of news management is to convince the public to accept those viewpoints and policies which are in step with administration objectives. There are as many different methods of managing the news as there are officials in the government.

News management is not new to the federal government. As early as 1909, Congress passed legislation prohibiting the Forestry Service from spending money to prepare articles for use in newspapers and magazines. In 1913, a law applying to all executive agencies was enacted to provide that "no money appropriated by this or any other act shall be used for the compensation of any publicity expert unless specifically appropriated for that purpose." More recently, several investigating committees of Congress have strongly criticized the publicity efforts of the executive branch. A House subcommittee issued a report in 1948 which bitterly condemned "techniques of government propaganda by which federal officials seek to perpetuate themselves in office, generate pressures on Congress for more and bigger appropriations, and sponsor job-building enterprises in the name of national emergency or by an artificially stimulated public demand."[1]

As the government has grown in size and complexity, federal officials have seen the need for corresponding increases in the scope of their information activity. In a report published in 1950, the first Hoover Commission estimated that the publicity programs of the executive branch were costing $105 million annually. By conservative estimates, this cost is now more than $450 million per year. The advent of television has been an especially big boon to government information specialists, facilitating instant communications to nearly every home in the nation.

In November, 1955, during the Eisenhower regime, the *New York Times'* James Reston noted the dangers of government news management: "I think in some ways it [news management] is more serious than the suppression of information because the power of the federal government here in Washington, with all of the instruments of communication at its command, to call press conferences and to put out themes . . . you can imagine the capacity to do things if they wish to do it. I am not arguing that suppression is a good thing but to keep a thing in is one thing, but to decide to use all of the powers at your command to put over a theme, then you move from the essentially negative to the positive realm, and you can do great damage, if you wish."[2] In March, 1963, during the Kennedy administration, columnist Arthur Krock wrote: "A news management policy not only exists but, in the form of direct and deliberate action, has been enforced more cynically and boldly than by any previous administration. . . . It has been employed with subtlety and imagination for which there is no historic parallel known to me."[3] In April, 1967, Bill D. Moyers, former press secretary to President Johnson, admitted that the Johnson administration manages the news. He warned: "Let us beware of believing things are going as well as those who hold public office would wish us to believe."[4]

The conventional processes for dissemination of news by the government include press conferences, news releases, speeches, reports, and on-the-record interviews. These processes are associated more with the government's responsibility to keep the public informed than with the government's desire to stage-manage events. News generated by these means is attributed to specific individuals or government bodies. Accountability is clear.

In addition to the conventional processes, however, there has grown up in recent years a number of other techniques for enlightening the public mind. These are the behind-the-scenes, don't-quote-me techniques. They encompass the leak, the trial balloon, and the backgrounder, among others. In each case, the information revealed is attributed only to "a reliable source," "an administration official," or "a White House spokesman." The purveyor of the information remains anonymous. He does not have to accept responsibility for what he says. Without fear of being quoted by name, he may divulge a national secret, advance a pet project, or undercut the positions of others. The not-for-attribution techniques enable government officials to spread information which, if it becomes desirable, can later be denied with impunity or dismissed as "idle speculation" on the part of the news media.

The leak has become an accepted way of doing business in Washington, D.C., at all levels, often for mutually conflicting purposes or counter to White House objectives. There has been so much leakage of information from government agencies that whole new security systems have been instituted to plug the holes. Some federal departments require employees to report to their superiors after all conversations with newsmen. Reporters are forced to seek official permission before entering certain government buildings, and, once inside, their movements are restricted to "approved" locations. Government telephones are monitored. Most security precautions fail because the preponderance of leakage takes place after working hours and off government property. Presidents Kennedy and Johnson became so concerned about leaks that they ordered the FBI to investigate in instances where disclosure of information reflected badly on administration programs. Richard Fryklund, who is currently Deputy Assistant Secretary of Defense for Public Affairs, was the subject of "the treatment" in 1963 when he was a reporter covering the Pentagon. Kennedy once told a group of State Department officials: "There is one area in which I need no help from you—and that is leaking to the press. We at the White House do a pretty good job of that ourselves."[5] On several occasions, Johnson has altered his plans after they have been leaked to the press.

While the primary purpose of the leak is to win public support for government programs, it is also used as a weapon in intragovernmental warfare. Here its purpose is negative. Two or more federal agencies competing for funds from Congress may closely examine one another's programs in the hope of discovering weaknesses. Once inadequacies are found, they are leaked to the news media or to members of Congress in the expectation that public disclosure will short-circuit funding of "opposition" programs. Disgruntled federal employees who lose out in struggles over policies are also prone to leak adverse information. Leaks resulting from internal conflicts often shed valuable light on executive deliberations, but they also endanger the conduct of foreign affairs when they involve United States relations with other nations.

The trial balloon has a more limited value as a device for managing the news. This technique comes into play when the government is faced with deciding between two or more courses of action, none of which promises complete success. In order to determine which course will be most acceptable to the greatest number of people, a government official "floats a trial balloon." He leaks word that the government has decided to adopt Policy A. Once this information is reported in the press, the government studies public reaction. If the reaction is hostile, the balloon is hauled down. If the reaction is either neutral or favorable, the policy is pursued. Sometimes it is necessary to float several balloons before an acceptable approach to a problem is found.

While essentially a method for testing the domestic political winds, the trial balloon is also useful in the diplomatic field. For the purpose of measuring foreign opinion concerning the contemplated bombing of the North Vietnamese harbor at Haiphong, the Johnson administration floated this story in April, 1967: "Top Johnson administration officials are engaged in a new, detailed study of whether to bomb Haiphong harbor in order to halt the flow into North Vietnam of aid from Communist countries. . . . The issue of bombing or possibly mining the harbor is under 'very lively discussion' within the Joint Chiefs of Staff, according to official sources."[6] The release of this balloon allowed the administration to debate and consider foreign reaction to a policy *before* it was finally established. Of particular importance were the reactions of the Soviet Union and other Communist countries supplying war goods to North Vietnam. The State Department makes frequent use of trial balloons. One newsman commented that there are so many balloons floating over the State Department that the building is in danger of soaring off into the air.

Another news management technique is the "backgrounder" or nonattribution briefing of newsmen by government officials. Backgrounders have a semiofficial status in Washington. No particular effort is made to keep them secret. They are staged regularly on Thursdays in midafternoon at the Pentagon and on Fridays in the early evening at the State Department. They are also held in hotels, private clubs, bars, and office buildings. There is hardly a reporter in Washington who does not participate in backgrounders.

The distinguishing characteristic of backgrounders is that identification of government participants is prohibited. During the late 1940's, newsmen discovered that White House aides, military officials, and foreign service officers would break secrecy if they could talk off the record. In return for nuggets of inside news, reporters agreed not to attribute the things they were told. The practice of blurred attribution became known as the Lindley Rule, named after former *Newsweek* correspondent Ernest K. Lindley, one of the first to suggest the backgrounder approach. "It was a system of compulsory plagiarism and it served us well," Lindley recalls.[7]

It was through a backgrounder that William McChesney Martin, chairman of the Federal Reserve Board, made the leak cited at the beginning of this chapter. In April, 1967, when the Senate Foreign Relations Committee voted a watered-down resolution for the President to take to a hemispheric meeting at Punta del Este, Uruguay, an unidentified White House spokesman (Walt W. Rostow) arranged a backgrounder to denounce the resolution as "worse than useless." By taking sanctuary in backgrounders, Martin and Rostow escaped having to answer to the public and to Congress for their statements.

In a recent speech to the American Society of Newspaper Editors, former Presidential adviser McGeorge Bundy pointed to a disadvantage of backgrounders: "The present rules are better for you [the press] and better for public officials than they are for the public. . . . The public very seldom knows what's going on." This view was supported by Bill D. Moyers, who told the ASNE that "the tendency to use background stories without attribution leaves the reader confused about the sources and therefore about the credibility of the information." Senator Robert F. Kennedy of New York agreed: "The unfortunate consequence of background briefings is the inability of an informed reader to make his own evaluation of the reliability, authority, and special interests of the official spokesman, forcing the reader to discount the news altogether or to accept it on faith." These public figures were articulating the dilemma faced by the citizen who reads news stories which have been based on statements made by anonymous government sources. How does the reader know whether the news comes from the President of the United States, from a minor bureaucrat with an ax to grind, or from Ho Chi Minh? Not knowing, the reader attempts to suspend judgment but, more often than not, he ends up becoming more confused or more cynical, or both.

In May of 1967, *Washington Post* editor Benjamin Bradlee made a move against spurious backgrounders. He drew up guidelines for his reporters which said: "First, we encourage every reporter to fight like hell to get it on the record. Second, he should insist that the absolute minimum he'll take is attribution to the government agency involved. Third, he should say in the story why it is background news. Finally, the reporter is free, at his discretion, to get up and leave a background session." The new rules were tested a few days later at a White House press conference. When an administration official announced that a part of the session was for "background only," *New York Times* reporter Max Frankel broke in: "I'm sorry, but if you're going to give me information on that basis, I'm authorized by my editors to say that the White House has no comment on this." So threatened, the official put much of the information on the record. However, when *Post* reporter Eric Wentworth tried to use the new rules a week later at a conference called by Secretary of Agriculture Orville Freeman, the Secretary refused to speak for the record. Wentworth left the conference. Other papers reported details of the meeting, but the *Post* carried nothing.

There are many other ways in which government manages the news. They include: saturation of the press with favorable items; strategic timing of announcements; social flattery; false weighting of facts; suppression; distortion; and threats. Favorable information is voluntarily disclosed and unfavorable facts are hidden. Officials hold hurry-up press conferences which happen to conflict with conferences previously called by those who may oppose administration policies. The President has distracted the public's attention from controversial events in the United States by taking publicity-laden trips abroad.

All the federal government's efforts in managing the news seem minuscule when compared to the campaign which succeeded in selling the American people on the urgent need to land a man on the moon by 1970. There is no parallel in United States history to the prodigious campaign carried out in 1961 to convince the public and Congress to commit some $30 billion to the moonshot program. There may never be another campaign like it.

When President Kennedy took office in January, 1961, he was faced with the imperative of developing an exciting and imaginative New Frontier program to "get America moving again." As a United States senator, Kennedy had shown little interest in the creation of the National Aeronautics and Space Administration (NASA) in 1958 or in its modest plans to conquer space. However, once in the White House, he took a new look at NASA. He asked the Vice President, Lyndon Johnson, to examine NASA's operations thoroughly with an eye to recommending an extension of the manned space flight program. As expected, Johnson filed a strongly affirmative report. Kennedy went to Congress to ask for a 61 percent increase in NASA's budget.

Then two history-making events occurred. On April 12, 1961, the Soviet Union's Major Yuri Gagarin orbited the earth in the Vostok I spacecraft. Gagarin's feet were hardly back on the ground when, on April 17, the humiliating failure at the Bay of Pigs handed the Kennedy administration a severe political setback. Now, more than ever before, Kennedy needed the moonshot program as a vehicle for attaining public confidence. He embraced the lunar landing as the only federal program which could possibly give Americans a feeling of forward movement, provide the required challenge to Soviet space feats, and distract the public's attention from the Cuban fiasco.

The President ordered a second review of the United States space budget to determine "which areas could be reasonably accelerated to attain certain objectives at a much earlier date."[8] He was determined to "step up our efforts" so that we might "prevail" in space. He asked NASA: "What can we do in space which will put us ahead of the Russians in *spectacular accomplishments* [emphasis added]?"[9] On May 22, 1961, Kennedy sent Congress a message on "Urgent National Needs" in which he promised a manned landing on the moon "within the decade." He said:

> Let it be clear . . . that I am asking the Congress and the country to accept a firm commitment to a new course of action —a course which will last for many years. . . . If we are to go only halfway, or reduce our sights in the face of difficulty, in my judgment it would be better not to go at all. . . . It is a most important decision that we make as a nation; but all of you have lived through the last four years and have seen the significance of space and the adventure in space, and no one can predict with certainty what the ultimate meaning will be of the mastery of space. *I believe we should go to the moon.* [Emphasis added.]

The American people were favorably impressed by the eloquence of their young President; they were inspired by his rhetoric and vision. He had captured their imaginations during the 1960 election campaign and now was drawing on a vast reservoir of personal popularity. He was not challenged when he equated the moonshot with winning "the battle that is going on around the world between freedom and tyranny" or when he suggested the program "may hold the key to our future on earth."

In Congress, where Kennedy was better known, he managed to get unanimous, if not enthusiastic, support. He effectively used the advantages of his office in obtaining congressional funding for the multi-billion dollar moon program. One of the President's special consultants, Richard E. Neustadt, explained: "A President's authority and status give him great advantages in dealing with the men he would persuade. . . . From the veto to appointments, from publicity to budgeting, and so down a long list, the White House now controls the most encompassing array of vantage points in the American political system. With hardly an exception, the men who share in governing this country are aware that at some time, in some degree, the doing of their jobs, the furthering of their ambitions, may depend upon the President of the United States. Their need for Presidential action, or their fear of it, is bound to be recurrent if not actually continuous. Their need or fear is his advantage."[10]

The late Dr. Hugh Dryden, deputy administrator at NASA, exhibited an unusual degree of candor in admitting that political expediency spurred the space program forward. In an interview in 1963, he said: "Purely on the basis of science, you cannot justify a program of this magnitude. The motivation was mostly political and it emanated from the White House. The responsibility for the decision was the President's. We just told him how it could be done and how soon."[11] Dr. Glen P. Wilson, a staff member of the Senate Aeronautical and Space Sciences Committee, noted: "Space is like motherhood; everybody's for it, and you're a heel if you oppose it."[12] A Democratic congressman, whose home district has reaped considerable benefits from the moon program, observed that Kennedy "needed a glamorous, even spectacular, program to get the New Frontier off the ground. He hitched his administration's star to the moonshot, so to speak. He sold the moon landing on the basis of glory; it was a 'sexy' program. He played down the tremendous costs involved." Astronaut John H. Glenn's ethereal justification for the moon program evidenced image-making at its best. Glenn said: "Why go? When they ask me about it, I am tempted to reply that it's because, in one very important sense, I have never grown up. . . . In space, as yet, there is only one enemy—space itself. It is an environment hostile to all men's greatest abilities. . . . The human race may never again have a similar chance to demonstrate that we can be the kind of people God intended us to be."[13]

Always conscious that history was being written, Kennedy encouraged his speech writers to uncover names and events out of the past to be used as analogies for the moon program. He alluded to Newton, Lindbergh, Chennault, Einstein, the Plymouth Bay Colony, the invention of the steam engine, and others in various space messages. A single speech in Texas contained the phrases "the new sea," "climb the highest mountain," "fly the Atlantic," and "pathfinders and pioneers." In a 1962 address at Rice University, Kennedy reasoned: "We choose to go to the moon in this decade and do other things, not because they are easy, but because they are hard; because that goal will serve to organize and measure the best of our energies and skills; because that challenge is one that we're willing to accept; one we are unwilling to postpone, and one we intend to win and the others too. . . . Many years ago the great British explorer George Mallory, who was to die on Mount Everest, was asked why did he want to climb it. He said: 'Because it is there.' "[14]

While Kennedy personally handled the emotional argument in favor of the moonshot, White House and NASA public relations personnel managed the more substantive arguments. They may be labeled as (1) Economic; (2) Military; and (3) Prestige.

The economic theory projected the idea that the United States moon program would produce tremendous "spin-off" benefits in the form of new industries, new jobs, and a general upgrading of the quality of American life. "It is estimated conservatively," Vice President Johnson reported in 1962, "that our space outlays will yield two dollars' return for every dollar invested; for every nickel we put into it, we get a dime back. . . . The real and legitimate goal of science is the endowment of human life with new inventions and riches. That is the goal of our space effort today." In a speech in Dallas, Johnson added: "Our space program is creating and helping to create new basic industries for our economy. The number of private companies and space research organizations participating in our space programs has grown in less than six years to more than five thousand." He reminded his audience that the space program was helping the economy of Texas and that it had "brought about a major rejuvenation to New England . . . is generating new growth and prosperity in the Deep South and Southeast, and will be an increasingly important source of contracts and jobs in economic activity for the Great Lakes, the Northwest, and the Rocky Mountain states."[15]

The expansion of facts concerning the economic benefits to be gained from the moon program soon caused, in James Reston's words, "a crisis in confidence in the administration's whole space program." The scientific and business communities were the first to question the economic argument. A formal editorial in *Science* magazine, published by the American Association for the Advancement of Science, called for "a re-examination of priorities" in the lunar landing program and questioned the accuracy of the economic argument. The editorial said: "The National Aeronautics and Space Administration has sought examples of technological fall-out from its program. To date, those cited have not been impressive. The problems of space are different from the problems of the earthly tax-paying economy. Not more than a small fraction of the cost of the moon program will be recovered through technological fall-out."[16] Economist William H. Meckling, writing in the *Bulletin of Atomic Scientists,* commented: "I would feel more comfortable if I could unveil a menu of exciting applications of space technology and with confidence predict both that they soon would be realized and that they would significantly affect all our lives. Unfortunately, the outlook is not that bright."[17] In a hearing held by the Senate Aeronautical and Space Sciences Committee, Dr. Simon Ramo, vice chairman of Thompson Ramo Wooldridge, Inc., a large space and missile firm, testified: "I doubt if one can make a strong case that 'fallouts' from these large, high priority [space] projects are very satisfying and furnish a strong basis for sponsoring the program." Franklin A. Lindsay, president of Itek Corporation, declared that government expectations from space research and development contracts have been greatly exaggerated. A NASA-sponsored study concluded: "Relatively little importance can be attached to the direct transfer of products from missile/space programs to the civilian sector of the economy. . . . The findings lead to the conclusion that product transfers have not been significant and that the term 'by-product' is misleading. . . . Failure to verify the authenticity of loose claims [has] caused others to exaggerate the [missile/space] contribution."[18] Aside from making rich corporations richer, the moon program has thus far failed to improve the quality of American life.

The military argument, today all but totally abandoned, arose out of United States discomfiture over the fact that Yuri Gagarin, a military officer, had orbited over the United States. The public was easily aroused by the suggested Russian threat to "national security." Air Force Brigadier General Homer A. Boushey was the first to observe publicly that the moon's "high ground" would be a military asset. He believed that the nation controlling the moon in the missile age would have a distinct retaliatory advantage. Another Air Force general, Curtis LeMay, was more explicit. He said: "Khrushchev himself has boasted publicly about 'fantastic weapons.' Suppose the Soviets were first to develop advanced weapons of this sort and to employ them aboard maneuvering spacecraft? If they could neutralize our ICBM's with such a system, they could change the balance of decisive power in their favor."[19]

Kennedy had never been able to work up much enthusiasm for the military argument. As soon as the moon program had been funded by Congress and sold to the public, he ordered administration spokesmen to play down the military aspects of a moon landing. In 1962, Secretary of Defense Robert S. McNamara told a reporter: "At this time I see no clear requirement for manned satellites for military purposes."[20] One scientist placed a missile launching from the moon, or from an orbiting satellite, in the same category as a hunter trying to shoot a rabbit from a railroad train traveling at 20,000 miles per hour. The passage of time has confirmed the inadequacy of the military argument.

The prestige theory was first advanced by the Eisenhower administration. Kennedy gave it zest. He made it clear that by setting a definite goal (1970) for reaching the moon, the United States had accepted the challenge of the Soviet Union. Our scientific and technological prestige was on the line. The race for world prestige was on. NASA administrator James E. Webb announced that although the Russians were likely to pass us on the first laps of the race, we nevertheless stood a fifty-fifty chance of beating them to the moon. When asked by a Senate committee what he expected to find on the moon, physicist Edward Teller answered: "The Russians." The esteemed Wernher von Braun trumpeted: "We are in a race for which the stakes are as big as space itself, and I suggest we must spit on our hands, haul in our belts, and get to work in earnest." It was not difficult to convince the American people that unless the United States was able to match Russia's space efforts, our prestige would suffer a drastic decline and world opinion would turn in favor of Russia.

The prestige theory disintegrated in 1962 when Kennedy himself proposed that the United States and Russia combine efforts in several areas of space exploration. NASA's Webb, previously the most outspoken advocate of the "get there first" policy, began to deny that a "race" ever existed. Administration officials quietly dropped the prestige argument once it became obvious that no United States space accomplishment, no matter how spectacular, could deprive the Soviet Union of its growing reputation for technological maturity. Former President Eisenhower said he did not see the need for continuing the space program as such a fantastically expensive crash program. "Why the great hurry to get to the moon and the planets?" he asked. "From here on, I think we should proceed in an orderly, scientific way, building one accomplishment on another, rather than engaging in a mad effort to win a stunt race."[21] In what was to be his last public statement on the space program, Kennedy reflected the administration's less competitive attitude toward the moonshot. He cited a story told by Irish author Frank O'Connor. In his boyhood days, O'Connor and his friends would make their way across the countryside and when they came to an orchard wall that seemed too high to climb, they would take off their hats and toss them over the wall. Then they had no choice but to follow them. "This nation has tossed its cap over the wall of space, and we have no choice but to follow it," Kennedy said.[22]

This analysis of the federal government's orchestration of public opinion in regard to the moon program should not be construed as denunciation of the program itself. The analysis is intended to illustrate how, with all the funds and mechanisms at its command, the government is able to manage public support for a particular program. There is little doubt that the moon program will benefit the United States. The doubt arises when consideration is given to the techniques used in getting the public to accept the program.

In creating an aura of goodness around the moon program, Project Apollo, the federal government also succeeded in wrapping it in a cloak of infallibility. In short, the government came to believe its own propaganda. Thus, when astronauts Virgil Grissom, Edward White, and Roger Chaffee died at Cape Kennedy's Pad 34 on January 27, 1967, Kennedy

Space Center director Kurt Debus was able to say: "Despite meticulous attention to the smallest detail, this tragedy occurred." Debus knew better. The Apollo program had been plagued by poor management, corner cutting, and faulty workmanship since its inception. But the mystique of the space program enabled NASA administrator Webb to admonish a House committee: "If any man in this room wants to ask 'For Whom the Apollo Tolls,' I can tell him. It tolls for him and for me, as well as for Grissom, White and Chaffee. It tolls for every astronaut who will lose his life on some lonely hill on the moon or Mars. It tolls for government and industrial executives and legislators alike." In translation, Webb was saying: "You [Congress] pay the fare, shut up, and leave the driving to us." He was using public sympathy for the dead astronauts and a fast-talking ability as weapons against the developing truth. He even tried to shift some of the blame to the news media by referring to the continuous evaluation of the space program by "opinion makers with little time for sober second thought." William Hines, science editor of the Washington *Evening Star*, commented:

> In these flack-ridden times it is perhaps not surprising that the taxpaying public should be hoodwinked, falsely propagandized, deliberately misled and, on occasion, even lied to by its servants. It is deplorable, however, and dangerous in the bargain, that NASA has deluded itself into believing the reality of its own Image.
>
> The Image is a myth 9 feet tall, compounded in equal parts of John Glenn and Dr. Robert H. Goddard, with just a dash of the Redeemer added for omniscience and omnipotence. . . .
>
> It is essential that The Image never show its feet of clay; everything NASA attempts must be crowned with success; probing the frontiers of technology and doing things never done before, NASA must always do them on schedule, within budgets, and just exactly right.[23]

The era of NASA's press-agent imagery was shattered when Webb was called to account before House and Senate investigating committees in May of 1967. Though he had previously stated that North American Aviation was the first selection of the 190-man NASA board to build the Apollo spacecraft, Webb changed his story in testimony before the Senate Aeronautical and Space Sciences Committee. Under questioning from Senator Margaret Chase Smith of Maine, he admitted that the Martin Company had been the first choice of the NASA board, but that he and three of his assistants had overruled the board in favor of North American. When Webb refused to disclose the contents of a report severely criticizing the handling of the Apollo program, Congressman John W. Wydler of New York snapped: "I think you have an obsession with secrecy, Mr. Webb." Commented Congressman Don Fuqua of Florida: "I get the feeling you haven't informed us of the state of this program." Webb still refused to give up the "Phillips Report." (The report was later made public by Congressman William F. Ryan of New York.) The reaction to Webb's performance by members of Congress was typified by a remark made by Congressman Ken Hechler of West Virginia: "I intend to be much more skeptical of NASA in the future." Despite the public airing of Webb's contradictory actions and misleading statements, the Congress failed to pass a measure introduced by Congressman Donald Rumsfeld of Illinois which would have required the NASA administrator to keep Congress "fully and currently informed." The Congress did, however, appreciably reduce NASA's appropriations for 1968.

In fiscal 1967, NASA spent some $20 million to maintain its image. Its public relations budget covered salaries for 400 publicity employees, production of television programs and motion pictures, news photo services, special exhibits, and scores of "supporting activities." None of these expenditures promises to change Washington reporters' view of NASA as a federal agency more concerned with propaganda than with truth. None will eradicate the saying among newsmen that NASA's initials stand for "Never A Straight Answer." Only new leadership and closer scrutiny from Congress will result in fundamental improvements in NASA's attitude toward its statutory obligation to inform the public honestly.

The executive branch of the federal government has no

qualms about bringing its resources to bear on Congress in order to influence legislation or to otherwise manage events. In April, 1967, Republican sponsors of a bill to amend the Elementary and Secondary Education Act were subjected to the full force of the "Johnson juggernaut." Playing upon educational leaders' fear of losing federal aid, administration officials spread the word from coast to coast that the GOP bill was designed to undermine the complicated formula under which private and parochial schools receive federal funds. United States Education Commissioner Harold Howe and Health, Education and Welfare Secretary John W. Gardner delivered speeches in which they misrepresented the intent of the bill. The administration aimed its attack at stirring up clergymen, particularly Roman Catholic, knowing full well that they have been sensitive to the church-state issue and that clergymen represent a powerful lobbying group. The President put the allegation of religious prejudice on the public record himself. In an April 27 speech at Camp Springs, Maryland, he said: "They [proponents of the bill] are reviving ancient and bitter feuds between church and public school leaders."

The administration's program of manipulating facts was so far-reaching and so thorough that many thousands of citizens were convinced that the Republican bill jeopardized aid to private and parochial schools. One congressman received 5,000 letters opposing the measure. Another member of Congress was telephoned by a hometown financial backer who threatened to oppose the congressman's reelection if he voted for the bill. Support for the amendment, which would have in no way impaired private and parochial school aid, faded rapidly. The proposal was defeated in the House.

Other attempts by the federal government to manage the news include:

—The discovery in 1967 that the Food and Drug Administration had been covertly distributing "news" articles to 400 trade-union newspapers under a heading "Good and Welfare."

—A 1966 memorandum from a Treasury Department official to Congressman Wright Patman of Texas which inadvertently carried an internal message confessing: "You'll note we have purposely not answered the question except in a very indirect way."

—The revelation in 1966 that the United States Information Agency had spent $90,000 the previous year to subsidize the publication of books which were sold in the United States without any mention of the USIA's subsidies.

—A program devised in 1967 by Office of Economic Opportunity units in Iowa to pay advertising rates to the news media in return for favorable news coverage.

In order to understand fully the problem of news management by the federal government, it is necessary to consider not only the methods available to government officials for exercising such management, but also the circumstances under which the news media are vulnerable to accepting and disseminating government information. There is a mutual dependency in the government-press relationship. The press is as dependent on the government for information as the government is on the press for communication of that information. Therefore, if news management is to be reduced, both the government and the press must initiate steps toward reduction.

NOTES TO CHAPTER 6

1. *Twenty-Third Intermediate Report,* Committee on Expenditures in the Executive Departments, House of Representatives, 80th Congress, Second Session, December 31, 1948, p. 15.

2. *Availability of Information from Federal Departments and Agencies,* Part I, Hearing before a Subcommittee of the Committee on Government Operations, House of Representatives, 84th Congress, First Session, November 7, 1955, p. 25.

3. Arthur Krock, "Mr. Kennedy's Management of the News," *Fortune,* March, 1963, p. 82.

4. Remarks by Moyers before the American Newspaper Publishers Association, New York, April 26, 1967.

5. "How Much Management of the News?" *Newsweek,* April 8, 1963, p. 61.

6. Chalmers M. Roberts and George C. Wilson, "Haiphong Harbor Eyed as Next Bombing Target," *Washington Post,* April 27, 1967, p. 1.

7. Richard Harwood, "On the Record About the Background Session," *Washington Post,* April 30, 1967.

8. *Washington Post,* April 25, 1961, p. 1.

9. "A Date with Diana," *An Analytical and Critical Study of the Decision by the United States to Land a Man on the Moon by 1970,* unpublished thesis by Stephen I. Danzansky, Washington, D.C., 1964, p. 11. (Hereafter referred to as "Danzansky Report.")

10. Richard E. Neustadt, *Presidential Power* (New York: Signet Books, 1964), pp. 43–44.

11. Danzansky Report, p. 14.

12. *Ibid.*

13. As quoted in *Newsweek,* October 8, 1962, p. 88.

14. Washington *Evening Star,* September 12, 1962, p. 1.

15. James Reston, "What Government Officials Do You Believe?" *New York Times,* April 24, 1963, p. 34.

16. *Science,* April, 1963.

17. *Reader's Digest,* January, 1964, p. 77.

18. *The Commercial Application of Missile/Space Technology,* Report of the Denver Research Institute, University of Denver, 1963.

19. *This Week Magazine,* September 16, 1962.

20. *Newsweek,* October 8, 1962, p. 78.

21. *The Saturday Evening Post,* August 11, 1962, p. 24.

22. Address by Kennedy at dedication of Aero-Space Medical Health Center, Brooks Air Force Base, Texas, November 21, 1963.

23. William Hines, "NASA: The Image Misfires," *The Nation,* April 24, 1967, p. 517.

CHAPTER 7

The Pentagon

In the councils of government, we must guard against the acquisition of unwarranted influence, whether sought or unsought, by the military-industrial complex. . . . We must never let the weight of this combination endanger our liberties or democratic processes. —DWIGHT D. EISENHOWER

At a rendezvous in a Washington, D.C., restaurant in mid-February, 1967, Chicago *Daily News* correspondent Charles E. Nicodemus was informed that the United States government had secretly authorized the sale of 20,300 hard-to-get M-16 rifles to the neutralist government of Singapore.

The informant, a professional weapons consultant, expressed the opinion that the sale was improper because of the "heavy demand" for M-16s by United States and allied fighting men in Vietnam.

Nicodemus was puzzled. He knew that Secretary of Defense Robert S. McNamara had been vehemently denying the existence of any shortage of weapons, ammunition, or other supplies in Vietnam. Could McNamara be mistaken? Was the M-16 in short supply? If so, how could the United States possibly afford to be permitting its export to places other than Vietnam?

Since his assignment to the *Daily News'* Washington

bureau in 1962, Nicodemus had wrestled with similar questions, and, in the process, had become an authority on defense procurement. He had developed and written several stories concerning the sale of arms, and as early as 1962 had been commended by United States Attorney General Robert F. Kennedy for his role in exposing an Army bribery ring at Fort Monmouth, N.J. At thirty-six, he had earned a reputation for thorough and incisive reporting of Pentagon affairs.

Nicodemus was familiar with the M-16's history. It had been developed in 1956 as the AR-15 by what was then the Armalite division of Fairchild-Hiller Corporation. The exclusive rights to manufacture and sell the rifle had been obtained by Colt Industries. Beginning in 1958, Colt made repeated attempts to sell the M-16 to the United States Army, but the Army—heavily committed to the Army-designed M-14 rifle—refused to buy. In July, 1960, Colt's Robert MacDonald managed to convince Air Force General Curtis LeMay to watch a demonstration of the M-16. On a farm outside Washington, MacDonald illustrated the rifle's authority by literally disintegrating a row of watermelons with it. Impressed, LeMay ordered twenty-five rifles for testing at Lackland Air Force Base.

The M-16 is a light, rapid-fire automatic rifle with a muzzle velocity high enough to inflict wounds similar to those made by soft-nose and exploding bullets outlawed by the Hague Conventions of 1899 and 1907. The high-speed bullet smashes bones and blood vessels, tears tissue apart, and transmits a shock which bursts vital organs. Because the M-16 is capable of a great volume of accurate fire at close range, it is considered an especially good weapon for nighttime and jungle fighting.

In 1961, Colt succeeded in getting the Pentagon's Advance Research Projects Agency to agree to begin testing the M-16 for possible use by United States Special Forces in Vietnam. President Kennedy was shown an M-16 while he was inspecting a Navy Seal Team at Norfolk, Virginia, in 1962, and he asked that it be demonstrated. He liked it so well that he ordered it adopted as standard equipment by the Secret Service. In 1963, after test quantities of the rifle proved to be extremely effective in jungle fighting in Vietnam, the Army reversed its position and contracted with Colt for 104,000 at a price of $13.3 million. Colt subsequently received Army orders for 404,000 additional guns. They were to be manufactured at a rate of 25,000 per month, with the final gun scheduled for delivery in December of 1967.

With this background, Nicodemus set out to gather information concerning the alleged plan to sell M-16s to Singapore. He first queried the Army Materiel Command to get details of existing M-16 production and delivery schedules. Next, he telephoned John Sipes, director of the State Department's Office of Munitions Control. Sipes acknowledged that Colt had been granted a license to export some 20,000 rifles to the former British colony. He said: "This is a private transaction over which the government has no control. All we did was issue an export license after we decided the sale would not be contrary to the national interest. I can't tell you anything more." Having confirmed that a sales agreement existed, Nicodemus called Colt's president, Robert Benke, who admitted the company had signed a "top secret" contract with Singapore. Benke referred further questions to Singapore's Secretary of Defense and Interior, Ge Bogaars. After he had sent a cablegram and made two unsuccessful telephone calls to Singapore, Nicodemus was advised that Bogaars was "out of his office" and that he had "no information to give anyway." The time had come to broach the subject at the Pentagon.

Major General David Liebman, speaking for the Assistant Secretary of Defense for Public Affairs, told Nicodemus that the Pentagon had approved the Singapore sale because the 25,000 M-16s the military was receiving each month were "all that the United States and its fighting allies can effectively utilize." In other words, Liebman said, the United States had no need for more than 25,000 rifles per month, and Colt was free to do anything it pleased with "excess production."

In a story distributed for release on March 6, 1967, Nicodemus laid the M-16 deal with Singapore before the public. The ninety-three newspapers subscribing to the Chicago Daily News Service also received seven follow-up stories during March and April. Each story revealed contradictory, misleading, and confusing statements made by Pentagon officials. The most flagrant discrepancies were:

—A Pentagon spokesman said that "most military needs for the M-16 have been met in Vietnam."[1] This was untrue. As of March 1, 1967, there was a backlog of orders for 350,000 M-16s for the Army, as well as orders for another 98,000 for the Air Force, Navy, and Marines. Under the then existing delivery schedules, the latter orders could not be filled until April of 1968. In addition, South Korean and South Vietnamese troops were anxiously awaiting 145,000 of the guns. General William C. Westmoreland, United States commander in Vietnam, had testified in Congress that he wanted every soldier under his command equipped with an M-16 to meet the growing firepower of Communist-made automatic rifles.

—Lieutenant Colonel Douglas Jones, the Pentagon's M-16 expert, declared that the sale to Singapore would not interfere with the "optimum delivery rate" of M-16s to Vietnam. This statement was misleading. At the time Jones spoke, the Pentagon was seeking to accelerate the delivery rate through inclusion in a Vietnam supplemental appropriations bill of an unpublicized request for $4 million to finance expansion of M-16 production facilities.

—Various Pentagon officials said the Department of Defense had "officially authorized" the Singapore sale. This was not the case. Because of a bureaucratic slip-up in the State Department, the sale was given the green light without advance clearance from the Pentagon. Had Pentagon officials been consulted, they probably would have vetoed the sale. Administrative procedures have since been changed to require Pentagon and CIA clearance of all major weapons exports.

—The Pentagon repeatedly attempted to confuse newsmen

by referring to the rifles destined for Singapore by their commercial designation, AR-15. These attempts met with some success. The designations AR-15 and M-16 both apply to the same weapon.

—Again in efforts to confuse the news media, the Pentagon gave out three different and conflicting versions of the M-16 delivery arrangement with Colt.

When Senator John C. Stennis of Mississippi, chairman of the Senate Armed Services Preparedness Subcommittee, and other members of Congress saw the Nicodemus stories, they expressed concern over the rifle sale. Singapore officials obstinately demanded the United States make good on its agreement. Singapore's Prime Minister, Lee Kuan Yew, had earlier announced that he had a letter from Secretary of State Dean Rusk guaranteeing Colt's delivery of the rifles "despite United States military needs." In South Korea, Defense Minister Kim Sung-Eun told a news conference that he had been begging the United States for M-16s and that it was urgent that the "outmoded small firearms of our boys" in Vietnam be replaced. *Hankok Ilbo,* a Seoul newspaper, said the sale of M-16s to Singapore "makes us feel as if we had been betrayed by a friend." South Vietnamese military leaders also restated their plea for M-16s.

In a hearing held on May 15, 1967, by a special House Armed Services Subcommittee named to investigate Pentagon assertions about the M-16 deal, Assistant Secretary of the Army Robert A. Brooks divulged that the Defense Department intended to prohibit any further sales of M-16s to foreign countries. "The sale to Singapore was the result of a defect in our procedures," he said. Congressman Richard Ichord of Missouri, subcommittee chairman, told Brooks that the sale "just defied all logic." Congressman Speedy Long of Louisiana said: "I can't see how you people in the executive branch could have, in good conscience, let this sale to Singapore go forward." Congressman Paul Findley of Illinois charged: "The Department of Defense has misled Congress and the public and prevaricated on every key fact involved in

the Singapore sale and in M-16 procurement." Nicodemus
wrote in a by-lined column that the Singapore sale could have
been stopped and the extra guns diverted to Vietnam "to help
out against the swelling tide of Chinese-made AK automatic
rifles, which badly outgun the M-14. But that would be an
admission that the Pentagon's rifle procurement program has
been deficient and shortsighted. And that would never do."[2]

As a result of the Nicodemus stories and the congressional
interest they stimulated, the Pentagon was prodded into
speeding up production of the M-16. Singapore got its guns.
However, the reluctance of the Pentagon to admit its foot-
dragging and procurement mistakes caused M-16 shortages
which hampered the allied effort in Vietnam. Our allies questioned our sincerity. The Pentagon's deceitful tactics widened
the credibility gap.

The Pentagon building, headquarters of the most powerful
military establishment on earth, was constructed in the early
1940's on the Virginia side of the Potomac River in a swamp-
land area known as "Hell's Bottom." The five-sided, fortress-
like structure is the world's largest office building. It has
7,000 offices, 1,900 toilets, and 17½ miles of corridors. A
source of discord from its conception, the Pentagon was criticized for its location (an original site adjoining Arlington
Cemetery was vetoed by President Roosevelt), for its cost (at
$83 million, cheaper than a battleship), and for its utility
(many saw it as another "empire building" move by the
military).

Today, the Pentagon is a self-contained "city" of 28,000
employees, a handful of whom direct the worldwide activities
of 3,500,000 men and women in the United States Air Force,
Army, Marines, and Navy. The declaration of the Continental Congress that "standing armies in time of peace are
inconsistent with the principles of republican governments,
dangerous to the liberties of a free people and generally
concerted into a destructive engine for establishing despotism"[3] has long been forsaken. The Secretary of Defense, a
civilian, administers the Defense Department's annual budget

of $75 billion (more than half of the total United States budget) and keeps track of military assets totaling $150 billion.

It is commonly recognized that the Pentagon derives its awesome power from two sources: money and the weapons money buys. Overlooked is a third source of power: control of information. With the vast resources at its command, the military establishment is in a position to do more controlling of information than any other single agency of government. Not only do Pentagon officials direct the flow of the greatest quantity of government information, but they also deal with data of the most significant quality. Daily decisions made in the Pentagon affect the security of our nation and the world, war and peace, life and death. There are no issues more vital than these. The responsibility of military leaders to inform the public fully and accurately is of paramount importance. And yet there are some who harbor a reluctance to let the people know what is going on in the Pentagon.

The complicated maze of the Pentagon was only partially simplified by the act of 1947 which reorganized the armed forces into three departments (Army, Navy, and Air Force) and which placed the Secretary of Defense in overall authority. The first Secretary, James Forrestal, remarked: "This office will probably be the biggest cemetery for dead cats in history." Overwhelmed by the immensity of his job, Forrestal leaped to his death in 1949. When President Kennedy took office in 1961, six secretaries later, he received a report which concluded: "Throughout all proposals, past and present, to make more effective the Defense Department organization, has run one central theme—the clarification and strengthening of the authority of the Secretary of Defense over the entire United States Military Establishment. . . . It is the conclusion of this committee that the doctrine of civilian control will be compromised as long as doubt exists on this point."[4] The report noted that for fifteen years it had been impossible to say who was master of the mighty forces gathered in the Pentagon. It recommended that Kennedy appoint a genuine "take-charge guy" as the eighth Secretary of Defense.

Kennedy obliged. He plucked a Republican, Robert Strange McNamara, from the presidency of the Ford Motor Company and asked him to do a job which—if he could handle it—promised to make him the second most powerful official in Washington. McNamara responded to the challenge with vigor. His rimless eyeglasses and slicked-down hair quickly became the symbols of fear among generals and admirals. He intimidated them with his IBM mind. Carl W. Borklund, author of *Men of the Pentagon: From Forrestal to McNamara*, offered this telling anecdote: "A colonel places an important, page-long cablegram in front of McNamara, who glances at it and returns it to the officer. 'Don't you want to read it?' asks the anxious colonel. 'I already have,' McNamara responds." An expert in statistical control, McNamara got a steel grip on the Pentagon's fiscal machinery and installed a bevy of Ivy League and West Coast "Whiz Kids" to keep it that way. He transferred numerous functions previously handled by the military services to his own office and he downgraded the authority of the military chiefs. He instituted a one-man rule which replaced collective military expertise with individual civilian judgment, smothered dissent, and forced the legions of the Pentagon to speak with one voice. He unleashed a force without precedent in the Pentagon—The McNamara Monarchy. He came on so strong, so fast that he was soon under sharp attack for exercising too much control at the Pentagon.

Hanson Baldwin, military editor of the *New York Times*, summed up McNamara's assumption of power this way: "The 'unification' of the armed services sponsored by Secretary of Defense Robert S. McNamara poses some subtle and insidious dangers—creeping dangers that are political, military and administrative. And they could present, in ultimate form, almost as great a threat to a secure and free nation as the attempted military coup envisaged in the recent novel, *Seven Days in May*."[5] Elvis J. Stahr, who was Secretary of the Army under McNamara and is now president of Indiana University, said McNamara is the ablest man he has ever worked with but "he has a tendency to overreach in exercising control and intrude in small details of administration." Stahr added: "The Defense Department is too big to be run by one man and there are just not enough McNamaras. . . . I'm afraid there is a tendency to neglect the accumulated wisdom and responsible toughness of the career officers."[6] Veteran Pentagon correspondent Jack Raymond observed that centralization of power in the hands of a civilian Secretary of Defense is equally as dangerous as too much power in the hands of a single "Prussian-style" chief of staff. He said: "The acknowledged excellence of a McNamara should not divert us from traditional precautions against centralized military authority outside the White House, whether exercised by a man in uniform or in civilian clothes. It is not the character of the man but the power he wields that should concern us."[7]

McNamara has tremendous confidence in his own abilities. Many construe this to be an air of superiority. He disconcerts his listeners by rattling off statistics in a glib, know-it-all manner. He is unwilling to admit mistakes, preferring to correct them without publicity through administrative channels rather than in public view. He is prone to defend his decisions, both good and bad, "at all costs." His apparent belief that the business of the Pentagon is somehow sacrosanct may account in part for his careless administration of military information programs.

In a closed-door appearance before the Senate Armed Services Committee in April, 1961, McNamara seemed to express a preference for misinforming the American people if, in his judgment, the circumstances warranted it. "Why should we tell Russia that the Zeus [guided missile] development may not be satisfactory?" he argued. "What we ought to be saying is that we have the most perfect anti-ICBM system that the human mind will ever devise. Instead the public domain is already full of statements that the Zeus may not be satisfactory, that it has deficiencies." Under this thinly-cloaked guise of discouraging the spread of information which might aid an enemy, McNamara was suggesting that the news media mislead the public.

A major blow to the United States government's credibility was struck on June 8, 1967, when the U.S.S. *Liberty* was attacked by Israeli aircraft and torpedo boats, killing 34 American seamen and wounding 75 more. A McNamara spokesman in the Pentagon offered the ludicrous explanation that the *Liberty* was a "research vessel" that was in the Arab-Israeli war zone "to assure communications between United States government posts in the Middle East and to assist in relaying information concerning the evacuation of American dependents and other American citizens." The truth was that the *Liberty*, an electronic ferret ship, had moved into the combat theater for the purpose of conducting sophisticated electronic espionage directed at both sides of the conflict. The insinuations, carefully circulated by Pentagon officials, that the attack was wholly without justification only served to defraud the American people. The *Washington Post* commented: "When, by some calamity, the cloak of secrecy is ripped away, then the government has an obligation to explain what happened in forthright terms, if only to maintain confidence in its integrity at home and abroad. . . . When the essentials of an espionage operation have been exposed, continued secrecy or obfuscation only serve to plant more seeds of doubt."

Another McNamara-directed credibility blunder occurred in June of 1967 when the Soviet Union charged that United States planes bombed and strafed one of its cargo ships on June 2 in the North Vietnamese port of Cam Pha. A spokesman for McNamara said the United States had no information confirming the allegation, but that an investigation had been ordered. On June 3, the Pentagon flatly denied the Soviet charges. However, after the Russians announced that one of seven crewmen wounded on the ship had died, the Defense Department lamely acknowledged that United States planes had been in the area at the time of the attack. The State Department sent a formal note of apology to the Soviet embassy. "As a result of this bungling," the Spokane *Spokesman-Review* observed, "the United States has suffered another blow to its prestige."

The still-smoldering controversy over the TFX jet fighter plane is a sad monument to McNamara's single-mindedness, his fallible judgment, and his compulsion to cover up errors. Contrary to recommendations of civilian experts and the Joint Chiefs of Staff, McNamara acted in 1961 to award a multi-billion dollar contract for the TFX (now named the F-111) to General Dynamics Corporation, a firm with good political connections and reported financial difficulties. He justified this singular action on the grounds that $1 billion would be saved because of "commonality," a McNamara word meaning the plane would be used by both the Air Force and Navy. It is now evident that, instead of $1 billion being saved, the TFX is going to cost nearly twice the original estimate of $7 billion. The plane has technical shortcomings which may never be corrected. But, even though his dollar-saving argument has been discredited, McNamara continues doggedly to defend the TFX deal. When Senator John L. McClellan of Arkansas, chairman of the Senate Investigating Subcommittee, demanded in early 1967 to be given the latest TFX cost estimates, McNamara refused. He conceded that costs have soared far above the original estimates, but declined to produce specific figures. He reasoned: "We should not release to the committee information which is ambiguous and could easily be misunderstood. . . . I don't believe the committee would want to receive information that affects so delicate a negotiation as this at this time."[8] McNamara's spurious logic failed to placate Senator McClellan, who noted that the Secretary had in the past told the committee "many things you do not want the Russians, the Chinese, or the Communists to know . . . but you cannot trust the committee to give it your estimates, our estimates of the cost of one of the largest weapons systems we have ever acquired."[9]

McNamara has widely heralded his cost effectiveness program. This balloon was deflated in August of 1966 by Congressman Charles Gubser of California, who said: "The public, and particularly Congress, is fast losing faith in the statistics of Secretary of Defense McNamara and the credibility gap is widening." Gubser, ranking minority member of the House Armed Services Special Investigating Subcommittee, pointed to a press conference in which McNamara had claimed Pentagon penny-pinching had saved the taxpayers $14 billion in five years. Gubser explained that he and the subcommittee chairman, Congressman Porter Hardy of Virginia, decided to look into McNamara's claims, and with the help of ten auditors from the General Accounting Office, discovered that more than one third of the announced savings were invalid and another third were questionable. In one case, McNamara claimed credit for a saving of $1.6 million for aircraft engineering changes which had been recommended by the Grumman Company before the Secretary ever took office. Another case involved McNamara's claimed saving of $51 million by having the Marines overhaul M-48 tanks instead of buying new M-60s. Close questioning by Gubser uncovered the information that the Marines were never authorized to purchase M-60 tanks and that they were not needed anyway. Gubser outlined still another case: "The Defense Department took credit for saving $83.5 million in 1965 by reducing the number of items it carried in inventory. The claim will be carried forward into each succeeding year so that in 1967 they will start with a saving of $83.5 million. This is about like going back to the year 1800 and continuing to claim savings for 166 years for not stocking bows and arrows. . . . Mr. McNamara has clearly played fast and loose with figures in his cost reduction program. Unfortunately, he has done so at a time when he needs public confidence and is losing it fast."[10]

The Hardy subcommittee urged McNamara to tell the truth in these terms: "The true accomplishments of the cost reduction program are its best recommendation. . . . Its continuing worth depends upon its acceptance as a valid indicator of results. Grossly inflated claims can only detract from its effectiveness." One leading newspaper editorialized: "If a housewife walks past the gourmet counter and doesn't buy a $5 can of imported truffles, does she have the right to boast to her husband that she has 'saved' this amount during the week? Few would blame the man in the house for raising an eyebrow at such a claim."[11] The newspaper expressed the hope that Congress would continue to swim through "the constant stream of propaganda flowing from the Pentagon" on the subject of "cost-avoidance." A Hardy subcommittee report also revealed that "some of the key documents . . . which support the above conclusion" were stamped "secret" by McNamara's office and the information concealed from the public. "Only a small portion of the content of these documents could be considered as classified information and, therefore, we have made repeated attempts to have the balance declassified," the report said. "Our efforts have been unsuccessful. OSD [Office of the Secretary of Defense] has taken the position that public disclosure would result in 'comfort to the enemy,' but, undoubtedly, the enemy derives more comfort from our attenuated military capability. . . . Public disclosure of the facts could do much to bring about an improvement in the decision-making process responsible for the above condition. A skeptic might question whether disclosure in such a situation could adversely affect the national defense or merely the public image of the decision-makers."[12]

McNamara's pretense as a money-saver was further destroyed in August of 1967 when Congressman Otis G. Pike of New York disclosed that the Defense Construction Supply Center at Columbus, Ohio, paid $194.30 apiece for gears that were priced by the manufacturer at $3.43 each. The Army Electronics Command, Pike added, bought 128 gear clamps, listed by the manufacturer at $1.80 each, for $18.75 apiece— a markup of more than 1,000 percent. Referring to Defense Department purchasing practices as "wasteful and appalling," Pike noted that the facts did not coincide with what

McNamara had been telling Congress about his "cost-conscious" administration of Pentagon buying.

Despite criticism from Congress and the press, McNamara has refused to admit any undue restraint upon the free flow of information from the Pentagon. However, he has continually erected new barriers to public scrutiny. In 1965, he established a new Defense Contract Audit Agency for the purpose of supplanting the role of the General Accounting Office (GAO) in auditing Pentagon operations. The GAO, a "watchdog" for Congress over executive branch spending, had issued reports which contained a great deal of information and some sharp attacks on Pentagon policies. By creating his own auditing agency, McNamara was able to contend that continued auditing by the GAO represented waste and duplication. In March of 1966, he presented this dubious argument to the House Government Operations Committee, and, with the acquiescence of committee chairman William L. Dawson of Illinois, succeeded in pressuring the GAO into drastically reducing its investigations of defense procurement, limiting the number of cases referred to the Justice Department for prosecution, and curtailing recommendations for the elimination of questionable practices. Further, the GAO was forced to "volunteer" to coordinate its activities with McNamara's self-appointed audit agency and to discontinue some of its public information functions. Less than a year after McNamara pulled the watchdog's teeth, the effect of his extractions was seen in the GAO's refusal to make public a report covering the entertainment of military procurement officers by defense contractors.

One of McNamara's most consistent critics, Clark Mollenhoff of Cowles Publications, Incorporated, told a Sigma Delta Chi convention in April of 1967 that the Secretary's whole cost effectiveness program is "a lot of public relations bunk." Pointing out that Pentagon expenditures have skyrocketed, Mollenhoff said: "McNamara came into office in 1961, immediately increased the defense budget by $8 billion, and then claimed to be the greatest economizer in history. His economy claims come from phony savings. He cancels a particular program, puts out a lot of publicity about the money 'saved,' and then turns around and spends that money on something else. It's gotten to a point where neither the conservatives nor the liberals in Congress believe what McNamara tells them. We don't like to think that the Secretary of Defense lies to us, but you tell me a better word for it." A more subdued McNamara critic is George C. Wilson, Pentagon reporter for the *Washington Post*. He observed: "Public confidence is the real mortar of our government. Lying erodes that confidence. If the Pentagon is going to take on a censorship responsibility, then it should also be responsible to the extent that it does not tinker with the truth." Donald L. Zylstra, a reporter for American Aviation Publications, has noted a "marked deterioration in the Department of Defense news climate . . . since the advent of the McNamara regime." He said that if McNamara's "speak-with-one-voice" policy were carried to its ultimate extreme, the public "might be permitted only 10 to 15 percent of the pertinent, unclassified news about government."[13]

In July of 1967, members of Congress began asking searching questions of McNamara after Neil Sheehan revealed in the *New York Times* that the United States had given away or sold $46.3 billion worth of arms to foreign governments in the last seventeen years. Congressional leaders had no knowledge of most of the sales. To make matters worse, it was discovered that $2 billion in camouflaged arms sales had been made through credits provided by the Export-Import Bank. In protest against the use of the Export-Import Bank as a "cover" for selling arms abroad, thirteen members of the House Banking and Currency Committee demanded a thorough investigation. They said: "The issue confronting us far transcends past failures to keep informed the Congressional committees with primary legislative jurisdiction over the Export-Import Bank's operations. On the contrary, the issue goes to the heart of the growing crisis in confidence surrounding the Johnson administration. . . . It's not so much that necessary covert operations must remain confidential as it is that these covert operations further are designed to deceive. . . . We believe that the justified disclosure of this activity . . . has seriously damaged the Bank's reputation. The main task before our committee is consideration of various means by which international confidence and trust in the Bank can be restored."

During the first six years of the McNamara reign, Pentagon information programs were directed by Arthur Sylvester, a heavy-handed and quick-tempered former reporter for the Newark *Evening News*. McNamara flew to New York in 1961 to personally offer Sylvester the post of Assistant Secretary of Defense for Public Affairs. After "walking the streets for three days," Sylvester—then fifty-nine years old— accepted the job. Until his resignation* in February of 1967, he ran the most controversial "shop" in Pentagon history. Yet, he lasted in the Defense Department hot spot longer than any other man.

Sylvester's stormy Pentagon career was most outstanding for its popularization of the terms "news management" and "right to lie." These terms grew out of the Bay of Pigs invasion and the Cuban missile crisis. In each instance, Sylvester employed stratagems of distortion in disseminating information which undermined the confidence of the public and the press. Many government officials today hold Sylvester in low esteem, not because of his questionable approaches to the handling of government news, but because of his audacity in articulating them. He violated the bureaucratic rule of "do it, justify it, shut up."

In an appearance before the House Subcommittee on Government Information, Charles S. Rowe, chairman of the Freedom of Information Committee of the Associated Press Managing Editors Association, testified: "In its efforts to deceive actual or potential foreign adversaries, the government has also deceived the American people. The credibility of their government has suffered in the eyes of many citizens.

* Sylvester is now reported to be writing his memoirs. Newsmen prophesy they will be printed on asbestos paper.

This erosion of faith in the veracity of government, if long continued, can result in serious harm to a democratic society."[14] Rowe was making reference to Sylvester's denial in October, 1962, that there were offensive missiles in Cuba, when, in fact, he had evidence that such weapons were present, and also to the Pentagon's statement that a scheduled amphibious exercise in the Caribbean had been canceled because of a hurricane when it had actually been canceled because the ships were needed in the blockade of Cuba. Doubts about the Pentagon's credibility increased when, two months after the Cuban missile crisis, Sylvester expressed his belief in the government's "inherent . . . right, if necessary, to lie to save itself when it's going up into nuclear war." Rowe commented: "If we should accept a premise that the government has a right to lie to the American people under one set of circumstances, there is a serious danger that this repugnant philosophy will be extended to more and more circumstances and we will find ourselves being lied to with increasing frequency. In the battle of democracy versus totalitarianism, let us not imitate the tactics of our adversaries. Let our weapon be the truth, not the lie."[15] The pattern of deception and manipulation of news established by Sylvester's office in the early days of the missile crisis so damaged the Pentagon's credibility that McNamara found it necessary to stage a televised intelligence briefing in an attempt to restore public confidence in government pronouncements.

Subsequent to making his right-to-lie statement, Sylvester frequently denied ever having made such a remark. "This I never said," he told a Senate Committee. However, the truth was established by Stanford Smith, general manager of the American Newspaper Publishers Association, who told a House committee: "When Mr. Sylvester appeared before the New York chapter of Sigma Delta Chi [December 6, 1962], of which I happen to be the vice president, the American Broadcasting Company had a tape recorder there. And as a service to all media who are vitally interested in this subject we [ANPA] borrowed the tape from the ABC and we had our office transcribe the exact words of Mr. Sylvester, and under the supervision of an executive of our staff who was present at the time. So I would like to testify to the fact that the quotation from Mr. Sylvester . . . is a verbatim transcript of what Mr. Sylvester said on that occasion."[16] Sylvester's unabashed denials on this matter only served to further cloud his reputation for veracity.*

Sylvester seemed to enjoy his "guerrilla war" with newsmen. His style was antagonistic. On one occasion, when he accused reporters of deliberately violating the rules of a backgrounder held by McNamara, two of them almost took a swing at him. He averted an embarrassing situation by saying he hadn't meant to use the word "deliberately." Other Sylvester encounters included his indignant scolding of labor columnist Victor Riesel for accurately describing inefficiency and corruption in the unloading of war materiel at the Port of Saigon; his intemperate berating of the *New York Times'* R. W. Apple, Jr., for refusing to relay an official Pentagon handout on an air raid in Vietnam; and his badgering of magazine reporter J. Richard Elliott, Jr., for writing an article highly critical of the TFX.

Sylvester's most heated battle was with Morley Safer of CBS News, winner in 1966 of both the Sigma Delta Chi and the Overseas Press Club awards for best television reporting. It started when Safer reported on Sylvester's conduct at a 1965 meeting in Vietnam arranged by Barry Zorthian, information chief at the United States embassy in Saigon, to discuss the credibility question. Noting that Zorthian had been concerned for a number of reasons about the Pentagon's credibility, Safer recounted the meeting's events:

* Writing in the *Saturday Evening Post's* "Speaking Out" column of November 18, 1967, Sylvester admitted that he *did* make the right-to-lie statement in 1962. He added: ". . . (T)he assertion that government information must always be truthful requires qualification. . . . For six years I watched cover stories go down smooth as cream." Sylvester also argued that the use of "no comment" as an alternative for lying would be no solution because it would require government spokesmen to take newsmen aside to acquaint them with the facts on the understanding that nothing would be printed. "After all," he jabbed, "newsmen *are* gabby."

Those of us involved in broadcasting were anxious to discuss the problems of communication. There was general opening banter, which Sylvester quickly brushed aside. He seemed anxious to take a stand—to say something that would jar us. He did:

"I can't understand how you fellows can write what you do while American boys are dying out there," Sylvester began. Then he went on to the effect that American correspondents had a patriotic duty to disseminate only information that made the United States look good.

A network television correspondent said, "Surely, Arthur, you don't expect the American press to be the handmaiden of government."

"That's exactly what I expect," came the reply.

An agency man raised the problem that had preoccupied Ambassador [Maxwell] Taylor and Barry Zorthian—about the credibility of American officials. Responded the Assistant Secretary of Defense for Public Affairs:

"Look, if you think any American official is going to tell you the truth, then you're stupid. Did you hear that? Stupid."[17]

In his report, Safer said that when one of the most respected of all the newsmen in Vietnam—a veteran of World War II, the Indochina War, and Korea—suggested that Sylvester was being deliberately provocative, the Assistant Secretary threatened: "Look, I don't even have to talk to you people. I know how to deal with you through your editors and publishers in the states."

As was his custom, Sylvester counterattacked by maligning Safer's report as a "gem of misrepresentation." He implied that Safer had had too many "cool drinks," hinted that his reporting had endangered American troops, and said "Safer is the only man I ever heard refer to another man as a 'handmaiden.'" Sylvester complained to Fred W. Friendly, then president of CBS News, who recalled:

Here's Arthur Sylvester from the Defense Department calling me up. "How can you use a Canadian correspondent [Safer is from Canada] to cover the war in Vietnam?" he said. Imagine . . .

> I got another call from Sylvester. He said, "You know, we checked into this Safer in Canada. And although he was very good, he was very tough on the military." Imagine . . .
> What Sylvester did was write letters all over the country vilifying Safer. He does that with anybody who does something he does not like. Absolutely tries to vilify the person. In this country, a man in the government doing a thing like that. Well, I wrote him a letter. A rough letter.[18]

Sylvester also publicly accused the Overseas Press Club editors who published Safer's account of practicing "editorial dishonesty." The editors—Arthur G. Milton, Jess Gorkin, and Edwin Kiester, Jr.—reacted by querying other correspondents present at the Saigon meeting. No fewer than eight of them confirmed the accuracy of the Safer report. Then the editors said: "[We] received a phone call from Mr. Sylvester. Like the original incident described by Safer, it had to be experienced to be believed. Much of it was conducted at the top of Mr. Sylvester's healthy lungs, and it showed us that all that has been said about Mr. Sylvester's being abusive, profane, combative and inaccurate was absolutely true in spades. Mr. Sylvester . . . described Safer as a 'moocher' and implied that he was drunk at the time, slandered two other correspondents ('Oh, Christ! If you believe him!') and once again noted that Safer was Canadian and therefore presumably disloyal."[19] The editors concluded that United States reporters were being "fed untruths and misleading information by their own government" and they recommended that "the entire matter of governmental lying and intimidation of the press" be investigated by the Overseas Press Club.

Sylvester did not confine his intimidations to the press. Barely twenty-four hours after stating in a radio interview that he doubted the Pentagon was fully reporting United States fatalities in Vietnam, Dr. Daniel M. Berman, a professor of political science at American University, received a telephone call from Sylvester. The Assistant Secretary demanded to know Berman's sources of information and berated him for thirty minutes for his not having first cleared his comments with the Pentagon. Sylvester then wrote

Berman a splenetic letter, sending copies to the president of American University and to the general manager of the radio station which had broadcast Berman's remarks. Firing back at Sylvester, Berman wrote: "[Your] letter proves to me only that you are not always willing to confess to the mendacities for which you are so well known. . . . I want to express my contempt for the obvious effort at intimidation implicit in your submission of a carbon copy of your letter to the president of the university where I teach." When Berman later repeated his suspicions about Vietnam fatalities over another radio station, that station's program director was also the subject of a tirade by Sylvester. Berman mused: "I can testify from personal experience that Mr. Sylvester does not limit his threats to newsmen. First he tries to intimidate newsmen, and now he goes after a professor. Who will be next?"

One of Sylvester's most controversial acts was his issuance of a directive on October 27, 1962, to all Pentagon personnel, requiring that "the substance of each interview and telephone conversation with a media representative . . . be reported to the appropriate public information office before the close of business that day. A report need not be made if a representative of the public information office is present at the interview."[20] Sylvester explained the monitoring directive by saying: "It is an attempt on our part, at least, to know what the heck is going on in the Department of Defense." The order severely limited the ability of Pentagon officials to talk freely with newsmen. This inhibition of officers' contacts with the press was the goal of Sylvester's directive. "The effect of such an order can only be to close up the flow of information except what is permitted through official channels," the Tulsa *Daily World* commented. "It means, simply, that the department is clamping a tight grip around every person under its control, to prevent any information from being given out that might be displeasing to somebody at the top."

Perhaps the best analysis of Sylvester's staying power in office was provided by Richard Fryklund, former Pentagon reporter for the Washington *Evening Star* who is now Deputy

Assistant Secretary of Defense for Public Affairs. Upon Sylvester's retirement, Fryklund explained: "Reporters used to wonder why McNamara and Presidents Kennedy and Johnson kept him. In part it was because Sylvester was only saying things that they would like to have said themselves. But the real secret, reporters eventually learned, lay in a phrase President Johnson used in his letter accepting Sylvester's resignation. He has served two Presidents, Johnson said, 'with total loyalty, resolute courage, and selfless dedication.' His loyalty was indeed total, and his superiors appreciated it. Much of the 'news management' blamed on Sylvester was the doing of the President and McNamara—but Sylvester took the blame without complaint and with apparent enjoyment."[21]

Sylvester was succeeded in February, 1967, by one of his deputies, forty-five-year-old Phil G. Goulding, a onetime reporter for the Cleveland *Plain Dealer*. While there have been few changes in Pentagon information policies under Goulding, open controversies with newsmen have declined. The younger, more sophisticated Goulding has refrained from baiting newsmen and taunting congressmen and senators. He devoted his initial months in office to obtaining businesslike performances from the Pentagon's more than 3,000 publicity employees and greater results from the $35 million annual public relations budget.

One of Goulding's first moves was to abolish Sylvester's monitoring directive. He then turned to the Pentagon-operated newspaper for servicemen, *Stars and Stripes,* which has been plagued for years by military censors and officers attempting to use it for personal and propaganda purposes. When *Stars and Stripes* was revived from Civil War and World War I editions in 1942, General George C. Marshall set its editorial guidelines:

> A soldier's newspaper, in these grave times, is more than a morale venture. It is a symbol of the things we are fighting to preserve and spread in this threatened world. It represents

the free thought and free expression of a free people. . . .
We have his [General John J. Pershing's] authority that no
official control was ever exercised over the matter which went
into the *Stars and Stripes*. It always was for and by the
soldier. This policy is to govern the conduct of the new publication.[22]

General Marshall's guidelines were supported by United
States Army Regulation 360-40 which reads: "It is not intended that the newspaper should become the mouthpiece of
the United States European Command or other command, or
any individual or group." The regulation also bars "arbitrary
censorship." Robert L. Moora, wartime managing editor of
Stars and Stripes, recalled: "In the process of publishing,
under military jurisdiction, a newspaper that would be representative of the American free press, some strange things
transpired. Not the least of these involved the staff's resort to
wit and wile, conspiracy and conniving, to provide a clean,
honest, accurate paper, free from propaganda and headquarters pressure—the kind of paper General Dwight D.
Eisenhower wanted and for which he had issued a firm 'hands
off' policy."[23] With the strong supprt of Generals Marshall
and Eisenhower, *Stars and Stripes* survived World War II.

Today, from its base in Darmstadt, Germany, the "Unofficial Newspaper of the United States Forces in Europe,
North Africa and the Middle East" publishes 150,000 daily
copies which circulate in fifty countries. Its far-flung operations are run by 1,800 employees under an annual budget of
$13 million. In 1966, *Stars and Stripes'* operations showed a
profit of $415,000 from the sale of newspapers, operation of
bookstores, and job printing for military organizations. Its
editorial staff, composed of both civilians and military
officers, subscribes to the AP and UPI wire services, the
North American Newspaper Alliance service, three photo
services, and a wide variety of other news sources. As far as
United States servicemen stationed abroad are concerned,
Stars and Stripes is "it," both because of its professional

format and because it is often the only United States news-paper available on military property.

As a result of charges of censorship of racial news during the rioting in Birmingham, Alabama, in August, 1963, Presidential press secretary Pierre Salinger ordered the Pentagon to undertake a full investigation of *Stars and Stripes'* news policies. The Army's inspector general, Major General Edward H. McDavid, went to Germany and conducted three days of hearings. After President Kennedy's assassination in November, 1963, however, the Pentagon refused to give Salinger the results of its investigation. Complaints of censorship by the military continued, but civilian editorial staff members were unable to find recourse for appeal other than to the officers doing the censoring.

In January, 1967, the Freedom of Information Committee of the Associated Press Managing Editors Association formally requested that the House Subcommittee on Government Information look into Pentagon plans to close the *Stars and Stripes* office in New York in favor of channeling news to Europe through a central office in Washington. The Pentagon argued that its consolidation plans would "eliminate duplication," but newsmen feared the plans represented a move toward greater military control of editorial matter. Under pressure from the subcommittee, the office merger plans were dropped. In March, 1967, *Stars and Stripes* broke into the headlines again when the Pentagon "reassigned" Colonel George E. Moranda, Army information chief in Europe, because Moranda failed to squelch an AP story reporting the arrest of the nineteen-year-old son of the United States ambassador to West Germany for driving under the influence of LSD in California. The Pentagon first said Moranda's transfer to Washington was "routine," but later stated it was "because of a loss of confidence in his suitability as public affairs officer, United States Army Europe." It was obvious to all that Moranda, who had served only seven months of a three-year tour of duty in Europe, had been sacked because he objected to military censorship of *Stars and Stripes*.

On March 16, 1967, the details of fifty-three specific instances of military censorship of *Stars and Stripes* were bared in the *Congressional Record*. They included the Pentagon's suppression or distortion of news items about the Joint Chiefs of Staff, the Warren report, speeches of military officers, foreign elections, motion pictures, military accidents, the Olympic games, the CIA, and racial incidents in the United States, among others. The Washington *Evening Star* declared: "If the Pentagon wants to distribute a house organ, completely laundered and reflecting only the official views of the administration, it is free to do so. But . . . it should make this clear to readers and state in each issue that *Stars and Stripes* is a controlled, censored, and managed publication. If soldiers are buying a trained seal, the label ought to carry this information."

In recognition of *Stars and Stripes'* censorship problems, Goulding prepared a memorandum for Secretary McNamara to distribute to all military personnel on May 1, 1967. The memorandum recognized the right of members of the armed forces "to the same unrestricted access to news as are all other citizens." It stated: "Interference to this access of news will not be permitted. The calculated withholding of unfavorable news stories and wire service reports from troop information publications such as *Stars and Stripes*, or the censorship of news stories or broadcasts over such outlets as Armed Forces Radio and Television Service, is prohibited. News management and meddling with the news will not be tolerated, either in external public information or internal troop information."[24] Thomas Morris, the Assistant Secretary of Defense for Manpower, was directed to personally supervise the "free flow of information" to United States troops.

To be sure, Goulding's work is cut out for him. In trying to restore some of the Pentagon's lost credibility, he will have to cope with: the unwarranted ban of the independent newspaper, *Overseas Weekly*, from military newsstands; Pentagon "terror tactics" in dealing with newsmen, including the use of lie detectors, secret listening devices, telephone monitoring, and FBI surveillance; overclassification of military information; deceit and manipulation of facts by Pentagon officials; and a host of other shortcomings in information procedures. Regardless of any good intentions he may have, Goulding will succeed only in direct proportion to the leeway given him by McNamara.

The American people deserve better-managed news than what they are now getting from the Pentagon. The enormous size and complexity of the military establishment loom as a continuous threat to a fully informed people, not to mention the greater danger to an uninformed people. The military must never be taken for granted and never considered too complicated for public inspection. We ought to be demanding the utmost in believability from the Pentagon, particularly in view of the clear and present dangers implicit in Vietnam.

NOTES TO CHAPTER 7

1. See United Press International story of March 6, 1967.
2. Chicago *Daily News,* March 21, 1967.
3. *Journals of the Continental Congress (1787),* XXVII, p. 433.
4. Report of preinauguration task force headed by Senator Stuart Symington of Missouri, December, 1960.
5. As quoted in Jack Raymond, *Power at the Pentagon* (New York: Harper & Row, 1964), pp. 280–281.
6. *Ibid.,* p. 289.
7. *Ibid.,* p. 293.
8. *Washington Post,* March 19, 1967.
9. *Ibid.*
10. Quoted in *The Republican,* publication of the Republican National Committee, August 23, 1966, p. 11.
11. Washington *Evening Star,* September 1, 1966, p. 12.
12. Quoted in the Report of the Freedom of Information Committee, Sigma Delta Chi, 1966, p. 8.
13. *Nieman Reports,* March, 1963, p. 10.
14. *Government Information Plans and Policies (Part I),* Hearings before a Subcommittee of the Committee on Government Operations, House of Representatives, 88th Congress, First Session, March 19, 1963, p. 23.
15. *Ibid.*
16. *Ibid.,* p. 60.
17. Morley Safer, "Television Covers the War," *Dateline 1966: Covering War* (Overseas Press Club of America, 1966), p. 71.

18. Jimmy Breslin, "Friendly's Day," New York *Herald Tribune,* February 18, 1966, p. 21.

19. "Dateline Editors: Their Side of Sylvester Dispute," *The Overseas Press Club Bulletin,* June 4, 1966, p. 4.

20. Memorandum for Department of Defense Personnel, October 27, 1962. Cited in Hearings before a Subcommittee of the Committee on Government Operations, House of Representatives, 88th Congress, First Session, May 27 and 28, 1963, p. 355.

21. Richard Fryklund, "Arthur Sylvester Quits as Pentagon News Chief," Washington *Evening Star,* January 1, 1967, p. 1.

22. As quoted in Peter Kuhrt, "Silver Anniversary for GI Joe's Paper," *The Quill,* May, 1967, pp. 20–21.

23. *Ibid.,* p. 21.

24. See Associated Press story of May 2, 1967.

CHAPTER 8

Vietnam

One cannot remember a more complete dissociation between words and responsibility than in the United States government today. . . . The dedication of the United States to the salvation of Asia represents a translation of rhetorical extravagance into national policy. . . . The fact is that our government just doesn't know a lot of things it pretends to know. —ARTHUR M. SCHLESINGER, JR.

A placard carried in an anti-Vietnam rally in New York City read: "Insufficient Data."

A magazine advertisement for a new book about Vietnam promised: "No other book can go as far in clarification of the confusion."

These two expressions, while seemingly unrelated, have the common characteristic of being symptomatic of the doubt and uncertainty about the war in Vietnam which prevails in the United States today. They point to a growing public concern that United States government pronouncements about the war have been marked by a lack of candor and laden with misleading and contradictory facts. They explain, in part, why the United States' third largest war is its least understood.

One of the most alarming aspects of the confusion over the United States role in Vietnam is that it has been prompted, not by ambitious military leaders eager to enhance their careers through battle, but by civilian leaders whose reputations for veracity and forthrightness ought to be beyond question. The President of the United States, the Secretary of Defense, and the Secretary of State, among others, have consistently misinformed the people about Vietnam and have thereby reduced the level of public confidence necessary for the achievement of a satisfactory conclusion of the fighting. The handling of Vietnam information by the government has accentuated the crisis in credibility.

For all practical purposes, the events leading up to the current dilemma in Vietnam began in 1954 on the day before the French army was destroyed at Dien Bien Phu in what was then known as Indochina. On May 6, 1954, Senator Lyndon B. Johnson struck a blow at bipartisanship in United States foreign policy by attacking Secretary of State John Foster Dulles' policies for settling the Indochina war. Johnson, who had earlier rejected Dulles' proposal for direct United States military assistance to the French, said: "What is American policy on Indochina? All of us have listened to the dismal series of reversals and confusions and alarms and excursions which have emerged from Washington over the past few weeks. . . . Our friends and allies are frightened and wondering, as we do, where we are headed."[1] Writing in the *New York Times* of May 8, 1954, Arthur Krock observed: "How critical to the non-Communist nations, striving at Geneva to repair their broken front, was the hour in which Senator Johnson [spoke], was stressed next morning by the fall of Dien Bien Phu."

As Vice President in 1961, Johnson toured Southeast Asia to reassure United States' allies that the Kennedy administration had no intention of withdrawing its influence from the area. While in Saigon, he somewhat imprudently compared South Vietnamese Prime Minister Ngo Dinh Diem to Winston Churchill; he seemed genuinely impressed with Diem's "admirable qualities." In reporting to Kennedy on his return, Johnson said: "There is no alternative to United States leadership in Southeast Asia. . . . The fundamental decision required of the United States is whether we are to attempt to meet the challenge of Communist expansion now in Southeast Asia by a major effort in support of the forces of freedom in the area or throw in the towel. . . . I recommend we proceed with a clear-cut and strong program of action."[2] He indicated that the failure of the United States to "help these countries defend themselves" would require the United States to pull back "our defenses to San Francisco and a 'Fortress America' concept."

On the advice of Johnson, General Maxwell Taylor, and White House aide Walt W. Rostow (now a top foreign affairs adviser to President Johnson), Kennedy ordered an American military task force of 15,000 men to South Vietnam. Unlike the few hundred United States advisers sent to the country by Eisenhower, the task force was authorized to conduct "self-defense" combat operations, to undertake perimeter security, and, if necessary, to act as a reserve force to the Vietnamese army. Kennedy had not acted without reservations. He told Arthur M. Schlesinger, Jr.: "They want a force of American troops. They say it's necessary in order to restore confidence and maintain morale. But it will be just like Berlin. The troops will march in; the bands will play; the crowds will cheer; and in four days everyone will have forgotten. Then we will be told we have to send in more troops. It's like taking a drink. The effect wears off, and you have to take another."[3] (Kennedy added the view that the war in Vietnam could be won only if it remained a Vietnamese war. If it became a white man's war, he said, the United States would lose as the French had lost earlier.)

Commenting on Kennedy's unpublicized decision to commit United States troops to Vietnam, Pierre Salinger said in a 1966 television interview: "I am highly critical, not only of my own role in our policies on information in Vietnam, but of the President's and most everybody connected with the administration—because I think that we attempted to disguise pretty much the growing American commitment in Vietnam over the period 1961–63. In so doing, I think we did a disservice, in a way, to the American people. I think if we had been more candid about our commitment at that time there would be a greater understanding of the need for American participation in Vietnam today." Other former Kennedy administration officials have echoed Salinger's view.

As a senator in 1954, Johnson opposed military intervention in Vietnam. As the Vice President in 1961, he uniformly endorsed it. As a candidate for President in 1964, he reverted to his nonintervention policy of ten years earlier. During the 1964 election campaign, he said: "Some others are eager to enlarge the conflict. They call upon us to supply American boys to do the job that Asian boys should do. They ask us to take reckless actions which might risk the lives of millions and engulf much of Asia and certainly threaten the peace of the entire world. Moreover, such action would offer no solution at all to the real problem of Vietnam."[4] Johnson delivered numerous other speeches which made clear his opposition to sending "American boys nine to ten thousand miles from home," to bombing North Vietnam, and to getting "involved in a nation with 700,000,000 people [China] and . . . tied down in a land war in Asia."

After his overwhelming election victory in November, 1964, Johnson altered course again, this time in the direction of accelerating United States involvement in the war. By 1968, he had authorized the dispatch of more than 550,000 United States troops to Vietnam, resulting in 15,000 dead and 100,000 wounded.

In the opinion of Walter Lippmann, dean of the Washington press corps, Johnson's position-switching on Vietnam stems from the fact that he is, by nature, a deceitful person. "Time after time Johnson's statements about our situation in Vietnam have proved to be misleading and untrue," Lippmann explained. "We need a better banker of the public trust. If I had been the editor of the *Washington Post* in early 1965 when Johnson was planning to move to a full-scale war in Vietnam, I'd have raised a great stink and told the people what was happening." Lippmann, the subject of bitter personal comments from Johnson and others in the White House, noted that after Johnson won the 1964 election on a platform promising "constraint and reason in regard to Vietnam," he secretly decided to escalate the war. According to Lippmann, Johnson carefully avoided telling the American people what he was doing and he did nothing which might have been construed as escalation. "Johnson avoided calling up the reserves, failed to make the necessary budgetary allowances, covered up the ordering of war materiel, and held off from taking other actions which might have led the people to believe that he was preparing for a major fight in Vietnam," Lippmann said. "He didn't even tell Congress what he was planning. The day before making his Baltimore speech [April 7, 1965, at Johns Hopkins University], Johnson told me that he agreed with me that the war had to be won on the nonmilitary side. The Baltimore speech reflected this view. He showed it to me before he delivered it. But a short time later, I found that he was telling other people other things. He was either lying to me or to the others. I resolved at that point never to go back to the White House again. I have not been there since."

A source of consternation has been the elusive nature of the United States commitment in South Vietnam. Originally, administration spokesmen said United States military involvement was based on a pledge made by President Eisenhower in a letter of October 1, 1954, to Prime Minister Diem. Then, the administration argued that our involvement resulted from the Southeast Asia (SEATO) Collective Defense Treaty signed at Manila on September 8, 1954. Next, it was suggested that United States commitment had sprung from the Tonkin Gulf Resolution of August 10, 1964. Let us examine these "commitments."

There was nothing in Eisenhower's letter to Diem which could legitimately be interpreted as a commitment of military aid to South Vietnam. Nevertheless, Johnson has sought to tie Eisenhower (and the Republican Party) to his Vietnam policies. On August 3, 1965, Johnson said: "Today, the most difficult problem that confronts your President is how to keep an agreement that I did not initiate—I inherited it [from Eisenhower]—but an agreement to help a small nation remain independent, free of aggression." He has frequently stated: "Our commitment is just the same as the commitment made by President Eisenhower in 1954."

The Eisenhower letter, as Secretary of Defense Robert S. McNamara admitted on March 26, 1964, was written in response to a request for "economic assistance."[5] The letter said: "We have been exploring ways and means to permit our aid to Vietnam to be more effective. . . . I am instructing the American Ambassador to examine . . . an intelligent program of American aid. . . . The purpose of this offer is to assist the government of Vietnam in developing and maintraining a strong, viable state, capable of resisting attempted subversion or aggression through military means. . . . The United States expects that this aid will be met by performance on the part of the government of Vietnam in undertaking needed reforms." Eisenhower also expressed the hope that this conditional offer of economic aid would "contribute effectively towards an independent Vietnam endowed with a strong government." Eisenhower has since made it clear that he did not consider his letter to Diem as a commitment to militarily defend South Vietnam. For six years he refused to permit the United States to fight in Vietnam. If Eisenhower had intended to make a military commitment, it is doubtful he would have done so by private letter and without consultation with Congress.

In testimony before the Senate Foreign Relations Committee on February 17, 1966, General Maxwell Taylor, former United States Ambassador to South Vietnam and now a special consultant to Johnson, denied that the Eisenhower administration made any commitment to use United States troops in combat in Vietnam. General Taylor engaged in this dialogue with Senator Bourke Hickenlooper of Iowa:

SENATOR HICKENLOOPER: Now, up until the end of the Eisenhower administration, we had only about 750 military personnel in South Vietnam, did we not?

GENERAL TAYLOR: It was very small, something like that.

SENATOR HICKENLOOPER: I think that is within 25 or 30 of the number, either way, and they were entirely devoted to giving technical advice on training to the South Vietnamese troops.

GENERAL TAYLOR: That is correct.

SENATOR HICKENLOOPER: To your knowledge, did we have any commitment or agreement with the South Vietnamese up to that time that we would put in active field military forces to conduct a war along with them?

GENERAL TAYLOR: *No, sir. Very clearly we made no such commitment. We didn't want such a commitment. This was the last thing we had in mind.* [Emphasis added.]

SENATOR HICKENLOOPER: When was the commitment made for us to actively participate in the military operations of the war as American personnel?

GENERAL TAYLOR: . . . insofar as the use of our combat ground forces are concerned, that took place, of course, only in the spring of 1965.[6]

Henry Steele Commager, professor of history at Amherst College, takes vigorous exception to the Johnson administration's "naked and ashamed" propaganda that Americans are dying in Vietnam in order "to keep American promises— indeed, 'to fulfill one of the most solemn pledges' in our history, a pledge made by three Presidents, no less." Commager says that such reasoning is nonsense. "President Eisenhower refused to make such a pledge; President Kennedy insisted that the Vietnamese should fight their own war. It is President Johnson who made the pledge (though not, it might be remembered, in the campaign of 1964), and who is now busy conferring retroactive solemnity upon it."[7] Clayton Fritchey, a former aide to the late Adlai Stevenson at the United Nations, says "the present policy [in Vietnam] is a far cry from the one that Kennedy, Eisenhower and Truman pursued. Not one of them thought Vietnam was of sufficient 'vital interest' to involve the United States in a land war in Asia."[8] Senator James B. Pearson of Kansas expressed the view of most of his Senate colleagues when he said: "President Johnson frequently implies that whether we like it or not President Eisenhower made a commitment to Vietnam which we are honorbound to observe. In point of fact, the so-called Eisenhower commitment is nothing more than a letter to the Diem government offering economic aid. . . . Continual harping on the notion of honoring commitments no one understands, ultimately destroys public confidence in our position there."[9]

The argument that the SEATO Treaty of 1954 represented a commitment of United States military force in Vietnam has been the favorite of Secretary of State Dean Rusk, among others. It is a fact that those who wrote the treaty specifically avoided the inclusion of any provision calling for an automatic armed response to aggression. In 1954, Secretary of State Dulles declared: "The agreement of each of the parties to act to meet the common danger 'in accordance with its constitutional processes' leaves to the judgment of each country the type of action to be taken in the event an armed attack occurs."[10] Dulles added that the treaty "does not attempt to get into the difficult question as to precisely how we act."

An even clearer explanation of the treaty was made by Senator H. Alexander Smith, a delegate to the Manila Conference who signed the agreement on behalf of the United States. Senator Smith testified: "Some of the participants came to Manila with the intention of establishing an organization modeled on the lines of the North Atlantic Treaty arrangements. That would have been a compulsory arrangement for our military participation in case of any attack. Such an organization might have required the commitment of American ground forces to the Asian mainland. *We carefully avoided any possible implication regarding an arrangement of that kind. We have no purpose of following any such policy as that of having our forces involved in a ground war* [emphasis added]. Under this treaty, each party recognizes that an armed attack on any country within the treaty area would endanger its own peace and safety. Each party, therefore, agrees to act to meet the common danger in accordance with its constitutional processes. That means, by implication, that if any such emergency as is contemplated by the treaty should arise in that area it will be brought before the Congress by the President and the administration, and will be considered under our constitutional processes. . . . For ourselves, the arrangement means that we will have avoided the impracticable overcommitment which would have been involved if we attempted to place American ground forces around the perimeter of the area of potential Chinese ingress into southeast Asia. *Nothing in this treaty calls for the use of American ground forces in that fashion* [emphasis added]."[11]

In addition to deceitfully using the SEATO Treaty as the basis for the United States military commitment in Vietnam, Johnson administration officials have confused the facts further by first citing one section of the treaty as specific authority for United States involvement and then switching to another section. Secretary Rusk, in particular, has shifted back and forth between paragraphs one and two of Article IV of the treaty. The first paragraph states that "aggression" against any of the parties to the treaty would endanger peace, and it pledges the signatories "to meet the common danger in accordance with its constitutional processes." The second paragraph, directed at the problem of "subversion," provides that if any of the signatories' territory "is threatened in any way other than by armed attack or is affected or threatened by any fact or situation which might endanger the peace," then the signatories will "consult" to discuss procedures for a common defense. Under these two paragraphs, the United States is obligated only to consider responses to aggression through constitutional processes, i.e., Congress, and to consult with its allies in the event of subversion by a hostile power. Neither paragraph commits the United States to a military response of any kind. In 1966, Senator J. W. Fulbright of Arkansas tried to get to the heart of the administration's ambiguous references to the treaty when he told Secretary Rusk: "I do not see the specific commitment. I do not see the

Southeast Asia Treaty [as a commitment]. I think it might be worthwhile for you to give us, maybe in writing, something to clarify this even further, with specific reference to that part of the treaty and the provisions which require it because I am not convinced of it." Rusk failed to present any clarification.

The Tonkin Gulf Resolution, rushed through Congress in just two days in August, 1964, has served as a third administration justification for broad military involvement in Vietnam. The resolution was passed without debate by a combined House-Senate vote of 502 to 2. It was considered to be a gesture of support for President Johnson after the North Vietnamese fired torpedoes at United States destroyers in the Gulf of Tonkin. It pledged support to the Commander-in-Chief in taking "all necessary measures to repel any armed attack against the forces of the United States, and to prevent further aggression." Members of Congress who voted for the resolution did so in the belief that it would evidence American unity at a particular time of crisis. "By voting out the resolution, we did not intend to give the President a 'blank check' to do anything he pleased in Vietnam," one senator said. "You might say the resolution seemed to represent good public relations at the time. Its purpose was to meet a specific problem, nothing more." Another senator said he was unclear as to which nation had been the aggressor in the Tonkin Gulf incident. "Yes, the administration told us that our ships were wrongfully attacked, but I'm not sure I believe it. I am told by other sources that our ships were within eleven miles of the North Vietnamese shore, inside the twelve-mile limit." Senator Gaylord Nelson of Wisconsin observed: "It would be mighty risky if Cuban PT boats were firing on Florida, for Russian armed ships or destroyers to be patrolling between us and Cuba, eleven miles out."[12]

A congressman who sat in on a White House briefing on Vietnam related: "The President pulled out of his pocket a crumpled piece of paper which was the Tonkin Gulf Resolution. He then proceeded to quote it practically from memory.

He said he had it in his pocket every day since it was passed. He repeated and repeated various phrases from it, such as, 'support and approve.' He said, 'That's two words, and they're both there.' He said the resolution committed practically every member of Congress to the effort in Vietnam, and that Johnson was not responsible for it, that previous Presidents and the Congress were responsible for it. . . . He said he, Johnson, is not to blame, that his advisers are doing the job and they were appointed by other people. To use a Johnsonian phrase, 'A stuck pig squeals,' and the President was indeed squealing today."

In a two-hour Senate debate over the Tonkin Gulf Resolution on September 26, 1967, Senator Clifford Case of New Jersey said many senators had been assured at the time the resolution was being passed that it was not intended to grant the unlimited authority its words appeared to convey. "For the President to take advantage of the restraint and responsibility of Congress has been highly irresponsible," Senator Case charged. "The people's anxiety, and that of Congress too, springs perhaps in greatest part from a growing conviction that the administration is not telling the truth. But the President has done more than to squander his credibility; he has dealt a grievous blow at the process by which we have arrived at the expression of national unity in the face of international crises." Senator Case was supported by Senator Jacob Javits of New York and a number of other colleagues. Less than two months after the Senate debate, CBS diplomatic correspondent Marvin Kalb revealed that Assistant Secretary of State William Bundy had told a closed session of the Senate Foreign Relations Committee that "we had contingent drafts [of the Tonkin Gulf Resolution] for some time prior to Aug. 2 [1964]," the date of the first attack on a United States destroyer. Kalb reported: "Many Senators now believe that the incidents served merely as pretexts for the administration to move the resolution through Congress on a wave of emotion about American ships being attacked on the high seas."

Johnson's flaunting of the Tonkin Gulf Resolution has now

all but stopped entirely. By constantly alluding to the resolution as blanket approval from Congress for military actions in Vietnam, the President found that he was losing congressional support. In April, 1967, when Johnson sought a similar open-ended resolution to take to a meeting of Latin American leaders, the Senate refused to grant it.

Considering the complicated and confusing nature of the Vietnam war, it would seem particularly essential that the American people be adequately and accurately informed about the war's status and about prospects for peace. Yet, in relating information about the war, the administration has only intensified public suspicion and doubt. Time and time again, government officials have concealed motives, denied the truth, and grossly overestimated progress in the war. One of the most important casualties of the war has been the accuracy of information about it.

Stewart Alsop has suggested that the President "fire out of hand all his chief advisers, starting with Secretary of Defense Robert McNamara," for giving advice which has been "consistently and totally wrong." McNamara has been to Vietnam nine times. He has returned to the United States after each trip and given the public inaccurate prophecies and faulty assessments. On his first visit to Vietnam in May, 1962, McNamara told newsmen: "There is no plan for introducing combat forces into South Vietnam. . . . The [South Vietnamese] government has asked only for logistical support." Upon returning from his second trip in October, 1963, McNamara said: "The major part of the United States military task can be completed by the end of 1965, although there may be a continuing requirement for a limited number of United States training personnel." After his third visit, in December, 1963, McNamara announced: "We have every reason to believe that [United States military] plans will be successful in 1964." In March, 1964, following his fourth visit, he declared: "We are confident these plans point the way to victory." After his fifth trip, in May, 1964: "This is a war for the confidence of the people and the security of these people. . . . Reliance on military pressure upon the North would not be a proper response." On returning from his sixth visit in July, 1965, McNamara said: "The overall situation continues to be serious." During his seventh visit, on November 29, 1965, he boasted: "We have stopped losing the war." After his eighth trip, in October, 1966, McNamara noted: "The rate of progress has exceeded our expectations. I saw nothing that in any way indicates a substantial change in the rate of operations, the tempo of operations, the type of operations in the months ahead." Finally, following his last visit to Vietnam in July, 1967, McNamara said: "Substantial progress has been achieved on virtually all fronts—political, economic, and military—since my previous visit to Vietnam."

Even as President Johnson announced on July 28, 1965, that he was sending 125,000 troops to Vietnam, he said the move did "not imply any change in policy whatever." Commented Los Angeles *Times* correspondent Jack Foisie: "Although the decision to commit large-scale American combat units in Vietnam is apparent, and is obvious to the enemy . . . authorities in Washington try to pretend that we really are not committed to land warfare in Asia."[13] Tom Wicker, Washington bureau chief of the *New York Times*, pointed out that the record of the Johnson administration is "sprinkled with overoptimistic and unwarranted claims, wrong or changed assumptions and justifications, and misleading simplifications, as well as with seemingly contradictory positions . . . a good part of the public does believe there is a suspicious gap between the administration's statements and the facts of the war."[14] CBS newsman Walter Cronkite told a Chicago audience: "I would like to suggest that one of the reasons for the great confusion which wracks this nation today over the Vietnam war is the fact that we were committed without a proper airing of the facts. . . . Half-truths or lies, even once indulged in, undermine the government's credibility and feed the fire of skepticism and cynicism that can destroy our democracy."[15] James Reston wrote that the administration's "official statements are still so confusing that nobody can quite make out what the official view of the war actually is."

Administration officials have drawn criticism from within their own ranks for their unwillingness to tell even top aides how much the Vietnam war is costing and how it is to be financed. Members of the Federal Reserve Board have warned that they aren't being told what they need to know in order to consider monetary policies. In 1965, the White House ridiculed reports that Vietnam spending would exceed $10 billion in 1966. The Federal Reserve, believing what little it was told, maintained its easy-money policy to the end of 1965. Then, in the spring of 1966, the Fed was forced into a crash program of monetary restraint in order to cope with burgeoning Vietnam spending. A few months later, the tight money policy was relaxed again. Fed officials don't know what to expect next. All they are told is that defense spending information must be kept from them because disclosure might somehow aid the enemy.

"The American people are being deliberately deceived about the cost of the war," said Congressman Richard H. Poff of Virginia. In a newsletter to his constituents in September, 1966, Congressman Poff pointed out that the 1967 defense appropriation bill asked for only $58 billion for Vietnam, $12 billion less than was needed. Poff said: "Obviously, the purpose of this fiscal sleight of hand is to hold back the money until all new domestic spending programs have been funded and then later, after the November [1966] elections, appropriate the $12 billion deficiency for the war effort. That way, national defense instead of welfare gets the blame for busting the budget." Syndicated columnist Richard Wilson has also criticized Vietnam fiscal policy. "The great deception of 1966 is now exposed," he commented. "Unfortunately, it will undoubtedly further condition the plausibility of the Johnson administration as long as it remains in office. Knowingly, and with guile and aforethought, the cost of the Vietnam war was understated by half. . . . The Johnson administration has ridden all through the year 1966 on a false budget projection showing a lowered deficit from the previous year when in fact the budget deficit was to become two or three times that big. This kind of deception has been characteristic of the whole Vietnam intervention, and those who are strongly for this intervention can regret most that the public and Congress were never given in advance full information on the nature of the commitment or its cost."[16]

In mid-1966, the administration told the people that it estimated the cost of the war at $1 to $1.5 billion a month. Privately, however, it was admitted that the cost was more like $2.5 billion per month. In September, 1966, Secretary McNamara repeated the official estimate that "incremental costs of Southeast Asia operations" were $1 billion a month. But Congressman Melvin R. Laird of Wisconsin, second-ranking minority member on the House Defense Appropriations Subcommittee, estimated the cost at $2 billion per month and forecast the cost would hit $2.5 billion a month by January 1, 1967. When President Johnson was pressed for information on war costs at a news conference on September 22, 1966, he admonished newsmen: "I think that the Congress, through the Appropriations Committee and Authorizations Committee, have had very full details on our expenditures, men, money and materiel in Vietnam. I would commend to you some homework. Read the hearings."[17] Reporters asked Robert Fleming, deputy White House press secretary, where such information appeared on the public record. Fleming answered: "We do not have the committee record available so that we can cite dates and pages." As it turned out, the hearings referred to by the President had been classified "secret" by the Defense Department. Congressman Laird questioned Pentagon Comptroller Robert N. Anthony. "When I asked him where the Vietnam war cost estimates were that the President referred to in his news conference," Laird said, "Anthony replied that there is nothing in the hearings that would tell you the cost of the war in Vietnam."

On April 25, 1967, Senator John Stennis of Mississippi predicted for the third straight year that defense spending would be considerably higher than White House and Defense Department estimates. Noting that Congress has been "required to legislate in the dark, in the absence of the facts," Stennis said Vietnam spending for fiscal 1968 would be $4 to $6 billion more than the amount budgeted. A good many people were inclined to put more faith in the Stennis figures than in those of the Johnson administration.

The unwillingness of the executive branch to present a full and honest picture of events concerning the war in Vietnam was exemplified by a memorandum issued on January 11, 1965, by Deputy Secretary of Defense Cyrus Vance. Under the classification "For Official Use Only," the memo directed Defense Department witnesses appearing before congressional committees to voice the official views of the department rather than their own considered judgments. Only if "pressed" for their personal opinions were witnesses to give them, and then with some qualifications. The Vance memo calls into serious question the utility of Congress listening to Defense Department witnesses, all of whom are under orders to reflect one official view.

Public confusion about the status of the war has been heightened by the revelation of the administration's rejection of peace initiatives and by a series of on-again, off-again "peace offensives." The President said in May, 1965: "For months now we have waited for a sign, a signal, even a whisper, but our offer of unconditional discussions has fallen on unreceptive ears. Not a sound has been heard. Not a signal has been sighted. Still we wait."[18] Two months later, Johnson told newsmen: "I must say that candor compels me to tell you that there has not been the slightest indication that the other side is interested in negotiation or in unconditional discussions although the United States has made some dozen separate attempts to bring them about."[19] In a refutation of the President's words, the State Department admitted on November 15, 1965, that the United States had received and rejected a 1964 Hanoi proposal that United States and North Vietnamese representatives meet in Rangoon, Burma, to discuss means of ending the war. State Department spokesman Robert J. McCloskey acknowledged these facts only after Eric Severeid* had reported most of the story in a *Look* magazine article in which he said United States officials could have written "the terms of the cease-fire offer exactly as they saw fit" and that "someone in Washington insisted that this attempt be postponed until after the [1964] Presidential election." The White House explained privately to United Nations Secretary-General U Thant, through whom the peace offer had been relayed, that it had denied receiving the offer because it considered the bid "procedural" rather than "substantive." The real reason for rejection of the peace feeler was that it was made at a time when the war was going badly for the United States. The administration opposed negotiations at a time when the United States military bargaining position was weak. Thus, United States officials felt it necessary to give the erroneous impression that Hanoi was not prepared to come to the conference table.

A crude example of the Johnson administration's attempts to divert public attention from the less hopeful aspects of the Vietnam war came in March of 1967. As Senator Robert F. Kennedy of New York was preparing to deliver a Senate speech in favor of negotiations and a pause in the bombing of North Vietnam, the President launched a series of moves designed to command the headlines and to otherwise black out the Kennedy speech. On the day Kennedy spoke, Johnson (1) delivered an unscheduled speech, (2) called an impromptu news conference, (3) announced the Russians had agreed to discuss methods of limiting the arms race, (4) ar-

---

* Severeid's acrount was backed up by Bernard S. Redmont, chief of the Paris bureau of the Westinghouse Broadcasting Company, who reported from Paris on November 17, 1965: "Two or three offers to negotiate peace were made by Communist North Vietnam a year ago and six months ago. One of these offers was made confidentially through the intermediary of the French government and reported to you by me at that time. Diplomatic denials were issued [by the United States], as often happens, but there was never any doubt here in Paris that Hanoi was ready to negotiate before the escalation of the war, and that the Johnson administration ignored or turned down these offers."

ranged for statements about the war's progress by General William C. Westmoreland and Secretary of State Rusk, and (5) sent a letter defending Vietnam bombing to Senator Henry M. Jackson of Washington, who caused its contents to be released to the press while Kennedy was speaking. Upon seeing the administration "treatment" given Kennedy, reporters recalled the President's sudden rush to Honolulu in 1966 at the same time Senator William Fulbright's hearings on Vietnam were attracting large television audiences.

Johnson's much-publicized trips to Honolulu, Manila, and Guam were billed by the administration as "peace offensives," but, in reality, they were efforts to boost public confidence in the administration's conduct of the war. Rather than resulting in new peace formulas, the President's Asian travels seemed to solidify the determination of the United States and its allies to win the war militarily. Commenting on Johnson's trip through the Far East in October, 1966, newsman Carl T. Rowan said: "There can be no doubt that Johnson will dominate American headlines for two weeks. There is also little doubt that the public stands a good chance of becoming just plain confused about what we are doing and what we plan to do in Vietnam. . . . There is not an important figure in the administration who believes that the Manila conference itself will move the world appreciably closer to peace in Vietnam." Columnist Crosby S. Noyes wrote: "All of a sudden everything seems to be coming up roses. The troubles are all packed away in the old kit bag and the word has gone out to smile, smile, smile. President Johnson, winging his way around his triumphal Far Eastern tour, has set the tone. . . . For the moment, euphoria is the order of the day, handed down by a President who believes firmly that the more voters there are who accept the proposition that they've never had it so good the happier the results will be on November 8 [date of the 1966 elections] . . . The current wave of orchestrated optimism adds to the credibility gap, which for some time has been one of the administration's major problems." In their column of January 23, 1967, Rowland Evans and Robert

Novak observed that "the real purpose" of the President's trip to Honolulu in January, 1966, "was to minimize the [resumption of] bombing" of North Vietnam. "Moreover, last fall during the election campaign, Mr. Johnson—wearing his politician's hat—wanted the voters to see a hopeful side of the conflict. His trip to Manila in late October was specifically designed for that end."

In a meeting with Democratic congressional leaders in 1966, Johnson confided that he felt the war could only be won militarily. He told one questioner: "Hanoi is the stud duck in this operation. Get Hanoi out of this and it's over. But Hanoi won't budge." He pleaded the military case by pointing out that many critics had been recommending numerous alternative solutions. "Well, we have done all those things—we have changed the generals, we have changed the head of the South Vietnamese government [an admission never made publicly], we have asked everybody in every capital. Finally, we decided we had done everything but take it to the U.N. So we took it to the U.N. But I'll bet you a speckled bird dog that the critics said we were wrong because we didn't take it there sooner, or later, or taller, or shorter, or hotter, or colder. Where were all the critics and experts when the commitments were being made?"

Many officials in Washington believe that the rapid fluctuations and inconsistencies in administration policy on peace negotiations have had a direct influence on Hanoi's attitude toward a peaceful settlement of the war. It is felt that leaders in North Vietnam are not convinced of the sincerity of United States invitations to discuss peace. Foreign observers have been confused by such actions as the administration releasing on the eve of the President's departure for Guam in March, 1967, twenty-three photographs to support earlier claims that the Communists moved twenty times the normal amount of supplies into South Vietnam during a bombing pause. This action convinced some that the United States was more interested in arguing war than in talking peace. Another United States move which tended to confuse was the release on May 1, 1967, of a list of twenty-eight "peace proposals" which Secretary of State Rusk said had been rejected by North Vietnam. The list included nearly every proposal ever made. It was intended to serve as proof of genuine United States interest in securing peace negotiations, but it fell short of its goal because many of the proposals listed had never been put forward, or pursued with any enthusiasm, and others had been made only to pacify anti-war critics in the United States. In the opinion of Arthur M. Schlesinger, Jr., there has been a lack of will on the part of the Johnson administration to approach realistically solutions to the war. Schlesinger said: "It cannot be said that the administration has pursued negotiation with a fraction of the zeal, imagination and perseverance with which it has pursued war. . . . Nor can it be said that the administration has laid fairly before the American people the occasional [peace] signals, however faint, which have come from Hanoi. . . . Nor, for all our declarations about 'unconditional' negotiations, have we refrained from setting conditions—such as, for example, that we won't talk to the Vietcong unless they come to the conference table disguised as North Vietnamese."[20]

In reporting to the American people on the ability and readiness of the United States to fight the war, government officials have contributed to confusion and doubt by indulging in fanciful explanations, evasive statements, and departures from the truth. Secretary of Defense McNamara, for example, has continually denied the existence of a shortage of military pilots in Vietnam. However, the Senate Preparedness Investigating Subcommittee reported on April 6, 1967, that Marine Corps leaders had made "unequivocal statements as to the existing pilot shortages, their significant effect on Marine Corps capabilities, and the fact that present programs do not alleviate the shortages, or their effects, for a long period of time."[21] On March 2, 1967, General Wallace M. Greene, Jr., commandant of the Marine Corps, told the subcommittee: "Our present shortage is 851 pilots. . . . Our projected shortage for fiscal year 1968 is 1,021 pilots."[22]

Chief of Naval Operations David McDonald admitted to "urgent pilot needs" in 1966. Air Force Chief of Staff J. P. McConnell has expressed concern over the "downward trend" in pilot retention. The growing demand of commercial airlines for pilots has contributed to the military shortages. In order to undercut this competition, the Navy recently proposed a three-year moratorium on airline hiring of military pilots.[23] On May 30, 1967, the Air Force announced that some 3,700 officers faced extended duty of up to a year; flying officers on desk jobs had earlier been ordered reassigned as pilots whenever possible. Senator John Stennis, chairman of the Preparedness Subcommittee, said: "Despite the apparent tendency on the part of some to minimize the gravity of the pilot problem, it is clear that it is real and serious. It is also clear that, upon the basis of present planning, it will continue for some time in the future."

After denying for months the charge that aircraft losses in Vietnam were being understated, the Pentagon admitted in February, 1967, that 1,172 fixed-wing aircraft had been destroyed—almost double the previously announced total of 621. In addition, actual helicopter losses were double the previously reported total of 255. The true figures brought into the open congressional concern over whether aircraft production was keeping pace with aircraft losses. In May, 1966, and again in March, 1967, various Air Force officials testified in closed Senate hearings that the Air Force "cannot, within existing resources, continue to support a large-scale augmentation" in Vietnam. General G. P. Disoway, commander-in-chief of the Tactical Air Command, complained of "a shortage of aircraft." Clearly, aircraft deliveries were falling behind losses, but Secretary McNamara continued to insist that production was sufficient. The facts were so obviously running counter to McNamara's words that Senator Margaret Chase Smith of Maine, ranking minority member of the Senate Armed Services Committee, was prompted to say to him: "Mr. Secretary, if I can't trust you on the little things, how can I trust you on the big things?"[24] Congressman

Glenard P. Lipscomb of California, top Republican on the House Defense Appropriations Subcommittee, accused McNamara of "fudging the figures." Lipscomb noted that McNamara was counting aircraft taken out of mothballs as "deliveries," and that one such delivery count included what the Navy called 141 "obsolescent A-4As and F-8A/Bs." The California Congressman said "deliveries" to him, and to the public, meant "new craft, modern, not obsolescent. . . . I do not feel whan you take an aircraft out of storage and put it back into the inventory you can consider it a delivery." He produced a Navy memorandum saying that aircraft taken out of storage were suitable only for training purposes. "It appears," the Senate Preparedness Subcommittee said, "that the Department of Defense has avoided taking prompt action to solve problems which clearly loomed upon the horizon in the apparent hope that the problems would somehow disappear." In order to cover up its failure to budget an adequate number of aircraft for Vietnam, the Pentagon resorted to the release of figures which showed only half of the actual number of plane losses. Once revealed, this deceit further diminished public support for the war.

At a backgrounder on April 14, 1966, McNamara attempted to rebut a charge by House Minority Leader Gerald R. Ford of Michigan that the United States was "running short of bombs despite all the billions we have voted for defense." In characteristic fashion, McNamara unleashed a barrage of statistics in the hope of proving that Ford's charge was "completely misleading." However, when pressed by reporters, McNamara had to admit that the United States had been forced to repurchase several thousand 750-pound bombs to meet military requirements in Vietnam. "I would certainly hope we aren't paying more for them than we sold them for," McNamara quipped. Two days later, newsmen learned that the Pentagon had repurchased more than 5,570 bombs from Kaus and Steinhausen, a German fertilizer company, at a price of $114,500. The bombs had been sold for $1.70 each and repurchased at a cost of $21 each. McNamara relied on subterfuge because of his earlier boast that "no shortages have impeded our combat operations in Southeast Asia." In fact, the shortage of 750-pound bombs had forced the curtailment of bombing strikes in Vietnam. Air Force General Thomas P. Gerrity testified that it was "literally true that we did not have sufficient 750-pound bombs to give them all they wanted . . . and support all the sorties in Vietnam." Senator Richard B. Russell of Georgia, chairman of the Senate Armed Services Committee, was "utterly astounded" by the bomb shortage. "I was assured no later than last week by Secretary of Defense McNamara . . . that we had adequate ammunition of every kind in Vietnam," he said.

The executive branch of the federal government has misled the public on numerous other matters related to Vietnam, including: the use of Thailand as a base for United States offensive operations; the degree of effectiveness of bombing raids in North Vietnam; the rate of infiltration of North Vietnamese into South Vietnam; the adequacy of South Vietnamese harbor facilities; the readiness of United States military reserves for combat; and the acceleration of troop commitments in Vietnam.

The administration's lack of candor about casualties in Vietnam has contributed to public confusion as much as any other single factor. It is this aspect of the fighting that has been seized upon by anti-war demonstrators as "evidence" that the United States is trying to make the world believe that the war is being won when it is really not. By misrepresenting casualty figures, the Department of Defense has provided fuel for the fire of protest.

In the early days of the war, military spokesmen understated both the number of troops and the number of casualties in Vietnam. This was done in order to minimize the extent of United States involvement in Southeast Asia. As the war continued and United States participation became more and more obvious, the reporting of casualty figures seemed to improve. A Pentagon official explained that, in addition to outright lying, the military "hedged" casualty figures from

1961 to 1965 by referring only to troops on permanent station orders, giving our figures only upon specific request, delaying responses to queries for statistics, overestimating enemy casualties, underestimating allied losses, and referring to United States losses as "light, moderate or heavy." Every man in a company might have been killed, but these United States casualties were still described as "light" under the premise that one company is only a small part of the full troop complement in a given battle area. This practice of measuring casualties against the total force was abandoned in 1966 in favor of disclosing the exact number of killed and wounded.

In a discussion of Vietnam press coverage sponsored by the Sigma Delta Chi journalism society in April, 1967, panelists agreed that there have been serious shortcomings in the reporting of casualties. "The counting of enemy bodies is ridiculous," said Dan Rather, White House correspondent for CBS News. "We have frequently overestimated the enemy's losses. Many of the dead we've reported as enemy killed are not enemy at all. They're civilians." Another panelist, Brigadier General Winant Sidle, director of information services for the Defense Department, observed: "Yes, body counting may be ridiculous, but we got started and now we're stuck with it." Ralph Kennan of the Baltimore *Sun,* recently returned from Vietnam, expressed his approval for the United States "getting out of the numbers game altogether." He said the North Vietnamese and Vietcong remove as many of their dead as possible from the battlefield, thereby forcing United States commanders to estimate enemy losses. Kennan also observed that many South Vietnamese officers report less than the total number of men killed under their commands. The officers continue receiving the dead soldiers' rations which they sell at a profit. "You can get very cynical and not believe anybody in Vietnam," Kennan said.

According to Major Martin B. Reilly, a Marine Corps information specialist in the Pentagon, a policy of "full disclosure and maximum candor" regarding casualties was adopted in 1965 at the time the decision was made to accelerate United States participation in the war. This policy, Major Reilly said, involved the institution of regular press briefings in Saigon, the daily release of battle data, the availability of combat officers to the press, the assignment of additional public information officers to Vietnam, and the reporting of United States personnel killed, captured, and wounded on both a daily and weekly basis. "Most of the material resulting from this policy would have been classified 'top secret' at an earlier time," Major Reilly said. "Today it's different. Now we honestly attempt to report all possible information without jeopardizing security."

Despite some improvements in government reporting of casualties, many inconsistencies still exist. For example, on May 5, 1966, Congressman Otis Pike of New York charged that the Department of Defense had "surreptitiously" reduced by half the total number of claimed Vietcong wounded since 1961. He said the figure of 365,000 wounded was replaced with one of 182,000 in secret reports given the House Armed Services Committee in 1966. In another case, Secretary of State Rusk gave out a figure for South Vietnamese casualties which was 50 percent higher than the figure released by the Defense Department just a month earlier. Such contradictions serve to feed the belief that casualty reporting by the government is not as straightforward as it might be.

The credibility problem has been complicated further by the strained and confusing circumstances under which newsmen have had to operate in Vietnam itself. In what should have served as a clear-cut warning of things to come, Carl T. Rowan, Deputy Assistant Secretary of State for Public Affairs, delivered remarks at New York University in September, 1961, in which he said that any contention that the people's right to know is an absolute and fundamental principle is "self-deception." Those concerned with the public's right to know, he said, are really more interested in the right of the news media "to make a buck." Despite his biased view, Rowan was selected in early 1962 to draft a "press guidance" directive telling United States officials in Vietnam how to deal with reporters. The directive was officially adopted by the State Department, the Defense Department, and the USIA. It stated that news stories criticizing the South Vietnamese (Diem) government could not be "forbidden," but observed that such stories increase the difficulties of United States officials in Saigon; that newsmen should be advised that trifling or thoughtless criticism of the South Vietnamese government would make it more difficult to maintain cooperation between the United States and South Vietnamese governments; and that newsmen should not be transported on military activities of the type that might result in "undesirable" news stories. When a storm of protest grew up against the directive, the only flaw the State Department could find in it was its "sloppy drafting." While State Department spokesmen insisted that later telegrams superseded the directive, no specific move was made to issue a clarification until mid-1963. The directive was amended only after the House Subcommittee on Government Information reported:

> In recent weeks the American public has been surprised by developments in Vietnam—developments which have been many months in the making but which the American people are just now discovering. The restrictive United States press policy in Vietnam—drafted in the State Department's public relations office by an official with an admitted distrust for the people's right to know—unquestionably contributed to the lack of information about conditions in Vietnam which created an international crisis. Instead of hiding the facts from the American public, the State Department should have done everything possible to expose the true situation to full view.[25]

Jack Foisie reported in 1962 that United States and South Vietnamese officials were providing newsmen with "only the most meager information" on American involvement in the war. "Officially there is no censorship," Foisie said. "But cabled copy is monitored and correspondents can be brought up on charges of spreading 'false information.' " In a report to his *New York Times* office in 1962, correspondent Homer Bigart complained: "Too often correspondents are regarded by the American mission as tools of foreign policy. Those who balk are apt to find it a bit lonely, for they are likely to be distrusted and shunned by American and Vietnamese officials. I am sick of it. . . ." The States' view of reporters in Vietnam during 1961–63 was summed up by a high-ranking United States official who said: "Why don't you fellows get on the team?" The "team" view was that any reporter who tended to detract from the impression of United States non-involvement was somehow disloyal. A case in point was the United States government's insistence that the Geneva Convention of 1954 was effective in Vietnam and that no more than 600 United States military personnel were in South Vietnam. Every reporter there knew this was not true. Anyone in Vietnam in 1963 could watch United States military personnel disembarking from ships docked at the foot of Saigon's main business boulevard. Thousands of United States servicemen were in the country. Nevertheless, the Geneva Convention fabrication was maintained and America's reporters were expected to support it. This was "team" play. In his eagerness to make "getting on the team" more attractive to newsmen, one United States press officer compiled and distributed a list of "available" girls in Saigon. "Things of this kind are to keep the correspondents happy in Saigon; take their minds off the war," the officer explained.

John Mecklin, a former public affairs officer in Vietnam, has seen the war from both the government and press points of view. "The history of United States public information policy in Vietnam is a long and sorry tale of petty deception, ineptitude and sometimes arrogance," Mecklin concludes. "The policy today is more enlightened than it was a few years ago, but it is still loaded with slanted euphemisms, e.g., a ban on official use of the word 'ambush' to describe an attack upon United States troops because it sounds as if they were outsmarted, and half-truths designed to paper over the fact that occasionally there is cause for concern about the state of things in Vietnam. The official attitude in Saigon is an unpleasant projection of a kind of instinctive reluctance of the

Johnson administration to level with the people—the so-called 'credibility gap'—and it is particularly annoying out there because it relates to events in which American soldiers are dying."[26]

Nowhere is the administration's "reluctance . . . to level with the people" more apparent than at the military briefings held at 5 P.M. each day in Saigon. Known as the "five o'clock follies," the daily briefings were originated to enable United States officials to relay information to the press and to give newsmen a chance to question American officials. But the briefings have chiefly turned into propaganda forums for the military and sources of indigestion for correspondents. They often dissolve into loud shouting matches. Ward Just of the *Washington Post* recently recounted how an Army colonel stormed down the briefing room aisle shouting to reporters "that's enough, shut it off." The colonel's tactless approach, Just said, inspired the New York *Daily News'* Joseph Fried to shoot back: "Just you wait a minute, buddy. I'm not in the Army." After Charles Mohr of the *New York Times* witnessed action in the field one day, he attended the 5 P.M. briefing. "There was nothing horrendously wrong with the briefing, except it was almost unrecognizable," Mohr remarked. "The information as dispensed at the briefings is worth little journalistically. Sometimes it is hardly coherent. Officials are more interested in policy than in facts, in the effect of a story rather than in its accuracy." NBC's Dean Brelis noted that United States briefing officers are inclined to "present a picture of Vietnam in pastel colors." Tom Tiede of the Newspaper Enterprise Association suggested that "some key military personnel apparently had studied public relations under Sonny Liston." Tiede cited the following exchange about casualties between a reporter and a military information officer:

> "I dunno," the GI replied.
> "Light, moderate or heavy?" the reporter persisted.
> "Said I dunno."

"Weren't you there?"

"Yup."

"Did you see anyone killed?"

"Yup."

"A lot or a few?"

"I dunno."

"Good grief, soldier, don't you know anything?"

"Yeah, I know I only got forty-eight days left on my tour and I ain't messing anything up by shooting my mouth off to no newspaperman."

Most newsmen who attend the 5 P.M. briefings in Saigon have a feeling of sympathy for the briefing officers. It is felt that the officers give out misleading and contradictory information not out of devious motives, but rather because they do not know what is happening themselves. Sometimes the briefing officers are "conned" by their superiors; often they are kept uninformed. The result of such practices is seen in these conflicting reports of July 14, 1964:

> *Associated Press, Saigon, July 14:* "A ranking United States military spokesman denied Tuesday that there were indications regular North Vietnamese Army units were moving into South Vietnam."
>
> *United Press International, Saigon, July 14:* "The headquarters of the United States military here announced tonight that Communist North Vietnam had accelerated its infiltration into the south."

While such outright contradictions are infrequent, the fact remains that the longer a reporter attends the "five o'clock follies," the more confused, cynical, and pessimistic he is likely to become. For this reason, a number of reporters in Vietnam no longer attend the 5 P.M. briefings. They prefer to ferret out the unadorned truth on their own.

In a confidential memorandum to his office in the United States, a foreign news analyst just returned from Vietnam reported: "Among newsmen and the military there is developing a deep distrust. On the side of the newsmen, at least, there is some cause. On the military side, some of the stupidities are being committed by men who know better. The only conclusion can be that they are carrying out orders from the Defense or State Departments in Washington, or both. There is also a reluctance to admit that sometimes our side does fall on its face." Columnists Evans and Novak corroborated the thesis that news policies in Vietnam are directed from Washington: "The repeated propaganda buildup of basically sound programs into instant panaceas of victory has sugar-coated the realities of this war for too long. It has also misled the American people and confused the President's operatives on the scene. What is needed is less propaganda and more willingness to tell the hard truth."[27] A *New York Times* editorial concurred: "The credibility of the United States government has been one of the numerous casualties of the war in Vietnam. Time after time high-ranking representatives of government—in Washington and in Saigon—have obscured, confused or distorted news from Vietnam, or have made fatuously erroneous evaluations about the course of the war, for public consumption."[28] James Reston commented: "In the Vietnamese war, from beginning to end, there has been a serious and widespread lack of trust in the government's statements about how well the war was going, what role our men were playing, and how well the South Vietnamese government was doing. The administration's first problem, therefore, is not how to talk to the North Vietnamese, but how to talk candidly to the American people. If there is a crisis, it is not a crisis of diplomacy abroad but of confidence at home."[29]

Evidence of the public's dwindling faith in the administration's Vietnam policies is found in the results of virtually every new public opinion poll. A recent poll by Louis Harris showed the administration's rating on the handling of the war had slumped from 47 percent to 33 percent in less than six weeks. A poll taken in October, 1967, by George Gallup indicated that 70 percent of the American people think the administration has failed to tell the public all it should know about Vietnam. "A natural consequence of the questioning attitude of many Americans today is the feeling that they have not been let in on the whole story of Vietnam," Gallup noted. Senator Charles H. Percy of Illinois reports his polls show that his mildly critical views of the war are meeting with an increasingly favorable response. The senior senator from Illinois, Everett M. Dirksen, who has generously supported the administration's conduct of the war, says he is convinced there is a "definite change" in the thinking of the average American about the war. Other polls indicate that the people are confused about United States intentions and goals in Vietnam, and that government equivocation has caused support for the war to diminish.

The Johnson administration may overcome the military hurdles in Vietnam, but it may never regain the confidence of the people at home. There are limits to the public's gullibility; public opinion in a free society has a way of developing an instinct for the truth. As a result of its misleading and deceptive information policies, the administration has needlessly weakened public support for the Vietnam war. The administration has failed to directly confront the people with the realities of a struggle which can only be sustained by increased public understanding. A great deal depends on whether or not the American people believe the pronouncements of their government, on whether or not the world believes the United States wants an honorable settlement of the war. As of now, too few believe.

NOTES TO CHAPTER 8

1. Rowland Evans and Robert Novak, *Lyndon B. Johnson: The Exercise of Power* (New York: The New American Library, 1966), p. 77.
2. *Ibid.*, p. 322.
3. Arthur M. Schlesinger, Jr., *A Thousand Days: John F. Kennedy in the White House* (Boston: Houghton Mifflin Company, 1965), p. 547.
4. Speech by President Johnson before the American Bar Association, New York, August 12, 1964.
5. Department of State Bulletin, April 13, 1964, pp. 563–564.

6. Hearings before the Senate Committee on Foreign Relations (Part I), 89th Congress, Second Session, February 17, 1966, p. 450.

7. Henry Steele Commager, "On the Way to 1984," *The Saturday Review*, April 15, 1967, pp. 69–80.

8. Clayton Fritchey, "Viet Policy Continuity Disputed," Washington *Evening Star*, January 20, 1967.

9. Remarks of United States Senator James B. Pearson, "The Credibility of the Administration on Vietnam," *Congressional Record*, May 27, 1966.

10. Hearings before the Senate Committee on Foreign Relations (Part I), 83rd Congress, Second Session, November 11, 1954, p. 4.

11. *Congressional Record*, February 1, 1955, p. 1053.

12. Quoted by Henry Steele Commager, "Our Vietnam Commitment," *Diplomat*, June, 1966, p. 24.

13. Los Angeles *Times*, July 25, 1965.

14. *New York Times*, August 12, 1966.

15. Speech by Walter Cronkite before the Inland Daily Press Association, Chicago, February 21, 1966.

16. Richard Wilson, "Great Deception of 1966—Cost of the War," Washington *Evening Star*, December 12, 1966.

17. George C. Wilson, "Laird Alleges Deception in Costs of War," *Washington Post*, September 27, 1966, p. 16.

18. As quoted in *Congressional Quarterly*, May 14, 1965, p. 941.

19. James Reston, "Washington: 'Candor Compels Me to Tell You,'" *New York Times*, November 17, 1965, p. 46.

20. *Congressional Record*, September 19, 1966, p. 22057.

21. *Investigation of the Preparedness Program*, Report by the Preparedness Investigating Subcommittee of the Committee on Armed Services, United States Senate, 90th Congress, First Session, April 6, 1967, p. 16.

22. *Ibid.*

23. "The Pilot Pinch," *Time*, April 14, 1967, p. 35.

24. Quoted by George C. Wilson at Sigma Delta Chi meeting in Washington, D.C., April 1, 1967.

25. *United States Information Problems in Vietnam*, Eleventh Report by the Committee on Government Operations, United States House of Representatives, 88th Congress, First Session, October 1, 1963, p. 3.

26. "Reporting Vietnam," *New Leader*, November 21, 1966, p. 8.

27. *Washington Post*, November 21, 1966.

28. *New York Times*, April 23, 1965.

29. *New York Times*, November 17, 1965, p. 46.

CHAPTER 9

The Moss Subcommittee

Secrecy—the first refuge of incompetents—must be at a bare minimum in a democratic society, for a fully informed public is the basis of self-government. Those elected or appointed to positions of executive authority must recognize that government, in a democracy, cannot be wiser than the people.

> —COMMITTEE ON GOVERNMENT
> OPERATIONS, UNITED STATES
> HOUSE OF REPRESENTATIVES

The post-World War II period gave rise to government secrecy on a scale never before seen in the United States.

In reaction to the uncertainties of the Cold War, literally tons of documents were classified "For Official Eyes Only." The censor's stamp was wielded by thousands of government employees at all levels of the burgeoning executive branch. The prevailing attitude toward government records was, "When in doubt, classify."

This practice produced the inevitable absurdities. The amount of peanut butter consumed by the armed forces was classified "secret" because the government feared this information might enable an enemy to determine the degree of our military preparedness. At the same time another government agency was publishing and selling reports that detailed the exact size of the armed forces.

Secrecy labels were placed on: a twenty-year-old report describing shark attacks on shipwrecked sailors; a study of the modern adaptation of the bow and arrow; a scrapbook about atomic energy compiled from newspapers and magazines by a group of college students; and a report on the use of public funds to send border inspectors to rifle and pistol matches.

It was at the height of postwar secrecy in 1953 that Congressman John E. Moss of California first confronted executive branch intransigence. As a freshman Democrat on the House Post Office and Civil Service Committee, the thirty-nine-year-old former businessman requested the United States Civil Service Commission to supply information in support of its claim that some 2,800 federal employees had been discharged for "security reasons." Moss felt the dismissals ought to be clarified because they reflected badly on the employees, on government service, and on the Truman administration which had originally hired most of those dismissed.

Moss explained: "I knew the majority of the people dismissed had not been let go because they lacked patriotism or because their allegiance to the country was in doubt. But these were the reasons implied. I had every confidence that the Truman administration had been diligent in administering the laws and had attempted to hire loyal Americans."

Pointing out that a person might have been dismissed for having a "drinking problem" or because of a misstatement, even unintentional, on his job application, Moss said: "Most people don't regard getting a parking ticket as an arrest, but it is a misdemeanor, and so when you get a parking ticket you have been arrested. If an employee failed to put that down correctly on his application form and he was subsequently dismissed, maybe for other reasons, a post-audit of the facts would cause that to appear as the 'security reason.' "

Moss insisted that the Civil Service Commission produce the facts. He wanted a precise breakdown of the reasons for the dismissals. The commission flatly refused to supply the information requested.

With the Republicans in control of both the executive

branch and the Congress, there was no one to whom Moss could appeal for assistance. He had run head-on into the wall of government secrecy.

In 1955, when the Democrats reclaimed a majority in Congress, Moss sought assignment to the House Committee on Government Operations. He asked the committee chairman, William L. Dawson of Illinois, a Democrat, to authorize a study to determine the extent of information withholding in the executive branch. Dawson, who was aware that secrecy in the Eisenhower administration was a potential political issue, selected a veteran member of the committee staff, Dr. Wallace J. Parks, to undertake the study. In a memorandum to Dawson on May 9, 1955, Parks concluded: "The trend toward suppression, non-availability, or denial of access to information appears to have been a general one affecting areas of government untouched by security considerations. Congress at large and the congressional committees have been deprived of information as well as the press, the government specialist, and leaders of public opinion."[1]

Backed by Parks' report, Moss next proposed that Dawson create a special subcommittee to monitor executive branch refusals to supply information. After consulting with then Majority Leader John McCormack of Massachusetts, Dawson decided to establish a Special Subcommittee on Government Information and to appoint Moss as its chairman.

In a letter to Moss on June 9, Dawson spelled out the subcommittee's assignment:

> . . . Charges have been made that Government agencies have denied or withheld pertinent and timely information from those who are entitled to receive it. These charges include the denial of such information to the newspapers, to radio and television broadcasters, magazines, and other communication media, to trained and qualified research experts and to the Congress. In many cases there is no apparent excuse for agencies of the executive branch of government either to withhold such information or to refuse to communicate it when requested. It has also been charged that pressures

of various sorts have been applied by Government officials to restrict the flow of information and the exchange of opinion outside the Government. . . . Accordingly, I am asking your Subcommittee to make such an investigation as will verify or refute these charges. . . .[2]

Why was Moss, a very junior member of Congress with no news media experience, no legal training, and no particular "influence," selected as chairman? "I was frankly quite surprised when I was asked to be chairman," Moss said. "I assumed I was selected because of the interest I had shown in the issue of government secrecy. I think Dawson determined that the man who had initiated the requests for the study and for the creation of the subcommittee should be offered the chairmanship. I was asked if I wanted it and of course I wanted it very desperately because I felt there was a job to be done."

The "job to be done" had been pinpointed earlier by the Freedom of Information Committee of the American Society of Newspaper Editors (ASNE). The FoI committee chairman, James Russell Wiggins, managing editor of the *Washington Post,* had challenged a directive issued in March, 1954, by Secretary of Defense Charles E. Wilson, which decreed that proposed speeches and statements by Pentagon officials would be scrutinized in advance not only for possible violations of security, but also to see whether or not their publication "would constitute a constructive contribution to the primary mission of the Department of Defense." A Pentagon public affairs officer, R. Karl Honaman, (formerly a public relations man for the Bell Telephone System), added insult to injury by writing Wiggins that the time of busy people in the Defense Department was being taken up by press questions which did not "truly meet the requirements of being useful or valuable." Wiggins rejoined: "In my book, the one to decide what is interesting or useful for the public is the people and not the government."[3] This clash between Honaman and Wiggins spotlighted for the news media and Congress the dangers of excessive government secrecy and military censorship.

Moss's first move as chairman of the new Subcommittee on Government Information was to appoint his administrative assistant, Samuel J. Archibald,* as staff director. Parks, a lawyer, was hired as counsel. A third member of the staff was J. Lacey Reynolds, a nine-year correspondent in Washington for the Nashville *Tennessean*.

Moss sent an 80-part questionnaire to 63 federal departments and agencies "to help determine their information policies and practices."[4] The Library of Congress was asked to prepare a report on all judicial decisions and statutory provisions pertaining to the availability of information in the executive branch. The news media were invited to make recommendations and to advise the subcommittee of difficulties they had experienced in gaining access to government information.

At a luncheon meeting with ASNE officers in July, 1955, Moss committed himself to "an objective establishment of facts, recognizing that the beginnings of secrecy were not in the Eisenhower administration." He paid particular attention to cultivating the "full cooperation" of the news media and, with the help of his staff, achieved remarkable success. Moss realized it was the press which was most handicapped by government officials' policy of "If in doubt, don't give out."

The first subcommittee hearings† were held in November of 1955. Prominent newsmen and information specialists were invited to air their philosophies on access to information and on existing government restrictions. Witnesses included: columnist Joseph Alsop; James Reston of the *New York Times;* James S. Pope, executive editor of the Louisville *Courier-Journal;* Theodore F. Koop, director of news and public

---

* Leaders of the freedom-of-information movement are quick to acknowledge that Archibald's contributions to the FoI cause have been second only to those made by Moss. Archibald, staff director until 1966, now serves the subcommittee as a special consultant.

† Moss preferred to call the initial hearings "panel discussions."

affairs for CBS in Washington; V. M. Newton, managing editor of the Tampa *Tribune;* and Harold L. Cross, ASNE counsel. Alsop summed up the tenor of the testimony when he said: "You have to begin by remembering that the boss in this country, thank God, is the American people. It is not the Secretary of the Security Council; it is not Mr. Wilson; it is not any of these people at all. The people is the master. And in our kind of society, we cannot hope to operate successfully unless the master of the society, the people, knows the essential facts."[5]

Another set of subcommittee hearings featured leading scientists and technological experts. They told the subcommittee that the federal government was so security conscious that a theory in basic science was classified "top secret" the moment it was born in the mind of the scientist. The witnesses testified that there would have been no atomic bomb if the security regulations then in existence had been in force in 1939. Dr. Lloyd V. Berkner, president of Associated Universities, Incorporated, testified: "In the case of radar, secrecy seriously delayed its development, and neither technical nor tactical progress was very appreciable. As a consequence, although it was technically and demonstrably adequate to have done this relatively simple job, radar failed to prevent Pearl Harbor. . . . Had they known our radar protection of Pearl Harbor, there is at least a reasonable doubt that the Japanese would have attempted a surprise. In any event, our own commanders certainly would not have been ignorant of the powerful tools at their command, and the outcome might well have been very different."[6]

Other first-year hearings were conducted with representatives of the Civil Service Commission, the Post Office, Treasury, Commerce, Agriculture, and Defense Departments, and five regulatory agencies. The official record revealed a pattern of secrecy and censorship so widespread that even members of the subcommittee were shocked.

By the end of the subcommittee's first year of operations, it was clear that federal officials were relying on three authorities as justification for withholding information. They were:

1. *Executive Privilege*—Eighteen departments and agencies cited a letter of May 17, 1954, from President Eisenhower to Secretary of Defense Wilson, as their authority for maintaining secrecy. The intent of the letter had been to forbid Army officers from testifying on matters relating to accusations made by Senator Joseph McCarthy of Wisconsin. A single sentence in Eisenhower's letter was construed as justification for refusing almost any request for information: "Because it is essential to efficient and effective administration that employees of the executive branch be in a position to be completely candid in advising with each other on official matters, and because it is not in the public interest that any of their conversations or communications, or any documents or reproductions, concerning such advice be disclosed, you will instruct employees of your Department that in all of their appearances before the subcommittee of the Senate Committee on Government Operations regarding the inquiry now before it they are not to testify to any such conversations or communications or to produce any such documents or reproductions."[7]

2. *5 U.S.C. 22*—This is the United States Code's so-called "housekeeping" statute (see p. 28). It was adopted in 1789 to provide for the "custody, use and preservation of the records" of the federal government. Twelve departments and agencies interpreted the words "custody" and "preservation" as their authority for withholding information.

3. *5 U.S.C. 1002, Section 3*—Known as the "public information section" of the 1946 Administrative Procedure Act, this section permitted the executive branch to withhold "in the public interest" any records for which it could find "good cause" for secrecy. It restricted access to "persons properly and directly concerned."

The Moss subcommittee concluded: "It is now incumbent upon Congress to bring order out of the present chaos. Congress should establish a uniform and universal rule on information practices. This rule should authorize and require full disclosure of information, except for specific exceptions defined by statute or restricted delegation of authority to withhold for an assigned reason. . . . The withholding should be subject to judicial review and the burden of proof should be on the official who withholds information. Most of the citation of authority for withholding by departments and agencies has been captious and equivocal. . . . Congress should clearly enunciate the fundamental principle that the public business is the public's business."[8]

Moss was hopeful he could "bring order out of chaos" without having to resort to a protracted program of amending federal statutes. He recognized the importance of legislative remedies, but he felt "the real source of the problem lies deeper. It concerns the spirit with which the agencies read the statutes, and the attitude taken by administrators toward the public's right to supervise the federal government."[9]

Moss considered the subcommittee's "watchdog" function as its primary and most effective role. When the subcommittee received a complaint of unwarranted secrecy, the first step was to determine whether or not the offending agency was exceeding its legal authority. If so, the agency head received a letter from Moss asking for conformity to the law. If the agency did not alter its policies, Moss proposed that a public hearing be held on the matter. Sometimes hearings were held, but in most cases the agencies voluntarily changed their policies or their regulations, or both. Finally, if the subcommittee felt an agency's regulations or a federal law did not allow sufficient access, alterations were recommended to the appropriate congressional committee. This "educational" process worked because federal officials were unwilling to persist in withholding information if the withholding threatened to cause a public uproar.

While continuing emphasis on the subcommittee's watchdog role, Moss did not neglect legislative solutions. In January, 1957, he introduced a bill (H.R. 2767) to amend the "housekeeping" statute. A companion bill was introduced in the Senate by Senator Thomas C. Hennings of Missouri. The nineteen word amendment simply stated that nothing in the statute (5 U.S.C. 22) should be construed as authority for withholding nonsecurity information. In 1958, the amendment passed both the House and Senate without a dissenting vote.

No sooner had the amendment become law, however, than federal departments and agencies switched to executive privilege and to the Administrative Procedure Act as their justifications for secrecy. Though there was little that could be done about executive privilege for the time being, Moss and other subcommittee members countered by introducing bills to close the loopholes in the Administrative Procedure Act. But a problem developed; the bills died in the House Judiciary Committee.

"It was impossible to amend the Administrative Procedure Act without the support of the Judiciary Committee," staff director Archibald noted. "It wasn't that the committee was opposed to the amendments. It was just that its members couldn't have cared less about them. They had no priority."

According to Archibald, the amendments also faced roadblocks in the Senate, where the leadership was reluctant to back measures which threatened to disrupt the status quo. "The Senate Majority Leader, Lyndon Johnson, could get all the information he wanted from the executive branch, so why should he reduce the power information brings by letting everybody have access to it?" Archibald asked. In the face of this opposition, Moss and Archibald decided it would be best to let Senator Hennings try to nurse a bill through the Senate. If Hennings could get a bill approved, then the Moss subcommittee would tackle the job of getting it through the House.

On July 2, 1960, the Moss subcommittee issued a "progress of study" report covering its work over the first five years. The report documented 173 cases of federal abridgment of freedom of information. Censorship was removed in 95 cases, continued in 68 cases, partially removed in 8, and partially continued in 2. The subcommittee achieved results in three out of five cases.

The report declared:

> The power to withhold the facts of government is the power to destroy that government in a democratic society. Such power is not to be lightly granted nor recklessly used. When the full light of publicity is thrown on the hidden operations of bureaucratic agencies, hitherto secret documents often become public records. In the majority of federal information cases during the past five years, agencies which have seen the light have divulged the information. Often the excuse of a "mistake" has been advanced to explain a refusal of information; a few times once-hidden records were disclosed after a simple reminder that public business is the public's business. Many times, however, the full weight of legislative authority combined with the pressure of public opinion is necessary—as was the case with the Death Valley documents hidden by the Interior Department—before self-centered bureaucrats will honor the people's right to know. . . . A continuing battle must be waged to wipe out the unnecessary pockets of secrecy in administrative regulations, longstanding custom, and bureaucratic attitudes.[10]

The Death Valley episode was a case in point. In March of 1960, the subcommittee was asked to look into the Interior Department's refusal of a Government Operations Committee request for a memorandum prepared by the department's legal experts on land and water exchange plans in the Death Valley National Monument area. In spite of five official letters and numerous telephone calls, the committee had not received even the courtesy of an acknowledgment of its request.

After a subcommittee staff interview with George Abbott, Interior Department Solicitor who had taken personal charge of the case, the subcommittee charged the department with a "conspiracy of silence." The charge was widely reported by the news media. As public interest began to develop in the case, Secretary of the Interior Fred A. Seaton broke silence by stating that he would not divulge the information.

Moss wrote to Seaton and pointed out that top department officials had received both free and cut-rate vacations at the plush winter resort owned in the Death Valley area by the same company with which the department was negotiating the water rights and land exchange. Under threat of a full-scale scandal in an election year, Seaton agreed to make the requested document available.

In another case, the subcommittee was successful in forcing the revision of an Air Force manual which attacked the National Council of Churches as Communist-infiltrated and which ridiculed the people's right to know. Moss threatened to conduct a thorough investigation unless Secretary of Defense Thomas S. Gates, Jr., ordered a review of all military manuals and a deletion of a statement on page 82 of Air Force Manual 205-5 which said: "Another rather silly remark often heard concerning security is that Americans have a right to know what's going on. Most people realize the foolhardiness of such a suggestion." The review was undertaken and the deletion made.

"I think the greatest accomplishment of the subcommittee in the first five years was its role in serving as a catalyst to generate public awareness of the need and the right to know," Moss said. "When we started out in 1955, you couldn't have gotten a discussion of the right to know except in the smallest group of professional journalists. We had to sell the term 'right to know.' Today government secrecy is a public issue. I think it will be an issue in every campaign in the future, regardless of which party is involved, because it has become part of the political dialogue. The subcommittee helped to call attention to this issue."

One of Moss's efforts to introduce the secrecy issue into the political dialogue was reported by subcomittee staff member Jack Howard, onetime reporter for the San Francisco *Chronicle,* in a letter on July 22, 1960, to another former *Chronicle* reporter, Pierre Salinger, then press secretary to Democratic Presidential candidate John F. Kennedy:

> John Moss has asked me to establish some sort of contact with your organization in order to make sure that anything we have that might be of possible use this fall will be channeled to the right places. . . .
> The Information Subcommittee will from time to time be generating material that may be useful, especially if Senator Kennedy plans any appearances before editors, publishers, or press groups.[11]

Moss had previously discussed the freedom-of-information issue with Kennedy and found a ready supporter. "Clearly, he [Kennedy] had followed the work of the subcommittee," Moss said. "He voiced a strong conviction that it was necessary work, that far too much secrecy had developed in the executive departments of government, and that Congress had to act to break it down."[12] Moss added that Kennedy also "showed a very keen understanding of the political capital" in discussing the Eisenhower administration's secrecy habits.

Moss got Kennedy to agree that if any "executive privilege" to withhold information existed, it was a privilege personal to the President and only the President could exercise it. Shortly thereafter, a major campaign issue developed over the refusal of the Eisenhower administration to release USIA public opinion polls. Moss explained:

> It was definitely arranged through my staff and the staff of the Kennedy campaign here in Washington, that the subcommittee would demand these polls. Nixon had very unwisely, I think, raised the question of the standing of the United States abroad, how well thought of we were. Kennedy, refuting the claims of Nixon, cited the results of a USIA poll. Senator Fulbright then requested the polls so that they could be public, so that the public could be in a position to evaluate the truth of Nixon's claim or the counter-charge of Kennedy.
> The Eisenhower administration, incredible to me, refused those polls. When they refused them to the Senate committee,

it was immediately referred to my subcommittee, and we went all out to get them. As a matter of fact, from the standpoint of political advantage, the refusal created an issue far more significant than whether or not we were well regarded abroad. Kennedy exploited that very effectively and, I think, with complete justification.[13]

Moss's efforts to stimulate Kennedy's awareness of the importance of open public records paid off handsomely on March 7, 1962. In a prearranged exchange of letters, Kennedy pledged: "Executive privilege can be invoked only by the President and will not be used without specific Presidential approval." True to his word, Kennedy did not permit subordinates to cite executive privilege as an excuse for withholding information. He personally exercised the privilege only once. This precedent that executive privilege could be used only by the President and only under special circumstances represented the second milestone* in the subcommittee's short history.

Despite Kennedy's personal belief in the propriety of free access to information, the subcommittee's fight against executive branch information policies continued unabated. The St. Louis *Globe-Democrat* commented that "a thin veneer of new leadership superimposed on the massive bureaucracy is not enough to prevent secrecy-minded career officials from equating secrecy with good government." While censorship and accompanying news management had in the past been conducted on the basis of Eisenhower's personal policy, they were now being carried out on the strength of long-established bureaucratic custom. In a speech before the American Bar Association in San Francisco, Moss warned: "Narrow as the use of executive privilege may be today, there easily can be abuse of this claim of authority for unjustifiable secrecy, or there can be abuse of any one of a dozen claims which have been advanced in recent years."[14]

Along with the Democrats' ascension to power in the execu-

* The first milestone was the successful amending of the "housekeeping" statute in 1958.

tive branch came the beginning of criticism that Moss was "taking it easy" on his political associates in the administration. In its 1961 report, the Advancement of Freedom of Information Committee of Sigma Delta Chi, the national journalism society, charged: "It was a gentle Moss who chided the Democratic bureaucrats for their secrecy instead of the old fire-eating Moss of 1955–60 who put scores of Republican bureaucrats on the witness stand and hammered them relentlessly and publicly in behalf of the American people's right to know about their government." *Editor & Publisher* magazine editorialized: "Under the Kennedy administration, the Moss Subcommittee (still controlled by Democrats) has taken a less critical attitude toward government information policies and Republicans say, 'We told you so.' "

Such criticism was justified. However, the critics* generally overlooked these points: (1) The subcommittee had, in its first five years, conducted exhaustive hearings in order to define and isolate the secrecy problem, and thus it was ready to move into a less colorful phase of operations aimed at a final legislative remedy; (2) the subcommittee had succeeded in amending the "housekeeping" statute and in exacting pledges of reform from President Kennedy, thus affecting reductions in executive secrecy; and (3) Moss had been able to establish a sound working relationship with the new Democratic administration, thus permitting "quiet persuasion" to take the place of public outcries.

Moss took the criticism in stride. He said: "I was always

* One of the most knowledgeable critics of the Moss Subcommittee is Dr. Robert O. Blanchard, chairman of the Department of Journalism, Public Relations, and Broadcasting at American University, Washington, D.C. Dr. Blanchard worked as a member of the subcommittee staff for five months in 1965, and, as a result concluded: "Despite its widely acknowledged achievements, the Moss Committee—as it has been known in the press—is now all but defunct. . . . There is a wealth of ideology and many platitudes, but little substance, left from the [Freedom of Information] movement's wave of the 1950's." An excellent account of Dr. Blanchard's views is found in the article, "A Watchdog in Decline," in the Summer, 1966, edition of the *Columbia Journalism Review*.

conscious when pressing the Eisenhower administration vigorously that I was exposing myself to the charge of being partisan. I tried carefully to avoid giving any support to that charge. I think it is frequently true that it's much easier to join an issue with your own family than with neighbors."[15] He also pointed to the subcommittee's continuing difficulties with the Kennedy-led bureaucracy: "We had a vigorous disagreement with Pierre Salinger. As a matter of fact, at one point Salinger demanded the resignation of Sam Archibald, and I had to acquaint him with the fact that the subcommittee was very much a part of the Congress and that we would preserve our independence. We had problems with the Secretary of Defense, Robert McNamara. I recall his calling on me at my office to try to explain a statement he had made which I had criticized rather strongly."

In 1961, the subcommittee collided with Carl Rowan, a State Department public affairs officer, over the wording of a directive that was intended to be the basic guideline for information policies in Vietnam. As a result of this collision, the directive was completely rewritten and its emphasis changed from one of withholding to one of disclosure. In 1962, the subcommittee sharply criticized the handling of news during the Cuban missile crisis. It clashed with the Federal Power Commission, the Federal Trade Commission, and other executive departments. Public hearings were held to examine overseas information policies, Defense and State Department information programs, and information procedures of the Office of Emergency Planning and the National Aeronautics and Space Administration. During the first six months of the Kennedy administration, the subcommittee investigated thirty-three complaints of executive secrecy.

An example of Moss's quieter efforts to combat secrecy in the Kennedy administration was an agreement worked out with USIA Director Edward R. Murrow in February, 1963. With the 1960 campaign issue over USIA polls still fresh in their minds, Moss and Archibald, along with subcommittee members Dante Fascell of Florida and George Meader of

Michigan, convinced Murrow to establish a four-step policy for making foreign public opinion polls available to Congress. The policy failed to provide for the release of the polls to the public or to minority (Republican) members of Congress, but it was nevertheless a step in the direction of disclosure.

In what must be construed as a vote of confidence in Moss's chairmanship, Dawson moved in 1963 to merge the Special Subcommittee on Government Information with the Subcommittee on Foreign Operations. Moss was named chairman of the expanded, permanent Subcommittee on Foreign Operations and Government Information. Membership on the subcommittee was increased from three to eight.

The year 1963 saw a renewed effort in the Senate to win approval of amendments to the Administrative Procedure Act. After the death of Senator Hennings, who had championed the amendments in the past, the cause was taken up by Senator Edward V. Long of Missouri. Through his Subcommittee on Administrative Procedures, Long succeeded in getting a bill to the floor of the Senate. It passed unanimously. Long's bill (S. 1666) moved to the House in 1964 and was referred to the Judiciary Committee, where it died again. *Editor & Publisher* observed: "Too many members of the House are involved in mending fences and running for office this fall to hope that anything might be accomplished in trying to pry the Long bill out of committee. But it might be worth a try if enough newspapers were to build a bonfire under that august body."[16]

The bonfire was built, not by the newspapers, but by Moss. He arranged a meeting with the chairman of the Judiciary Committee, Emanuel Celler of New York, and asked Celler to waive his committee's jurisdiction over the bill to amend the Administrative Procedure Act. Perhaps because of the heavy workload already before the Judiciary Committee—civil rights, immigration, Presidential succession, and reapportionment—Celler consented. It was agreed that Moss would introduce a bill in the House as an amendment to the "housekeeping" statute, with a provision that its passage would

automatically nullify Section 3 of the Administrative Procedure Act.

Moss introduced the bill (H.R. 5012) on February 17,
1965. It was referred to the Government Operations Committee and then passed on to the Moss subcommittee for action.
The objectives of the bill were to make "all records" available
to "any person" requesting them and to provide for appeal to
the courts. The bill specified eight categories of government
information which would be exempt from disclosure. In a staff
memorandum, Archibald noted that the Moss bill had vital
points in common with Senator Long's bill and also with
earlier bills drafted by Jacob Scher, a lawyer and professor of
journalism at Northwestern University who had ably assisted
the subcommittee until his death in 1961. Each of the bills:

> states that public records, which are evidence of official
> government action, are public property; establishes a pro-
> cedure to guarantee the individual's access to specific public
> records; designates those categories of official records which
> must, to maintain the processes of government and protect the
> nation, be exempt from disclosure.[17]

Long reintroduced his bill in the Senate as S. 1160, and on
February 17, Long and Moss issued a joint press release for
the purpose of associating the House and Senate bills. The
message that the two bills were directed at the same goal was
successfully communicated.

Now, with the jurisdictional problem in the House resolved
and with fresh bills introduced, Moss concentrated on another
difficult question: How to sell the legislation to the new
administration of President Johnson? In the past, every executive agency testifying on the legislation had opposed it.
Moss knew that Johnson would be under pressure from the
executive bureaucracy to block the bills. One telephone call
from the White House to the Democratic leadership in Congress could effectively obstruct the legislation.

Through discussions with his staff and various freedom-of-
information leaders, Moss decided to hold hearings on H.R.

5012 and to invite as witnesses both executive branch spokesmen and news media representatives. As in the 1957–58 hearings, testimony from the executive branch (in opposition) was scheduled first and statements by press representatives (in support) slated last. This order of appearance would allow executive branch testimony to be rebutted, point by point.

The administration's main presentation was made on March 30, 1965, by Norbert A. Schlei, assistant attorney general in the Justice Department, who outright rejected the idea that legislation could be written to protect the public's right to know. He said: "The problem is too vast, too protean, to yield to any such solution." He stated, in effect, that any disagreements between the executive branch and the public, or Congress, would have to be resolved at the pleasure of the executive. He offered no constructive suggestions for improving the legislation. In the days that followed, other administration witnesses took the same approach. The testimony was interpreted as an implied threat of veto of any bill Congress might pass.

Why was the Johnson administration opposed to a right-to-know law? First, the power of the executive branch to withhold information would be diminished. Second, Johnson had received a strongly worded memorandum in opposition to the legislation from Lee White, a Presidential adviser. White's interest dated back to 1962 when he and Pierre Salinger had been stung by Moss's criticism of the administration's handling of news during the Cuban missile crisis. White had not forgotten.

In early April of 1965, when House Speaker McCormack, Majority Leader Carl Albert, and Majority Whip Hale Boggs arrived at the White House for a weekly meeting of the Democratic leadership, President Johnson asked them to explain the status of Moss's bill. When advised it was at the hearing stage in the House, the President said he thought it was "terrible" legislation. "What's Moss trying to do to me?" he asked. He implied that Moss ought to be "brought into line." Within an hour, Moss was summoned out of a hearing by McCormack and told of Johnson's displeasure over the bill. "Clearly the executive branch had no enthusiasm for the bill, but I felt we had to move ahead," Moss said.

He arranged for a series of meetings with representatives of the Justice and Treasury Departments, the bill's most outspoken opponents, to consider areas of compromise.* Archibald and subcommittee counsel Benny Kass met with Bill D. Moyers, the President's press secretary, and with other White House aides. Moss personally explained the bill to Johnson during at least two social events which both attended.

Moss had no reason to believe the bill would ever be acceptable to the White House, but neither had he been explicitly told it would be vetoed.

"When we secured modification of the 'housekeeping' statute in 1958 we had no firm indication the Republican administration would accept it," Moss noted. "Suddenly, without any warning, the amendment moved without opposition and was signed into law by the President. I hoped the same thing would happen again. The most important part of H.R. 5012 was the establishment of the right of judicial review. I made it very clear in every conference with the executive branch that this point was not negotiable. This was the one that seemed to worry them the most. I think that's why we couldn't get any indication of Presidential attitude."

Moss's progress bogged down when he was unable to muster a quorum of subcommittee members to consider the bill. A meeting scheduled for May 24 was attended only by Moss and one other member: Donald Rumsfeld of Illinois, a thirty-two-year-old second-term Republican who had requested assignment to the subcommittee the previous January, was a co-sponsor of H.R. 5012, and, next to Moss, the bill's strongest supporter. The two alone could not consider and act upon the bill, and subsequent efforts to get a quorum failed. In July, Moss replaced two of the absentee subcom-

---

* The bill eventually underwent nine revisions.

mittee members with Democrats David S. King of Utah and Henry Helstoski of New Jersey.

Meanwhile, word was circulating throughout Washington that the White House had turned thumbs down on the freedom-of-information bill. In a July 11 column for the Albuquerque *Journal*, correspondent Paul R. Wieck explained: "The chill breeze that, on occasion, sweeps up from 1600 Pennsylvania Ave. to 'the Hill' now threatens to kill, in the bud, the 'freedom of access' bill that has been so long maturing. It took Rep. John Moss' government information subcommittee 10 years of digging about the federal bureaucracy before formal hearings were held last April on a first draft. But, hardly had the hearings started before it was denounced by President Lyndon B. Johnson in a closed-door session with his party's leadership in Congress. . . . Rep. Moss has been unable to get a quorum to continue the mark-up of his bill."[18]

Wieck said that Johnson was insisting that executive privilege be written into the bill and that the court review provision be removed. The *Journal* column continued: "A young . . . crew-cut member from a strong GOP district in suburban Cook County—Rep. Donald Rumsfeld—has taken a personal interest in the 'freedom of access' bill and quickly impresses any reporter with his grasp of the problem. He is unalterably opposed to the change in the first exception, the change that would allow material to be withheld by direction of the President. . . . Like others interested in the bill, Rep. Rumsfeld is aware of President Johnson's opposition. . . . The *Journal* correspondent asked Rep. Rumsfeld if he feels White House opposition is in any way responsible for the inability of Rep. Moss to summon a quorum of the subcommittee. He smiled just a trifle, paused a moment, and said: 'We always managed to meet before.' "[19]

On July 31, columnists Robert S. Allen and Paul Scott reported the administration was pushing to rewrite the bill to give the "heads of all government agencies authority to bar publication of official information they wanted to suppress."[20]

An Associated Press story said the President had passed down the word to jettison the bill.

"John Moss was doing battle—quietly, because it was his party in the White House—but he was doing battle with the administration all the time," Rumsfeld said. "Apart from the hearings, apart from the subcommittee, Moss was trying to work it out 'within the family.' Sure, there were times when it appeared like Moss was letting down—the time lag after the hearings, the canceling of subcommittee meetings, the adjourning of meetings. But these things were beyond Moss' control. He needed help."

On October 13, the Senate passed S. 1160, the Long bill. It was sent to the House and referred to the Moss subcommittee. In order to save time and to avoid conferences between the House and Senate to iron out differences in the bills, Moss scrapped H.R. 5012 and concentrated on the Senate bill, Long's S. 1160.

But the 1965 legislative session came to a close without any House action being taken on the bill.

When he returned to Washington for the opening of the second session of the 89th Congress in January, 1966, Rumsfeld had resolved to provide the only kind of "help" that could possibly spring the bill loose—political pressure. "It seemed to me that the thing that had to be done to get the bill moving was to try to interest the American people in it," Rumsfeld said. Early in the session, he asked Benny Kass to bring a copy of the latest redraft of the bill and to meet him in the Rayburn Room of the Capitol. "I read the draft and told Kass that he could tell John Moss, and I would tell John Moss, that in the event this version was put before our subcommittee I would oppose it. It codified the concept of executive privilege. It wasn't even worth amending. It would have been far worse than no bill at all."

Rumsfeld huddled with House Minority Leader Gerald R. Ford of Michigan to stress the significance of Republican support for the bill. Ford promised to help. Rumsfeld then met with Clark Mollenhoff of Cowles Publications and Julius

Frandsen of UPI, both leading freedom-of-information advocates. They agreed that "outside assistance" would be helpful. Next Rumsfeld conferred with Congressman Robert P. Griffin of Michigan,* the ranking Republican on the Moss subcommittee. Griffin, overburdened with other work for the Education and Labor Committee, asked Rumsfeld to take the initiative on the freedom-of-information bill.

"I then began to insert in the *Congressional Record* literally dozens of statements, articles, columns, and examples of news management," Rumsfeld said. "I inserted anything I could find to give other people ammunition to use in speeches, to ask questions about, to point up the problem of government secrecy. I encouraged other members of Congress to interest themselves in the subject and I got the word to the Republican National Committee and the Republican Congressional Committee."

In a speech in Chicago on February 21, Rumsfeld posed four questions which were heard, if not answered, in the White House:

> How could an Administration which claims to be interested in encouraging the participation of all citizens in government stand in opposition to this legislation?
>
> Why should President Johnson have asked the Congress to pass the Voting Rights Act of 1965, for example, if his Administration is intent on denying the public access to the information it needs to draw informed conclusions?
>
> Why should the Administration have any objection to the goal of assuring the people's right to know about the conduct of government?
>
> Why should the President on the one hand speak frequently of his interest in people and on the other hand deny those people their constitutional right to information on the conduct of government?

Moss recognized that Rumsfeld and other Republicans were fashioning an issue which could become a potent weapon for the GOP in the November general election. It was the issue

* Griffin was elected to the United States Senate in November, 1966.

of the "credibility gap." Moss advised the White House that agreement on the freedom-of-information bill had now become a political necessity. This argument impressed the White House. Objections to the bill began to fade.

On Wednesday, March 30, 1966, the Moss subcommittee voted unanimously to refer S. 1160 to the full Government Operations Committee with a do-pass recommendation. It was the first time the subcommittee had ever voted on a freedom-of-information bill.

On Wednesday, April 27, the Government Operations Committee approved the bill. The forward momentum was now such that a plan was devised by Moss and the Democratic leadership for the bill to bypass any possible complications in the Rules Committee. The plan called for a suspension of the House rules to permit the bill to go directly to the floor of the House. Moss predicted it might pass the House unanimously.

Notwithstanding these optimistic signs, Rumsfeld persisted in promoting the bill. On May 17, the Republican House Policy Committee officially endorsed the proposal, on May 18, Rumsfeld, Ford, and other GOP leaders held a press conference to call on the Johnson administration to support the bill; on May 25, nineteen Republicans extolled the bill's virtues in speeches in the House.

Monday, June 20, 1966, was a proud day for the proponents of the freedom-of-information concept. On that day, in a rare mood of total harmony, the House voted 307–0 to pass S. 1160 and to send it to the President for signature.

The only question remaining was whether or not Johnson would sign it. Moss said he had no guarantee either way. Without ceremony and without advance notice to anyone, Johnson signed the bill on July 4 while vacationing at his ranch in Johnson City, Texas. The President issued a statement saying:

> The measure I sign today, S. 1160, revises Section 3 of the Administrative Procedure Act to provide guidelines for

the public availability of the records of Federal departments and agencies.

This legislation springs from one of our most essential principles: A democracy works best when the people have all the information that the security of the nation permits. No one should be able to pull curtains of secrecy around decisions which can be revealed without injury to the public interest.

. . . This bill in no way impairs the President's power under our Constitution to provide for confidentiality when the the national interest so requires. There are some who have expressed concern that the language of this bill will be construed in such a way as to impair Government operations. I do not share this concern.

I have always believed that freedom of information is so vital that only the national security, not the desire of public officials or private citizens, should determine when it must be restricted.

. . . I am instructing every official in this Administration to cooperate to this end and to make information available to the full extent consistent with individual privacy and with the national interest.

Apparently, the President had some difficulty in arriving at words appropriate for the occasion. Two statements were released. The first draft was withdrawn after Johnson decided he wanted to make some changes. A substitute was then issued. The last paragraph of the original version had read: "I signed this measure with a deep sense of pride that the United States is an open society in which the *decisions and policies—as well as the mistakes—of public officials are always subjected to the scrutiny and judgment of the people* [emphasis added]." The final paragraph of the second statement said: "I signed this measure with a deep sense of pride that the United States is an open society in which the *people's right to know is cherished and guarded* [emphasis added]."

Moss had this to say: "We made some compromises and the legislation is, in my judgment, far from perfect. But it's a beginning. I have learned in nineteen years of legislating that if you can get a beginning point, or a foundation, it's easy to lay the next brick. It's easy to modify, to affect the changes that perfect the product."

The Federal Public Records Law (5 U.S.C. 552) became official on July 4, 1967. Its authors allowed a twelve-month "grace" period, from July 4, 1966, to July 4, 1967, to give all departments of the executive branch time to adjust to a new way of doing business. In June, 1967, Attorney General Ramsey Clark issued a 47-page memorandum to all government agencies to guide them in rewriting their information policies to conform to the new law. Most government officials have recognized and accepted the inevitability of adhering to the law. Some have not. In the first four months of the law's life, ten cases challenging government secrecy were filed in federal district courts. Half were decided on the side of disclosure and half on the side of withholding. In some instances, the mere threat of a court suit influenced government officials to take a second look at their information practices and to rule in favor of disclosure.

In a speech before the Federal Bar Association in Chicago on November 3, 1967, Congressman Rumsfeld said any fair assessment of progress since the new law's inception "must be somewhere between the extremes of it being an immediate cure-all or a wholly meaningless instrument." He added: "If the law is to have any affect at all on the 'credibility gap,' it will surely be a long-range affect. No law can force a man to be honest, or truthful, or candid in his remarks. However, the new law will affect the credibility problem in two ways: first, it will arouse public sentiment and create a demand for integrity in government; second, it will make more information available so that the public and the press will have to rely less upon what government officials tell them, they will have independent means of checking for the truth. This law deals with secrecy; it does not pretend to come to grips with the problems of deceit and lack of candor in government pronouncements. The political system, the ballot box, may be the only real answer for the credibility problem."

What does the future hold for the Moss subcommittee?

"I think we need to keep on auditing information policies in the executive branch," Moss said. "I feel it is much more important now than it was when we started. There is so much information generated in government today that it is difficult for people to get the facts even when they're freely available. If someone started locking up the facts, our people couldn't be effective governors of themselves. That's why we've got to continue the watchdog function."

NOTES TO CHAPTER 9

1. Memorandum in files of the Subcommittee on Foreign Operations and Government Information. See "Miscellaneous C (Charter and Its Background)."
2. *Ibid.*
3. William Stringer, *Christian Science Monitor,* June 27, 1955.
4. Letter from Moss to Archibald of July 22, 1955. See Subcommittee files.
5. *Availability of Information from Federal Departments and Agencies,* Part I, Hearings before a Subcommittee of the Committee on Government Operations, House of Representatives, 84th Congress, First Session, November 7, 1955, p. 22.
6. *Availability of Information from Federal Departments and Agencies,* Hearings before a Subcommittee of the Committee on Government Operations, House of Representatives, 84th Congress, Second Session, March 7, 1956, p. 757.
7. *Twenty-Fifth Intermediate Report,* Committee on Government Operations, House of Representatives, 84th Congress, Second Session, July 27, 1956, p. 65.
8. *Ibid.,* pp. 93–94.
9. *Harvard Law Record,* March 7, 1957.
10. *Availability of Information from Federal Departments and Agencies,* Twenty-Fourth Report by the Committee on Government Operations, House of Representatives, 86th Congress, Second Session, July 2, 1960, p. 37.
11. Letter from Howard to Salinger of July 22, 1960. See Subcommittee files.
12. *Oral History, Interview with John Moss,* by Philip M. Stern, John F. Kennedy Oral History Project, National Archives and Records Service, United States Government, April 13, 1965.
13. *Ibid.*
14. Speech by Moss before the Administrative Law Section, American Bar Association, San Francisco, August 7, 1962.
15. *The Moss Subcommittee, 1955—,* Freedom of Information Center

Publication No. 110, School of Journalism, University of Missouri, October, 1963, p. 13.

16. *Editor & Publisher,* August 29, 1964, p. 72.

17. Memorandum from Archibald of August 2, 1965. See Subcommittee files.

18. Paul R. Wieck, "Chill Threatens Press Bill," Albuquerque *Journal,* July 11, 1965.

19. *Ibid.*

20. Robert S. Allen and Paul Scott, "More Press Controls," Tulsa *World,* July 31, 1965.

CHAPTER 10

Closing the Gap

*Those who expect to reap the blessings of freedom
must, like men, undergo the fatigue of supporting it.*

—THOMAS PAINE

Sooner or later, the American people will have to face the fact
that the ever-growing authority of the executive branch of the
federal government will have to be checked, if the democratic
dialogue is to be preserved.

The President, leader of the vast executive sprawl, has
taken unto himself powers so great that a serious threat is
posed to the constitutional philosophy of checks and balances
among the three branches of government—the legislative,
executive, and judicial. Today, the checks and balances are
out of order. Even though the First Amendment of the
Constitution set forth the principle that the widest possible
dissemination of thought from diverse but equal sources is
essential to the well-being of the people, there is doubt that
our system of government is any longer dependent on the free
flow of ideas in the marketplace of democracy. This doubt
was anticipated by Judge Learned Hand, who said: "The
First Amendment pre-supposes that right conclusions are

more likely to be gathered out of a multitude of tongues, than through any kind of authoritative selection. To many this is, and always will be, folly; but we have staked upon it our all."

High among the President's powers is his control over the information which influences government decision-making and, ultimately, the course of our nation at home and abroad. The Constitution provides that the President "shall from time to time give to the Congress information on the state of the Union,"[1] but—as we have seen in foregoing chapters—the President enjoys wide discretion in fulfilling this informational role, and, in cases of unjustified withholding of information, neither the legislative nor the judicial branches has the means to force compliance. Further, the President's ability to command the attention of the news media maximizes his power to sway public opinion; yet, there is no guarantee that the President's influence of public opinion will satisfy more than his personal whim. In reporting to the people, the President is free to say what he likes and to omit what he dislikes. There is nothing to preclude his intermingling the "national interest" with concerns of a partisan or political nature.

The inclination of the executive branch to hide its actions from the Congress and the public has never been more pronounced than under the administration of President Johnson. Secrecy alone, however, has failed to satisfy the President's needs. To secrecy he has added the ingredients of deceit and news management. The result: the three-dimensioned "credibility gap."

The tendency of the executive to operate in secret has long been woven into the fabric of government bureaucracy. As stated by sociologist Max Weber:

> Every bureaucracy seeks to increase the superiority of the professionally informed by keeping their knowledge and intentions secret. Bureaucratic administration always tends to be an administration of "secret sessions": in so far as it can, it hides its knowledge and action from criticism. . . . The

tendency toward secrecy in certain administrative fields follows their material nature: everywhere that the power interests of the domination structure toward the outside are at stake, whether it is an economic competitor of a private enterprise, or a foreign, potential hostile polity, we find secrecy.[2]

Weber notes that the "official secret" is the specific invention of bureaucracy and that nothing is so fanatically defended by the bureaucracy as this attitude. In facing a parliament, Weber observes, the bureaucracy—out of a sure power instinct—fights every attempt of the parliament to gain knowledge by means of its own experts or from interest groups. "Bureaucracy naturally welcomes a poorly informed and hence a powerless parliament—at least in so far as ignorance somehow agrees with the bureaucracy's interests," Weber concludes.

Walter Lippmann, a friend of Presidents for forty years, substantiates the Weber theory as it is applied to the current credibility problem:

> The credibility gap today is not the result of honest misunderstanding between the President and the press in this complicated world. It is the result of a deliberate policy of artificial manipulation of official news. The purpose of this manipulation is to create a consensus for the President, to stifle debate about his aims and his policies, to thwart deep probing into what has already happened, what is actually happening, what is going to happen.
>
> In its press relations the Administration does not hold with the fundamental American principle that true opinion arises from honest inquiry and open debate and that true opinion is necessary to free government. For this Administration, the right opinions are those which lead to consensus with the leader, and to create such true opinion it is legitimate to wipe out the distinction between patriotism and patrioteering and to act on the assumption that the end justifies the means.[3]

Lippmann attributes the decline of confidence in the candor and reliability of the President to two causes: "One . . . is that Mr. Johnson is a pathologically secretive man. The other is that he believes in his right to manipulate the news in his own political interest and does not hold with the American tradition about the importance of an independent press."[4] Lippmann submits: "It is sophistry to pretend that in a free country a man has some sort of inalienable or constitutional right to deceive his fellow man. There is no more right to deceive than there is a right to swindle, to cheat, or to pick pockets."[5]

James Reston, a proponent of the adversary relationship between the government and the press, also takes a dim view of current information practices in the executive branch. He says: "It is much easier . . . for the President to manipulate the Congress than to persuade it; easier to overwhelm the press with statements, pronouncements, propaganda meetings, private interviews, messages to the Congress, trips to Asia—an endless avalanche of activity which dominates the news—rather than to convince the press that the President is following a clear line of policy, and saying the same thing in private that he says in public."[6] Reston believes the President's technique of manipulation is applied at high cost; the people want to understand and believe in the actions of their government, but they cannot. "The Congress is told that it is the 'partner' of the President in critical foreign policy decisions, but knows that it is not. The press is invited everywhere, urged to report and criticize, but is given the forms of participation without really participating and condemned for the criticism it is invited to make."

Senator Mark O. Hatfield of Oregon is of the opinion that there is an absolute necessity for the people to be sufficiently and honestly informed if they are to judge their own fates. "In order to function effectively as citizens," Hatfield says, "the people must have access to the unfettered truth. Without this access, our whole foundation of government will crumble." Hatfield believes the American people must vigorously resist the trend toward the government making available only information of a noncontroversial nature. "Of course there are certain qualifications to the right of access, such as security matters, national defense, and international crises, but the government has been relying on these qualifications too often. The people are being asked to accept government on faith. Our leaders have taken the position that an issue is far too complicated for the people to understand even if full information is provided. The government restricts information and says 'have faith in us; we're doing what's best for you.' This method is used on Members of Congress, as well as on the public. It is an extremely dangerous practice."

The Congress has, from time to time, attempted to bring the business of government into the open through special legislation. In 1928, a law was passed to provide that every executive department shall, upon request of the Committee on Government Operations of either the House or Senate, furnish any information requested of it relating to matters within the broad jurisdiction of the committees. The new Federal Public Records Law, discussed in Chapter IX, extends the 1928 doctrine and further provides for review by the courts in cases where information is arbitrarily withheld by the executive branch. While these and other federal laws have been adequate in expressing the desire for information on the part of the Congress and the public, they have so far been of little practical value in increasing the flow of information from executive agencies.

Can anything be done about the crisis in credibility? If so, who is to do it?

In theory, the legislative branch—the Congress—is in a position to exercise a great deal of control over the executive. But, in recent times, the Congress has acted much like a dog at the foot of the master's table, waiting for a bone to be tossed its way. The Congress has paid little heed to its constitutional obligation to serve as a check and balance on the executive. Joseph and Stewart Alsop analyze the diminished role of Congress this way:

Congress . . . does not initiate policy, as the House of Commons may be said to initiate policy through the leaders of its majority. Congress adapts, adopts or rejects the policies initiated by the executive. Its role is female; the executive has the male role.

. . . In the days of the first Senator Lodge, the problems confronting the nation were not too complex for the average man—which means for the ordinary Senator or Representative. With its battalions of lawyers to do the drafting, the Congress in those days could and did propose its own solutions for those problems. But now the problems have grown infinitely too complex, because our society has grown too complex. So the Congress today must let the executive branch study the problems and propose the solutions; and after the executive has proposed, the Congress duly adapts, adopts or rejects the proposal. Thus we have come to have what may be called a fully Presidential system of government.[7]

Coupled with Congress' self-adopted "female role" is the fact that the congressional house is in disarray. In 1966, the House-Senate Committee on the Organization of Congress received estimates that 90 percent of all decisions in Congress are made in secret committee meetings. A compilation by *Congressional Quarterly* showed that congressional committees held 386 (45 percent) of their 861 meetings during the first months of 1967 behind closed doors. When a member of the House Committee on Government Operations offered a resolution in 1967 to provide that a record of the committee's votes be made available to the public, committee members quickly rejected it. The same committee recently voted to limit drastically the authority of the General Accounting Office in securing information from the executive branch. The Congress also stubbornly refuses to allow radio and television coverage of its sessions.

If the Congress is to regain its station among the separate powers and begin to play a truly significant role in shaping effective, far-sighted solutions to the nation's problems, it must correct the appalling imbalance between the information it receives and the information available to the executive branch. In moving to correct this imbalance, the Congress faces a number of obstacles. They include:

1. *The fact that the preponderance of information about the day-to-day operations of the federal government is controlled by the executive branch.* While the Congress is responsible for authorizing and funding federal programs, it has no responsibility for administering them. The executive branch is the administrator. Thus, the Congress is dependent on the executive for information about government operations. It can be assumed that the executive branch will continue to resist attempts by the Congress to gain access to information in the executive's control.

2. *The decentralized organization of the Congress itself.* Authority in the Congress is widely dispersed among 535 individual members, two houses, thirty-six standing committees, and two political parties. As a result, it is extremely difficult for the Congress to bring its full weight to bear on the executive branch. The problem is compounded by the fact that congressional leaders, who are kept well informed by the executive branch, privately oppose efforts of their colleagues to secure information. These leaders understand that "information is power," and they are disinclined to share that power. Members of the minority party are not only unable to get assistance from the majority in acquiring information, but they are also stymied by some of their own leaders, who achieve personal security through "friendly relationships" with the executive branch and with the majority leadership in Congress.

3. *The fact that, in conflicts between the Congress and the President, the people tend to side with the President.* The late Senator Joseph McCarthy learned the hard way that the President has inordinate powers for rallying public opinion to his cause. More recently, Senator J. W. Fulbright has learned the same lesson. The President can readily command the attention of the news media; the Congress cannot. In addition to being at a distinct advantage in communicating with the

people, the President also reaps benefits from the "age of Presidential government." In the eyes of millions, the President is above reproach.

In order to reduce the extent of its reliance on the executive branch for information, the Congress should develop its own information storage and retrieval system through the purchase of automatic data processing (ADP) equipment. The executive branch currently operates 2,500 electronic computers; the Congress installed its first computer in 1967. Remarked Congressman Fred Schwengel of Iowa: "With the introduction of more than 13,000 measures in the House alone last year, it is difficult to comprehend how Congress could fail to take advantage of computer technology for the storage and retrieval of this most fundamental information while it allowed the executive branch to spend more than one billion dollars for automatic data processing in the departments and agencies."[8] Because of its failure to adopt modern information techniques, the Congress has fallen behind the executive branch throughout the entire policy-making process.

The Congress can further expand its independent sources of information by bolstering the authority of the General Accounting Office. The GAO was established in 1921 for the purpose of providing the independent examination and evaluation of executive branch programs. In 1963 and 1964, the GAO submitted 668 audit reports and other communications to the Congress on fiscal and related operations of the executive branch. However, after an executive branch official complained in 1966 that the GAO was "overzealous" in its investigations, the Congress voted to restrict the agency's authority. This unfortunate vote should be reconsidered and the GAO's responsibilities expanded.

Another major source of information for the Congress is the Legislative Reference Service (LRS) of the Library of Congress. In existence for more than fifty years, the LRS today is functioning under severe handicaps—insufficient personnel, outmoded resources, and cramped working facilities.

In 1946, the LRS staff of 95 handled 16,444 Congressional inquiries. Nineteen years later, with a staff of 200, the Service answered 113,628 requests, a workload increase of almost 700 percent. If the Congress expects to continue to receive timely and objective information, research, and evaluation of legislative matters from the LRS, it must provide the funds necessary for a thorough reorganization and modernization of the Service.

The Congress can extract substantially more information from the executive branch if it will exercise cautious control over the appropriations process. This is the Congress' "ace in the hole." Article I of the Constitution provides for congressional control of revenues and expenditures: "All bills for raising revenue shall originate in the House of Representatives [Section 7, Clause 1]"; "The Congress shall have the power to lay and collect taxes [Section 8, Clause 1];" and "No money shall be drawn from the Treasury, but in consequence of appropriations made by law [Section 9, Clause 7]." Without the funds provided annually by Congress, the executive branch would be helpless. The power of the purse is an ultimate power reserved for the exclusive use of the legislative branch, but it is rarely, if ever, used to force executive compliance with Congressional demands. This power ought to be employed as often as is necessary to convince the executive that "cooperation" is a two-way process.

Some changes in the committee organization in Congress would aid appreciably in overcoming the fragmentation of congressional authority and enable the Congress to be a more effective overseer of executive branch operations. One desirable change would be to place the Committees on Government Operations of the House and Senate in the hands of the political party other than the party of which the President is a member. Under minority control, the major congressional investigating committees would be considerably more diligent in seeking facts from the executive branch. Another proposed change, put forward by three members of the Joint Committee on the Organization of Congress, is for the House and

Senate each to establish a new Committee on Procedures and Policies to monitor executive activities, with the committee chairmen being from the minority party. Congressmen Thomas B. Curtis and Durward G. Hall of Missouri and James C. Cleveland of New Hampshire explained: "This is not an original idea in representative government either here or abroad. The House of Commons in Great Britain has a committee known as the Committee of Public Accounts whose chairman is by convention a leading member of the opposition. . . . If the minority [in Congress] had control of an investigatory committee, the 'credibility gap' could not have gained the serious proportions which it has today when an immense majority of the American public literally does not believe the pronouncements of its own government."[9] There is precedent in United States history for minority control of committee investigations. In 1923, when the Teapot Dome oil reserve scandal erupted, both the Congress and the executive branch were controlled by the Republican Party. Yet, at the urging of Republican Senator Robert LaFollette of Wisconsin, Senator Thomas J. Walsh of Montana, a Democrat, was prevailed upon to conduct the Teapot Dome investigation.

Another means for improving the congressional oversight function is to amend the rules in Congress to insure the minority party an adequate supply of committee staff positions. Too many congressional committees list no personnel responsible to the minority. Without sufficient professional staff assistants, the minority party cannot successfully perform the adversary role which is vital to the two-party system. Thoughtful members of the present majority party agree. Congressman David S. King of Utah, a Democrat, testified: "A formula must be found for balancing the personnel of the committee staffs more equitably between the majority and the minority parties. . . . In my opinion, the balance of personnel between the two parties on the committee staffs should more nearly approximate the division of party strength in the House itself."[10] Dr. James A. Robinson, professor of political science at Ohio State University, writes: "The best argument [for adequate minority staff] is that the improved performance of the minority members helps to strengthen the legislative way of life. If the majority party becomes increasingly aligned with the executive branch . . . then we must look to the minority to check the majority and in so doing to provide the necessary counterbalance to executive power."[11]

The seniority system in Congress ought to be altered. This system, in use for 121 years in the Senate and 57 years in the House, dictates that members with the most tenure (read: *oldest*) shall be chairmen of the congressional committees. The Congress is the only legislative body in the entire free world which uses such a system. The selection of committee chairmen on the basis of their skills, their dedication, or their promise is prohibited by the seniority system. It perpetuates weak and tired leadership. The Congress should seriously consider the election of committee chairmen by the members of the committees or by election within the respective party caucuses. With committee chairmen more responsive to the national interest than to sectional favoritism, and with genuine ability, the Congress will be imminently more productive.

Finally, if the Congress is to compete on equal terms with the executive branch, it must abandon the cherished congressional belief that if something has been done a certain way for one hundred years it must be good.

The nation's news media can also contribute to the demise of the credibility problem if they will be more attentive to their independent watchdog role. A mere handful of newsmen regularly guards the press's right of access to government information; the majority do nothing. First, publishers and network officials can increase their now-modest investment in manpower in Washington, D.C., the world biggest and most important news center. Washington news bureaus are understaffed and overworked to the point where only the most obvious news stories are being treated. Second, reporters can avoid involvement in the government's not-for-attribution and for-background-only press briefings. The service performed for the participants in these secrecy rites is far outweighed by the disservice they do the public. Reporters will be surprised to find how quickly their refusal to indulge in off-the-record sessions will prompt government officials to agree to speak for attribution. Third, newsmen can fortify their defenses against seduction by administration officials. "I think there are certain rules of hygiene in the relationship between a newspaper correspondent and high officials," Walter Lippmann noted a few years ago. "Newspapermen cannot be the cronies of great men. . . . I think there always has to be a certain distance between high public officials and newspapermen. I wouldn't say a wall or a fence, but an air space, and that's very important." Fourth, the press can be more alert to the news potential of the minority party. The minority has traditionally found it difficult to compete with the White House for news space. A minority with an improved communications line to the people would serve as a much more effective check upon the majority. Fifth, the news media can be less concerned with preserving the status quo and more concerned with raising hell.

The people, the first repository of the nation's strength, can do more than the Congress and the news media combined in assuring adequate and honest reporting from the executive branch. The American constitutional theory is that the people know best how to deal with their common problems. If well informed, the people can exercise their judgment and bring forth solutions far superior to those offered by any group of ordained leaders. As the 1960 report of the President's Commission on National Goals concluded: "Improvement of the democratic process requires a constantly better-informed public. . . . What America needs is not more voters, but more good voters, men and women who are informed, understanding, and reasonable. To produce such men and women in ever larger numbers should be a major goal of all labors to preserve American democracy."[12] The people can vigorously and angrily express their disapproval when the government is caught in a lie or when the truth is withheld. They can keep abreast of public issues, make their views known to their representatives in the federal government, refuse to accept unacceptable answers, familiarize themselves with the records of candidates for public office, and—above all else—exercise the precious right to vote. To do less is to abdicate the responsibilities of citizenship. In the last analysis, the solution for correcting the ills of democracy is more democracy. Those who say nothing can be done are clearly wrong.

NOTES TO CHAPTER 10

1. Article II, Section 3, United States Constitution.
2. H. H. Gerth and C. Wright Mills, eds., *From Max Weber: Essays in Sociology* (New York: Oxford University Press, 1946), p. 233.
3. Walter Lippmann, "The Credibility Gap—I," *Washington Post,* March 28, 1967.
4. Walter Lippmann, "The Credibility Gap—II," *Washington Post,* March 30, 1967.
5. Walter Lippmann, *The Public Philosophy* (New York: New American Library, 1955), p. 99.
6. James Reston, *The Artillery of the Press* (New York: Harper & Row, 1966), p. 104.
7. Joseph and Stewart Alsop, *The Reporter's Trade* (New York: Reynal & Company, 1958), p. 36.
8. Mary McInnis, ed., *We Propose: A Modern Congress, Selected Proposals by the House Republican Task Force on Congressional Reform and Minority Staffing* (New York: McGraw-Hill Book Company, 1966), p. 312.
9. *Organization of Congress,* Final Report of the Joint Committee on the Organization of the Congress, 89th Congress, Second Session, July 28, 1966, pp. 85, 86.
10. McInnis, *We Propose: A Modern Congress,* p. 7.
11. *Ibid.,* p. 8.
12. *Goals for Americans,* The Report of the President's Commission on National Goals (New York: Prentice-Hall, Inc., 1960), p. 77.

Selected Bibliography

Abel, Elie. *The Missile Crisis*. New York: J. B. Lippincott Company, 1966.

Alsop, Joseph and Stewart. *The Reporter's Trade*. New York: Reynal & Company, 1950.

Bolling, Richard. *House Out of Order*. New York: E. P. Dutton & Company, 1965.

Byrnes, James F. *Speaking Frankly*. New York: Harper & Brothers, 1947.

Campbell, L. R., and R. E. Wolseley. *Newsmen at Work: Reporting and Writing the News*. Boston: Houghton Mifflin Company, 1949.

Cater, Douglass. *The Fourth Branch of Government*. New York: Vintage Books, 1959.

CBS News Special Report. *Vietnam Perspective*. New York: Pocket Books, Inc., 1965.

Chafee, Zechariah, Jr. *Freedom of the Press in the United States*. Chicago: University of Chicago Press, 1947.

Cornwell, Elmer E. *Presidential Leadership of Public Opinion.* Bloomington, Ind.: Indiana University Press, 1965.

Coyle, David Cushman. *The United States Political System and How It Works.* New York: The New American Library, 1954.

Cross, Harold L. *The People's Right to Know.* New York: Columbia University Press, 1953.

Dos Passos, John. *Mr. Wilson's War.* Garden City, N.Y.: Doubleday & Company, 1962.

Eisenhower, Dwight D. *The White House Years: Waging Peace, 1956–1961.* Garden City, N.Y.: Doubleday & Company, 1965.

Evans, Rowland, and Robert Novak. *Lyndon B. Johnson: The Exercise of Power.* New York: The New American Library, 1966.

Fulbright, J. William. *The Arrogance of Power.* New York: Vintage Books, 1967.

Gerth, H. H., and C. Wright Mills, Editors. *From Max Weber: Essays in Sociology.* New York: Oxford University Press, 1946.

Gettleman, Marvin E., Editor. *Vietnam: History, Documents, and Opinions on a Major World Crisis.* New York: Fawcett Publications, Inc., 1965.

Geyelin, Philip. *Lyndon B. Johnson and the World.* New York: Frederick A. Praeger, Inc., 1966.

Goodwin, Richard N. *Triumph or Tragedy: Reflections on Vietnam.* New York: Vintage Books, 1966.

Halberstam, David. *The Making of a Quagmire.* New York: Random House, 1964.

Hiebert, Ray Eldon, Editor. *The Press in Washington.* New York: Dodd, Mead & Company, 1966.

Hohenberg, John. *Between Two Worlds: Policy, Press and Public Opinion in Asian-American Relations.* New York: Frederick A. Praeger, Inc., 1967.

Lasswell, Harold D. *National Security and Individual Freedom.* New York: McGraw-Hill Book Company, 1950.

Lawrence, David. *Diary of a Washington Correspondent.* New York: H. C. Kinsey & Company, 1942.

Leech, Margaret. *In the Days of McKinley.* New York: Harper & Brothers, 1959.

Lippmann, Walter. *The Public Philosophy.* New York: The New American Library, 1955.

Martin, John Bartlow. *Overtaken by Events.* Garden City, N.Y.: Doubleday & Company, 1966.

McInnis, Mary, Editor. *We Propose: A Modern Congress, Selected Proposals by the House Republican Task Force on Congressional Reform and Minority Staffing.* New York: McGraw-Hill Book Company, 1966.

Mecklin, John. *Mission in Torment.* Garden City, N.Y.: Doubleday & Company, 1965.

Morris, Christopher. *The Day They Lost the H-Bomb.* New York: Coward-McCann, 1966.

Murphy, Robert. *Diplomat Among Warriors.* Garden City, N.Y.: Doubleday & Company, 1964.

Neustadt, Richard E. *Presidential Power.* New York: The New American Library, 1964.

Newman, Bernard. *Background to Vietnam.* New York: The New American Library, 1966.

Noggle, Burl. *Teapot Dome: Oil and Politics in the 1920's.* New York: W. W. Norton, 1965.

Padover, Saul K., Editor. *Thomas Jefferson on Democracy.* New York: Penguin Books, Inc., 1946.

Pickerell, James H. *Vietnam in the Mud.* Indianapolis: Bobbs-Merrill Co., 1966.

Pollard, James E. *The Presidents and the Press.* Washington, D.C.: Public Affairs Press, 1964.

Phillips, Cabell. *The Truman Presidency.* New York: The Macmillan Company, 1966.

Randall, Henry S. *Life of Thomas Jefferson,* Vol. III. New York: Derby & Jackson, 1858.

Raymond, Jack. *Power at the Pentagon.* New York: Harper & Row, 1964.

Reston, James. *The Artillery of the Press.* New York: Harper & Row, 1966.

Rivers, William L. *The Opinionmakers.* Boston: Beacon Press, 1965.

Roberts, Charles W. *LBJ's Inner Circle.* New York: Delacorte Press, 1965.

Rockefeller, Nelson A. *The Future of Federalism.* Cambridge: Harvard University Press, 1962.

Rossiter, Clinton. *The American Presidency.* New York: The New American Library, 1956.

Rourke, Francis. *Secrecy Versus Publicity.* Baltimore: Johns Hopkins Press, 1960.

Salinger, Pierre. *With Kennedy.* Garden City, N.Y.: Doubleday & Company, 1966.

Schlesinger, Arthur M., Jr. *A Thousand Days: John F. Kennedy in the White House.* Boston: Houghton Mifflin Company, 1965.

Shils, Edward A. *The Torment of Secrecy.* Glencoe, Ill.: Free Press, 1956.

Smith, A. Merriman. *Thank You, Mr. President: A White House Notebook.* New York: Harper & Brothers, 1946.

Snow, C. P. *Science and Government.* Cambridge: Harvard University Press, 1961.

Szulc, Tad. *Dominican Diary.* New York: Dell Publishing Company, 1965.

Tacheron, Donald G., and Morris K. Udall. *The Job of the Congressman.* Indianapolis: Bobbs-Merrill Co., 1966.

Wise, David, and Thomas B. Ross. *The Invisible Government.* New York: Bantam Books, 1964.

Index

234 | Index

About the Author

After graduating from Northern Illinois University in 1958, Bruce Ladd spent six years as editor of award-winning newspapers in Illinois. In 1964, he was granted a leave of absence as associate editor of Paddock Publications, Inc., publishers of sixteen suburban newspapers in Arlington Heights, Illinois, to serve as press secretary to Illinois gubernatorial candidate Charles H. Percy. In 1965, he was named the first suburban journalist to receive the coveted Congressional Fellowship of the American Political Science Association. While under the Fellowship in Washington, D.C., he served as correspondent for the Suburban Press Foundation, Inc., and authored a penetrating study of the Republican Party's press relations. Since August, 1965, except for a six-month period spent writing this book, he has been Legislative and Special Assistant to Congressman Donald Rumsfeld of Illinois. Mr. Ladd is a Lecturer at the Washington Journalism Center and an active member of Sigma Delta Chi journalism society, serving on the Freedom of Information committees of both the Chicago and Washington chapters.